# NEW
# FORMS
# OF
# DEMOCRACY

LIU SJL

# NEW
# FORMS
# OF
# DEMOCRACY

**Edited by**
**David Held and Christopher Pollitt**

**⑤ SAGE Publications**

*in association with* The Open University

© The Open University 1986
First Published 1986

SAGE Publications Ltd
28 Banner Street
London EC1Y 8QE

SAGE Publications Inc
275 South Beverly Drive
Beverly Hills, California 90212

and 2111 West Hillcrest Drive
Newbury Park, California 91320

SAGE Publications India Pvt Ltd
C-236 Defence Colony
New Delhi 110 024

**British Library Cataloguing in Publication Data**

New forms of democracy.
 1. Democracy
 I. Held, David  II. Pollitt, Christopher
 III. Open University
 321.8    JC423

ISBN 0-80398-012-4
ISBN 0-80398-013-2 Pbk

**Library of Congress catalog card number 86-062642**

Typeset by System 4 Associates, Gerrards Cross, Buckinghamshire
Printed in Great Britain
by J. W. Arrowsmith Ltd, Bristol

First printing

# Contents

# List of Contributors

**John Burnheim** is Associate Professor in the Department of General Philosophy at the University of Sydney, Australia. He is author of *Is Democracy Possible?* (1985).

**Allan Cochrane** is a Lecturer in Urban Studies at The Open University. In the mid-1970s he was involved in action research with the Birmingham Community Development Project. More recently his research has focused on local economic policies and notions of municipal socialism. His publications include *Economic Policy Making by Local Authorities in Britain and West Germany* (with N. Johnson) and *City, Economy and Society* (edited with C. Hamnett and L. McDowell), as well as several related articles.

**David Held** is Senior Lecturer in Social Science at The Open University. His publications include: *Introduction to Critical Theory: Horkheimer to Habermas* (1980); *Habermas: Critical Debates* (edited with John B. Thompson, 1982); *Classes, Power and Conflict* (edited with Anthony Giddens, 1982); *States and Societies* (edited with colleagues at The Open University, 1984) and *Models of Democracy* (1987).

**Margaret Kiloh** is Lecturer in Interdisciplinary Social Science at The Open University. She has written on industrial relations in Africa and Australia and is an active trade unionist in Britain.

**Iain McLean** is Fellow and Praelector in Politics at University College, Oxford. He has been a Labour (1973–9) and SDP (1982–6) local councillor and has campaigned in numerous elections as well as his own. In his spare time he drives steam trains in Wales.

**Christopher Pollitt** is Senior Lecturer in Government at The Open University. A Whitehall administrator until the mid-1970s, he is author of *Manipulating the Machine* (1984) and editor of *Public Policy in Theory and Practice* (1979) and several other works on public policy-making. His current research concerns attempts to measure 'performance' in a variety of public services, especially education and health care.

**Sheila Rowbotham** has been involved in the women's movement since it began in the late 1960s. She has written extensively on the history of women's movements and socialism and in contemporary politics. Her books include *Women, Resistance and Revolution* (1972), *Hidden from History* (1973), *Women's Consciousness, Man's World* (1973), *Beyond the Fragments* (with Lynn Segal and Hilary Wainwright, 1979), and *Dreams and Dilemmas* (1983).

**Steve Smith** is Senior Lecturer in Politics at the University of East Anglia, where he teaches courses in international relations. He has also taught at Huddersfield Polytechnic and the State University of New York. He writes mainly in the areas of foreign policy analysis, international relations theory and nuclear weapons/arms control. He has written *Foreign Policy Adaptation* (1981) and edited *Politics and Human Nature* (with Ian Forbes, 1983), *Foreign Policy Implementation* (with Michael Clarke, 1985) and *International Relations: British and American Perspectives* (1985). He has also written a large number of articles in journals and collections of essays.

**Alan Ware** is Lecturer in Politics at the University of Warwick. He is the author of *The Logic of Party Democracy* and *The Breakdown of Democratic Party Organization 1940–1980*, and the editor of *Political Parties* (to be published in early 1987). He is currently engaged in research on parties and the modern state, and on a study examining the relationship between non-profit organizations, the market system and the state in England and America.

# Acknowledgements

Authors and editors frequently emphasize the extent to which the books they generate are actually products of a number of contributions. This commonplace is doubly true in the case of a book such as this, which has been conceived and put together in the context of the development of an Open University course, *Democratic Government and Politics*. We must, in particular, register our thanks to those people whose daily efforts to fulfil a demanding timetable made it possible for the book to appear on time. These included Mike Dawson, Mary Dicker, Anne Hunt, Sue How and Nigel Draper. We believe that the book that has resulted offers a timely re-assessment of one of the most central concepts in the study of politics. As such we hope that it will find a readership both among Open University students and far beyond. Democracy, one might say, is too important to be left to the politicians.

DH
CP

# 1 Introduction:
# New Forms of Democracy?
*David Held*

On both the right and left of the political spectrum today contemporary developments underline the urgency of the search for new political policies, strategies and institutional arrangements. In the West the crisis of the welfare state, of unemployment and inflation and of escalating demands on the polity has provided an enormous impetus to rethink the relation between the economy and the state, and between the sphere of private initiative and public regulation. Liberal political thought appears to have come to a major point of transition as pressures for state intervention conflict with traditional emphases on individual liberty. In the East the crisis of state-dominated societies, of bureaucracy and of ever greater pressures for democratic institutions have led to a questioning of the connections between planning institutions, bureaucracy and democracy. Eastern or Marxist political orthodoxy is vulnerable in the face of demands for, among other things, a free public sphere safeguarded by a polity that respects human rights. [1]

In this context renewed concern about the direction of contemporary politics has given way to fresh consideration of the very essence of democracy. But the renaissance of reflection on possible political futures has been handicapped by many things, including widespread cynicism, scepticism and mistrust of politics. Politics is frequently experienced today as something distant and remote from everyday life. [2] The affairs of government and national politics are not things many people claim to understand, nor are they a source of sustained interest. Not surprisingly, perhaps, those closest to both power and privilege are the ones who have most interest in and are most favourable to political life. But for many people, the fact that something is a recognizably 'political' statement is almost enough to bring it instantly into disrepute. Politics is often linked with self-seeking behaviour, hypocrisy and 'public relations' activity geared to selling policy packages. There are, of course, many highly specific single-issue campaigns, as well as a variety of powerful social movements and political parties which have clear-cut political objectives and which are well supported. But surveying contemporary politics – including the politics of the protest movements – one is struck by its seemingly contingent, fragmented and 'directionless' nature when taken as a whole. There is considerable doubt about appropriate alternatives to existing institutions. There is uncertainty not only about what kinds of institutions there might be but also about what general political directions should be taken. Thus, as possibilities for antagonistic stances against existing institutions are realized, so too are the germs of a variety of other kinds of political movements, e.g. movements in support of threatened institutions. Anxiety about 'directionless' change can fuel a call for the re-establishment of tradition and the authority of the state. This is the foundation for the appeal by the 'new' conservatives – or the new right – to the people and the nation, to many of those who feel so acutely unrepresented.

It is important to say something more about contemporary controversies over alternative political futures before introducing the main themes of *New Forms of Democracy*, for recent political debate has generated many of the key questions upon which *New Forms of Democracy* seeks to focus.

## Current controversies

The new right (or neo-liberalism as it is sometimes called), is, in general committed to the view that political life, like economic life, is – or ought to be – a matter of individual freedom and initiative (see Hayek, 1960, 1976, 1982 and Nozick, 1974). Accordingly, a *laissez-faire* or free market society is the key objective along with a 'minimal state'. The political programme of the new right includes: the extension of the market to more and more areas of life; the creation of a state stripped of 'excessive' involvement both in the economy and in the provision of opportunities; the curtailment of the power of certain groups (for instance, trade unions) to press their aims and goals; the construction of a government capable of enforcing law and order.[3]

In the late 1970s and 1980s, the governments of Margaret Thatcher and Ronald Reagan advocated 'rolling back the state' on grounds similar to those of the new right and of some of the theorists of 'overloaded government' (see Held, 1984 and McLennan, 1984). They insisted that individual freedom had been diminished because of the proliferation of bureaucratic state agencies attempting to meet the demands of those involved in group politics. In so arguing, they committed themselves to the classic liberal doctrine that the collective good (or the good of all individuals) can be properly realized in most cases only by private individuals acting in competitive relation with one another and pursuing their sectoral aims with minimal state interference. This commitment to the market as the key mechanism of economic and social regulation has a significant other side in the history of liberalism: a commitment to 'strong government' to provide a secure basis upon which, it is thought, business, trade and family life will prosper.

At root, the new right is concerned to advance the cause of 'liberalism' against 'democracy' by limiting the possible uses of state power. A government can only legitimately intervene in society to enforce *general rules* – rules which broadly protect 'life, liberty and estate'. Hayek, one of the leading advocates of these ideas, is unequivocal about this: a free, liberal order is incompatible with the enactment of rules which specify how people should use the means at their disposal (1960, pp. 231–2). Governments become coercive if they interfere with people's own capacity to determine their objectives. The prime example Hayek gives of such coercion is legislation which attempts to alter 'the material position of particular people or enforce distributive or "social" justice' (1960, p. 231). Distributive justice always imposes on some another's conception of merit or desert. It requires the allocation of resources by a central authority acting *as if* it knew what people should receive for their efforts and how they should behave. The value of individuals' services can, however, only justly be determined by their fellows in and through a decision-making system which does not interfere with *their* knowledge, choices and decisions. And there is only one sufficiently sensitive mechanism for determining 'collective' choice on an individual basis – the free market. When protected by a constitutional state, no system provides a mechanism of collective choice as dynamic, innovative and responsive as the operations of the free market.

The free market does not always operate perfectly; but, Hayek insists, its benefits radically outweigh its disadvantages (1960, 1976 and see Rutland, 1985). A free market system is the basis for a genuinely *liberal* democracy. In particular, the market can ensure the co-ordination of decisions of producers and consumers without the direction of a central authority; the pursuit by everybody of their own ends with the resources at their disposal; the development of a complex economy without an elite who claim to know how it all works. Politics, as a governmental decision-making system, will always be a radically imperfect system of choice when compared to the market. Thus, 'politics' or 'state action' should be kept to a minimum – to the sphere of operation of an 'ultra-liberal' state (Hayek, 1976, p. 172). An 'oppressive bureaucratic government' is the almost inevitable result of deviation from this prescription.

Thinkers like Hayek, along with the movement of the new right more generally, have contributed significantly to a discussion about the appropriate form and limits of state action (see Held and Keane, 1984). They have helped to make once again the relationship among state, civil society and subject populations a leading political issue. Conceptions about the proper character of this relationship are more unsettled now perhaps than at any point during the post-war years. But the new right, of course, is not the only tradition with a claim to inherit the vocabulary of freedom. The 'new left' has developed profound claims of its own to this lexicon. It is worth stressing that the new left did not develop principally as a 'counter-attack' on the new right. While the presence of the new right has in recent times sharpened new left views, the latter emerged primarily as a result of the political upheavals of the 1960s, internal debates on the left and dissatisfaction with the heritage of political theory, liberal and Marxist.[4] I shall focus the brief discussion below on the work of two people who have contributed, in particular, to the re-thinking of left conceptions of democracy: Pateman (1970, 1985) and Poulantzas (1980).

The extent to which individuals are 'free' in contemporary liberal democracies is questioned by the new left figures. To enjoy liberty means not only to enjoy equality before the law, important though this unquestionably is, but also to have the capacities (the material and cultural resources) to be able to choose between different courses of action. As Pateman puts it, 'the "free and equal individual" is, in practice, a person found much more rarely than liberal theory suggests' (1985, p. 171). Liberal theory – in its classical and contemporary guises – generally assumes what has, in fact, to be carefully examined: namely, whether the existing relationships among men and women, working, middle and upper classes, blacks and whites, and various ethnic groups allows formally recognized rights to be actually realized. The formal existence of certain rights is, while not unimportant, of little value if they cannot be exercised in everyday practice. An assessment of freedom must be made on the basis of liberties that are tangible, and capable of being deployed within the realms of both state and civil society. Without a concrete content – as particular freedoms – liberty can scarcely be said to have profound consequences for everyday life. If liberals or neo-liberals were to take these issues seriously, they would discover that massive numbers of individuals are restricted systematically – for want of a complex mix of resources and opportunities – from participating actively in political and civil life. Inequalities of class, sex and race substantially hinder the extent to which it can legitimately be claimed that individuals are 'free and equal'.

Furthermore, the very liberal claim that there can be a clear separation between 'civil society' and 'the state' is, Pateman argues, flawed, with fundamental consequences for key liberal tenets (1985, pp. 172 ff.) If the state is separate from the associations and practices of everyday life, then it is plausible to see it as a special kind of apparatus which the citizen ought to respect and obey. But if the state is enmeshed in these associations and practices, then the claim that the state is an 'independent authority' or 'circumscribed impartial power' is radically compromised. In Pateman's judgement (and that of many contemporary Marxists and neo-pluralists), the state is inescapably locked into the maintenance and reproduction of the inequalities of everyday life. Accordingly, the whole basis of its claim to distinct allegiance is in doubt (1985, pp. 173 f.) This is unsettling for the whole spectrum of questions concerning the nature of public power, the relation between the 'public' and the 'private', the proper scope of politics and the appropriate reach of democratic governments.

If the state is as a matter of routine neither 'separate' nor 'impartial' with respect to society, then it is clear that citizens will not be treated as 'free and equal'. If the 'public' and 'private' are interlocked in complex ways, then elections will always be insufficient as mechanisms to ensure the accountability of the forces actually involved in the 'governing' process. Moreover, since the 'meshing' of state and civil society leaves few, if any, realms of 'private life' untouched by 'politics', the question of the proper form of democratic regulation is acute. What form democratic control should take, and what the scope of democratic decision-making should be, becomes an urgent matter. However, the 'traditional' left response to these issues needs to be treated with caution. For 'new left' thinkers generally accept that there are fundamental difficulties with orthodox Marxist theory (cf. Macpherson, 1977).

Poulantzas has tried to develop a position, in common with other new left thinkers, which moves beyond a rigid juxtaposition of Marxism with liberalism. For Poulantzas, the development of Stalinism and a repressive state in Russia is not just due to the peculiarities of a 'backward' economy – as many Marxists today still argue – but can be traced to problems in the thought and practice of Marx and Lenin. Their belief that the institutions of representative democracy can be simply swept away by organizations or rank and file democracy is erroneous. Lenin, above all, mistook the nature of representative democracy when he labelled it simply as bourgeois. Underlying this typical Leninist view is a mistaken distrust of the idea of competing power centres in society. Moreover, it was because of distrust of this kind that Lenin ultimately undermined the autonomy of the Soviets after the 1917 revolution, and put the revolution on an 'anti-democratic' road. Poulantzas affirms the view that 'without general elections, without unrestricted freedom of press and assembly, without a free struggle of opinion, life dies out in every public institution' (Rosa Luxemburg, quoted by Poulantzas, 1980, p. 283).

Poulantzas argues that the whole relation between socialist thought and democratic institutions needs to be rethought in light not only of the reality of Eastern European socialism but also of the moral bankruptcy of the social democratic vision of reform. Social democratic politics has led to the adulation of 'social engineering', proliferating policies to make relatively minor adjustments in social and economic arrangements. The state has, accordingly, grown in size and power, undermining the vision that social democratic politics might once have had. But what, then, is the way forward? Institutions of direct democracy or self-management cannot simply replace the state; for, as Max Weber predicted, they leave a co-ordination vacuum readily filled by bureaucracy. Poulantzas emphasizes two sets of changes which he believes are vital for the transformation of the state in West and East into forms of what he calls 'socialist pluralism'. The state must be democratized by making parliament, state bureaucracies and political parties more open and accountable while new forms of struggle at the local level (through factory-based politics, the women's movement, ecological groups) must ensure that society, as well as the state, is democratized, i.e. subject to procedures which ensure accountability. But how these processes interrelate Poulantzas does not say, stressing instead that there are 'no easy recipes'.

While the new left theorists have highlighted a number of fundamental difficulties with liberal accounts of democracy and, in particular, with the new right position, the new left conception of democracy as it is and as it could be cannot simply be accepted. For fundamental issues are left unaddressed. Little is said, for instance, about how the economy is actually to be organized and related to the political apparatus, how institutions of representative democracy are to be combined with those of direct democracy, how the scope and power of administrative organizations are to be checked, how those who wish to 'opt out' of the political system might do so, or about how the problems posed by the ever-changing international system could be dealt with. Moreover, the arguments pass over the question of how the 'model' could be realized, over the whole issue of transitional stages, and over how those who might be worse off in some respects as a result of its application (those whose current circumstances allow them to determine the opportunities of others) might react and should be treated. To leave issues such as these unaddressed is to leave significant theoretical lacunae – a particularly acute problem during a time, like our own, of disenchantment with 'visionary politics'.

### New forms?

*New Forms of Democracy* certainly affirms that there are 'no easy recipes' when thinking about the issues posed about the future of democracy by either the right or left. Current political controversy has generated a range of pressing questions, the responses to which are by no means straight-forward. If the new right has posed important questions about the proper form and limits of state action, the new left has succeeded in highlighting severe problems about the extent to which there can be freedom and accountability in a world marked by vast inequalities between races, sexes and economic groupings. The issues that arise concern, on the one hand, the *re*form of state power and, on the other, the restructuring of 'civil' power centres which disrupt and distort democratic life. The questions posed, in sum, are: how, and in what ways, might state policy be made more accountable and effective? How, and in what ways, might 'non-state' relations be re-ordered to create the possibility of a citizenry that is 'free and equal'?[5]

The constellation of issues which emerge in the current debate about the desirable form of 'state power' and 'civil society' is the focus of *New Forms of Democracy*. In particular, the book is addressed to the questions: can 'democracy' be extended in scope, and developed in nature, in order that networks of arbitrary and/or unregulated power be brought under 'popular control'? Is democratization the key to solving problems posed by asymmetries of power? Which spheres of 'state' and 'society' can be democratized, and how and to what extent? Are there trade-offs between democracy and other important ends? The new right theorists would clearly be wholly sceptical about the prospects of deepening the grasp of democracy on social and political life. By emphasizing questions about the desirable limits of state power, they tend to disregard – if not dismiss altogether – those issues which are central to new left political philosophy: above all, the problems posed by the relation between liberty and (political, social and economic) inequality. *New Forms of Democracy* does not claim to resolve or settle the major differences between these positions. But by embracing some of the concerns of both sides, and by examining critically the prospects of change in the scope, methods and nature of democracy, it offers a contribution to the debate that is currently raging between left and right.

What are 'new forms' of democracy? There are, in very general terms, two broad types of democracy: direct or participatory democracy (a system of decision-making about public affairs in which citizens are directly involved) and liberal or representative democracy (a system of political rule embracing elected 'officers' who undertake to 'represent' the interests and/or views of citizens). From ancient Athens to the present day, there has been an array of conceptions of these two broad types (see Held, 1987). A remarkable diversity of democracies has existed and there has been an extraordinary number of experiments with democracy. When judged against this background, it must be said that there are few, if any, genuinely new forms of democracy today. What, then, is meant by 'new forms'? The authors of this book take 'new forms' to mean all those new initiatives from 'below' as well as new developments on formal political and policy agendas which seek to alter systematically the dominant form of contemporary democracy – that is, which seek to alter liberal or representative democracy by either increasing the *scope* or transforming the *methods* of democratic decision-making. Not all the 'new forms' examined below, it should be emphasized, are aimed at a total replacement of national representative democratic institutions – far from it. Some are aimed at modifying the function and operation of these institutions in certain respects. Some are aimed at developing a complementary range of democratic institutions in the spheres of everyday life – the workplace or the local community, for instance. But others do champion a substantial transformation of key aspects of contemporary democracy. Before reflecting on the positions taken by the authors of this volume with respect to these innovations, it is useful to have an overview of the issues addressed in each chapter.

In Chapter 2, Margaret Kiloh examines the application of mechanisms of democratic decision-making to the workplace: industrial democracy. Kiloh shows that there are a variety of forms of industrial democracy, sponsored by many different interest groups, each with different conditions for their survival and development. Analysing these conditions with the help of extensive case study material, Kiloh argues that the prospects of industrial democracy cannot be separated from a number of structural and ideological factors which systematically constrain its successful development. But, she concludes, the potential for industrial democracy has not yet been fully explored: industrial democracy might flourish, extending fundamentally the meaning of citizenship, if other spheres of society – including the local community and regional power centres – were subject to more stringent democratic control.

The idea that the 'community' might be a (if not the) proper locus of democratic decision-making is examined in Chapter 3 by Allan Cochrane. Governments of left and right have recently proclaimed themselves champions of greater community control. What precisely is meant by this? Why is the community the centre of so much political attention? Drawing on a range of empirical studies, Cochrane seeks to assess whether a more locally based politics can be developed and with what consequences. He ends with a sympathetic but sobering account of the successes and failures of democracy at the local level. While there is abundant evidence that those excluded from central political decision-making are quite capable of developing alternative programmes to those of 'public decision-makers', there is also evidence that involvement in community politics can leave local people trapped in 'political backwaters' isolated from wider national concerns. The promise of community politics remains difficult to realize.

Among the most significant challenges to contemporary forms of representative democracy is that posed by the women's movement. Sheila Rowbotham in Chapter 4 examines this challenge. More than any other recent development, feminism has set out arguments to suggest that the successful development of democracy depends on creating egalitarian, non-hierarchical relations between people in 'private' as well as 'public' life. The feminist slogan 'the personal is political' draws direct attention to this special emphasis. Rowbotham affirms the classic feminist view that the public sphere will never be fully democratic while the sexual division of labour undercuts the capacity of women to participate in social, economic and political activities; the transformation of sexual inequalities in households and workplaces is a prerequisite for the enhancement of democracy in 'public life'. But after tracing the background to modern feminism and its rapid development in the 1960s, Rowbotham argues that many original feminist concepts should not be regarded as sacrosanct. The success of the feminist challenge depends on a more divergent range of ideas than many feminists initially anticipated. For instance, the women's movement has frequently advocated participatory or 'expressive' forms of democracy as the only suitable models for the transformation of the spheres of the public and the private. But recurring difficulties in the women's movement itself – including painful patterns of personal conflict, inadequate decision-making procedures and a lack of willingness to appreciate certain types of skill – testifies to the necessity of combining elements of seemingly different political models. If feminism is to achieve a sustainable extension of democracy, ways will have to be found of linking participatory forms of politics with effective representative organizations.

Examining one of the most important set of political forces to mediate the relation between citizens, collectivities and 'the state', Alan Ware directs attention in Chapter 5 to political parties as democratic institutions. The chapter focuses on three issues which have become prominent in recent political debates: attempts to democratize well established parties, initiatives to provide democratic control of new parties, and the changing relationship between parties and pressure groups. One major case study is used to illustrate each of these issues. Ware argues that 'parties remain a source of frustration to democrats because, while they seem so central to the creation of more democratic societies, devising new structures for the realization of this objective has been relatively unsuccessful'. Assessing the few experiments there have been to alter party forms (the Parti Québécois in Quebec and the Greens in Germany) leads one to be cautious, Ware concludes, about the prospects of 'democratizing parties'. However, there is much to be learnt from the difficulties encountered in these recent initiatives which might help inform future political strategies to alter party structures.

New technology offers the opportunity of taking votes and sounding opinions by new means. For instance, opinion polls can be much more accurate and quicker than they were; votes can be cast by telephone or over a computer network; and potentially ordinary citizens can take a more prominent part in public decision-making than ever before. Analysing these possibilities in Chapter 6, Iain McLean argues that they put the possibility of direct democracy back on the political agenda. Assessing traditional arguments between direct and representative democrats, McLean maintains that new technology helps to solve some but not all of these arguments. The conclusion he draws is that new technology can facilitate a variety of processes which used to be physically impossible, but it cannot get over all the *logical* difficulties of direct democracy envisaged by the latter's critics. New technology offers a number of remarkable political opportunities, but it does not offer a new lease of life to direct democracy as a *general* political system; logic not technology undermines this option.

One of the central constraints on the development of democracy is said frequently – by both left and right – to be bureaucracy. Chapter 7, by Christopher Pollitt, explores this constraint, focusing centrally on public bureaucracies. Explicating a number of competing theories of the bureaucracy/democracy relation, Pollitt shows that there is no consensus as to its nature. After offering guidance through the myriad of scholarly debates about bureaucracy, Pollitt examines the possibility of 'alternatives' to bureaucracy, advocated by a number of contemporary writers. He shows that bureaucracy need not be regarded as a wholly rigid, monolithic entity: alternatives to existing types of public organizations can be envisaged and do sometimes exist, usually in experimental form. But, Pollitt concludes, all strategies of change must be cautious, experimental and guided by 'modest' expectations. For beyond a certain point strategies to find alternatives to bureaucracy will hit ' "buffers" where co-ordination would seriously be impaired, and effectiveness catastrophically undermined'. Yet there still remains, Pollitt suggests, wide scope for institutional innovation. The chapter ends with the elaboration of one strategy for organizational change.

The idea of extensive citizen participation in public decision-making faces, furthermore, a severe challenge from the very structure of relations among states. States face not only 'inward' – towards their citizens – but also 'outward' – towards the international political system. The latter is frequently characterized as 'anarchic', a sphere in which a war of all against all is a constant threat. In this international world, states are confronted by a security dilemma – the problem of how to secure their borders and interests without unduly antagonizing others and thereby risking their very security. This dilemma has created a domain of policy in which national governments have come to enjoy unique freedom to define what is in 'the national interest'. In Chapter 8, Steve Smith assesses the functioning of democracy under international as well as national pressures. Comparing the way decisions have been taken on central defence issues in Britain and the USA leads him to the view that, although there are significant differences between each country, executive management of information and a wide network of security controls leave minimal opportunities for legislatures and citizens to participate in defence and foreign policy decisions. The barriers to democratic control of these decisions are formidable. The question is: can democratic decision-making be extended to the sphere of foreign and defence policy? Smith is sceptical about the possibility of radical schemes to transform the whole basis on which current policies are made; the system of international states is, he believes, a 'limiting factor'. But institutional changes to create greater freedom of information, more effective divisions between different branches of the state and the mobilization of public opinion (through the peace movements) give some hope for establishing in the future greater accountability of foreign and defence affairs.

It cannot justifiably be claimed that democracy exists at the world level. World affairs are conducted between states, only some of which are 'democratic' even in the limited, conventional sense. Moreover, most of the issues which determine the fate of humankind are entirely beyond the control of ordinary citizens. This has led some to advocate a system of world government. John Burnheim, in Chapter 9, assesses this possibility critically, and warns in particular of an uncontrollable bureaucracy that might develop in the wake of such a system of government. Nonetheless, he argues, a promising basis exists for more accountable and effective world government based on 'functional authorities', each independent of the other, co-ordinated by negotiation or arbitration, with specific powers over specialized problem areas. Burnheim unpacks this vision in some detail, linking it to radically new proposals for establishing democratic regulation: the new functional authorities could be placed under the control of committees of people chosen by a 'statistical procedure so as to give a representative, regularly replaced sample of those most affected by the decisions of the body in question'. The difficulties faced by such a scheme cannot be underestimated, but Burnheim concludes that it offers a way forward in a world where there are desperately few opportunities for establishing democratic decision-making over some of the most central problems of our time – the problems of war and peace, hunger and food distribution, and the issues posed in general by radical asymmetries in resource distribution within and between countries.

The essays in this volume attempt to assess the prospects of democracy from both a theoretical and empirical point of view. In conducting a substantial survey of possible changes in the scope and methods of democracy, they offer an assessment of some of the alternative ways in which democracy might be developed in the late twentieth century. Together, they pursue an important range of questions. What kind of a response do they offer? Do the authors share a view of the possibilities of and limits to democratic innovations? In the first instance, it must be stressed that there are considerable divergences in approach and opinion among the contributors to this volume. This is hardly surprising in a collection of essays about matters as controversial as those addressed here. But there is a common note sounded by all the contributors; for they are both optimistic *and* pessimistic about the future of democracy and the opportunity of establishing new democratic forms. They envisage many possibilities for the development and enhancement of democracy, but also many difficulties, obstacles and dilemmas. Accordingly, *New Forms of Democracy* does not offer a wholly unambiguous set of answers to all the questions it sought to address. However, there is another common note worth emphasizing: in the debate between left and right neither position can be simply affirmed. For the message of this volume is that while, on the one hand, the right hopelessly underestimates the opportunities that exist for the development of democracy and effective democratic decision-making, the left, on the other hand, risks severely underestimating the difficulties of establishing 'new forms' on a sustainable basis.

*New Forms of Democracy*, then, rejects the view that humans are either essentially self-interested, and thus unable to sustain co-operative endeavours (as maintained frequently by the right), or basically altruistic, and thus unquestionably capable of becoming dedicated to the 'common good' (as presupposed often by the left). The position that emerges here is that people are able to *learn* to participate by participating and are more likely to seek participation *if* they can be confident that their input into decision-making will actually count; that is, will actually be weighted equitably with others and will not simply be side-stepped or ignored by those who wield greater power. How one translates this idea into particular arenas – the household, the workplace, the local community, branches of state agencies – is pursued in this volume, although the conclusions that are reached by no means amount to an unambiguous programme of democratic transformation. The possibility of changing the scope and methods of democracy is affirmed, but the difficulties involved in such changes are never lost sight of.

## Notes

1. I have discussed these issues at greater length in *Models of Democracy*, Cambridge, Polity Press, 1987. Some of the material in this introduction is adapted from Chapter 8 of *Models*.
2. The evidence for Britain is summarized in my 'Power and legitimacy in contemporary Britain', in McLennan *et al.* (eds) (1984).
3. It might be noted that the fourth item of this programme is arguably inconsistent with items one and two. In fact, a tension exists in conservatism generally and in the new right in particular between those who assert individual freedom and the market as the ultimate concern, and those who believe in the primacy of tradition, order and authority, because they fear the social consequences of rampant *laissez-faire* policies. My account of the new right concentrates on the former group, who have been most influential in current politics. See Levitas (1986) for an analysis of different elements in new right thinking.
4. The new left, like the new right, consists of more than one strand of political thought: at the very least, it consists of ideas inspired by Rousseau, anarchists and a variety of Marxist positions. A number of figures have contributed to the reformulation of left conceptions of democracy and freedom. See Pierson (1986) and Held (1987, Chapter 8).
5. The theoretical implications of these questions are explored more fully in Held (1987, Chapter 9) and Keane (1987).

## References

HAYEK, F. A. (1960) *The Constitution of Liberty*, London, Routledge and Kegan Paul.

HAYEK, F. A. (1976) *The Road to Serfdom*, London, Routledge and Kegan Paul.

HAYEK, F. A. (1982) *Law, Legislation and Liberty*, Vol. 3, London, Routledge and Kegan Paul.

HELD, D. (1984) 'Power and legitimacy in contemporary Britain', in G. McLENNAN, D. HELD and S. HALL (eds) *State and Society in Contemporary Britain*, Cambridge, Polity Press, pp. 299–369.

HELD, D. (1987) *Models of Democracy*, Cambridge, Polity Press.

HELD, D. and KEANE, J. (1984) 'Socialism and the limits of state action', in J. CURRAN (ed.) *The Future of the Left*, Cambridge, Polity Press, pp. 170–81.

KEANE, J. (1987) *Socialism and Civil Society*, London, Verso.

LEVITAS, R. (ed.) (1986) *The Ideology of the New Right*, Cambridge, Polity Press.

MACPHERSON, C. B. (1977) *The Life and Times of Liberal Democracy*, Oxford, Oxford University Press.

MCLENNAN, G. (1984) 'Capitalist state or democratic polity? Recent developments in Marxist and pluralist theory', in G. MCLENNAN *et al.*, pp. 80–109.

MCLENNAN, G. *et al.* (eds) (1984) *The Idea of the Modern State*, Milton Keynes, Open University Press.

NOZICK, R. (1974) *Anarchy, State and Utopia*, Oxford, Blackwell.

PATEMAN, C. (1970) *Participation and Democratic Theory*, Cambridge, Cambridge University Press.

PATEMAN, C. (1985) *The Problem of Political Obligation: a Critique of Liberal Theory*, Cambridge, Polity Press.

PIERSON, C. (1986) *Marxist Theory and Democratic Practice*, Cambridge, Polity Press.

POULANTZAS, N. (1980) *State, Power, Socialism*, London, Verso/New Left Books.

RUTLAND, P. (1985) *The Myth of the Plan*, London, Hutchinson.

# 2  Industrial Democracy
*Margaret Kiloh*

## 2.1  Introduction

Industrial or workplace democracy is frequently canvassed as a new form
or new application of the democratic principle, but the extent to which
industrial democracy is, in practice, either new or democratic depends
ultimately on the motivations of those proposing such schemes and on their
interpretation of the concept of democracy. Industrial democracy can only
be accepted as a new form in so far as it extends the practice of democratic
decision-making and control beyond the realm of the relationship between
individuals as *citizens* and the state into the realm of the relationship
between individuals as *workers* (or groups of workers) and their employers.

Unfortunately, discussion of industrial democracy suffers from even
more ambiguity than that of civic democracy. It is generally agreed that
industrial democracy is 'a good thing', but agreement as to the meaning
of the term, its justification, practical application and limitations is hard
to find. *What* is proposed is intimately connected with *why* it is proposed
and *who* is proposing it. For this reason it is necessary first to look at
the values and ideologies which lie behind different interpretations of
industrial democracy.

The discussion in this paper is divided into three sections. In the first
section (Section 2.2) I outline some of the arguments that have been put
forward for industrial democracy and the antecedents of the concept
in democratic theory. In the second (Section 2.3) I describe different
definitions and forms of industrial democracy and ways in which they may
be categorized, in terms of both institutional approach and relationship
to theoretical models of democracy. In the final section (Section 2.4) I
attempt to come to terms with the vital question, 'what are the prospects
for a genuine democratization of work?'

## 2.2  Why industrial democracy?

*The arguments*

Why industrial democracy? Arguments can be divided into those propounded
by what one might call democrats and those which are essentially
managerial. In the first case it is argued that, since work occupies so much
of our lives, it is at work that we are most qualified to contribute to decision-
making and most immediately affected by its results. However, with the
increasing size of firms, the concentration of economic power and the
centralization of decision-making, management has become more remote

and people have become unable to determine the shape of their own economic existence in the way that those who worked in pre-industrial societies were able to do (see Mills, 1959). This has as its consequence a feeling of powerlessness and alienation which in turn affects other aspects of life so that 'ordinary people are apt to resort to "world views" of an essentially passive, fatalistic and dependent kind' (Poole, 1978). In this way, the argument continues, the electorate are essentially 'disenfranchised' even when there is a democratic political system. They accept that they can exercise little or no influence over political decisions and none at all over economic ones; as a result, control remains in the hands of a minority and individuals fail to reach their full potential. Advocates of industrial democracy maintain that if the democratic ideal is to be fulfilled, social institutions, starting with the workplace, should be democratized. Industrial democracy will, it is claimed, produce better, more moral citizens and improve the quality of democratic government in a variety of ways.

Much of this advocacy is based upon an evolutionary view of the progressive development of industrial relations and a belief that there is an increasing demand for more participation in decision-making within society in general and the workplace in particular (Pateman, 1970; Bullock, 1977; Guest and Knight, 1979; Radice, 1978). According to this argument, improvements in education and the level of economic prosperity and security have led to a 'new era' of rising expectations and a crisis of legitimacy in which industry, as one of the last bastions of undemocratic behaviour within democratic society, is under siege. Evidence for this groundswell of democratic fervour is somewhat thin. Although there is certainly survey evidence which testifies to a general dissatisfaction with work and a desire for a greater say in decision-making (for example, Hanson and Rathkey, 1984; Heller *et al*. 1979), this shows that the desire for more say falls far short even of joint decision-making. Most studies point to a preference for day-to-day involvement in on-the-job decisions rather than a demand for widespread democracy.

Indeed, the belief that a demand for more democracy exists seems to rest to a large extent on a change in trade union policy in the early 1970s from hostility to a more positive attitude to certain forms of industrial democracy. Another important influence was the increased level of official and unofficial industrial disputes, many concerning issues of control, which were a feature of a relative period of full employment which characterized Western economies from the late 1950s until the early 1970s.

It was during this same period that the second group, whom I call managerialists, became interested in industrial democracy for quite different reasons. Like the democrats, managerialists recognize alienation and disaffection, but they are interested in the effect of this on economic performance rather than in its significance for the working of a democratic political system. They believe that 'Britain's industrial problems can only be successfully remedied by concerted action to improve the performance of industry' (Bullock, 1977). Industrial democracy is advocated as a means of promoting employee commitment and improving industrial relations, although there is little actual evidence that this is the case (Heller *et al.*, 1979).

These arguments are closely allied with those put forward by the 'human relations' school of industrial psychology, which explains human motivation in terms of a 'hierarchy' of needs, the highest of which is self-actualization (Maslow, 1954; Likert, 1961). According to this view, many problems, such as absenteeism, high labour turnover, low productivity, poor quality workmanship and strikes, can be attributed to inadequate consultation with workers and an over-authoritarian management style. Participation in decision-making is therefore seen as important not in terms of genuine power-sharing but of individual psychological needs or group dynamics: the key objective of industrial democracy is to improve job satisfaction and thence job performance and efficiency.

Proponents of this view include both members of the business community and elements of all the major political parties. The official 'business' view is epitomized by the response of the Confederation of British Industry to the recommendations of the Bullock Committee on Industrial Democracy (CBI, 1977). According to the CBI, the purpose of industrial democracy could be summed up in five basic objectives, none of which went further than discussion, information sharing, and the encouragement of a consensus perspective on the operation of capitalist production. Since then the Confederation has consistently opposed proposals for worker directors and the statutory enforcement of worker representation, and has proposed instead what it calls 'a flexible and realistic development of participation' (Cressey *et al.*, 1985).

In recent years the Commission of the European Community has proposed directives supporting both disclosure of information and the development of worker representation in decision-making. In the United Kingdom this has encouraged all four major parties to develop policies in this area, all of which to some extent emphasize the immediate benefits in terms of industrial efficiency and industrial relations. Such policies tend to be system-maintaining rather than system-transforming, combining managerial arguments with democratic rhetoric – or perhaps simply trying to have the best of both worlds. Such arguments, linking democratic decision-making with increased social consensus and improved economic performance, were put forward in Sweden during the debate which preceded the introduction there of legislation on industrial democracy, in the evidence to the Bullock Committee in Britain, and in the discussions in 1985 and 1986 on the formulation of Australian government policy on the issue. Whether or not industrial democracy lives up to this kind of rhetoric depends, however, on the theoretical underpinnings of proposals and the overall institutional framework in which they are set.

*The theoretical background*

At first sight many of the arguments put forward for industrial democracy have little connection with democratic theory. With the exceptions of Pateman and Dahl, whose contribution will be discussed later in this section, most contemporary discussion has taken place in the context of the study of management and industrial relations rather than of political philosophy. As a result, exhortation in terms of increased productivity or efficiency is more common than any mention of democratic rights or responsibilities. This is not to say, however, that democratic theory is of no relevance in understanding the ideological and normative background to contemporary proposals. On the contrary, there is a considerable body of ideas contributed from both liberal democratic and socialist perspectives with which it is useful to compare current policies and practices. Such ideas, although concerned with broad questions about human nature, the role of government and the relationship between the political and the economic spheres of society, provide alternative conceptual frameworks within which we can place industrial democracy (Held, 1987). Nineteenth-century liberal democratic theory has contributed a belief in the explicit separation of the 'private' economic and the 'public' political spheres and an interpretation of liberal democracy in terms of the protection of the right of all to pursue individual interests according to the rules of economic competition and free exchange. This interpretation forms the basis of the liberal democratic philosophy of the modern capitalist state and therefore has an important bearing on the debate about industrial democracy. To this, however, must be added the legacy of J. S. Mill and other 'developmental' democrats.

Mill believed that *participation* in decision-making was vital. Like Rousseau, he believed that it was an essential means of integrating individuals into the society to which they belong. He also thought that it would lead to the 'moral transformation' of individuals and of the community as a whole. While on the one hand he continued to emphasize the importance of a competitive market economy with private possession and control of the means of production, on the other he recognized the key role of industry and saw that as long as relationships of super- and subordination were retained in that field, the transformation could not be completed and the development of the individual and of the moral state would be constrained (Pateman, 1970).

This theme forms the basis of the socialist contribution to democratic theory. Liberal democratic theorists see private property as the cornerstone of social order; democratic political forms are advocated as a necessary means of protecting individual rights against state tyranny on the one hand and revolutionary demands from the lower classes on the other. Socialist theorists, in contrast, see private property and the political system which sustains it as the chief bulwark against the achievement of a genuine economic and political democracy in which each individual is free to develop his or her own talents and to make decisions without being prevented by economic and social constraints. A recurring theme among socialist theories is that of *industrial* democracy, with co-operative production as the main form of democratic participation in society. There are, however, considerable disagreements about how this is to be achieved and in particular about the role of the state in this transformation.

In the twentieth century, the actual experience of the working of representative forms of democracy in industrialized capitalist nations and of socialist 'people's democracies' has led to both conservative and radical critiques of each system which in many ways echo the discussions of the previous century, albeit in a new and infinitely more complex context. Without dwelling on the vast body of contemporary theory that is available, it is necessary to look at particular developments which either inform or engage explicitly in the current debate regarding the extension of democracy to the workplace.

One of the principal progenitors of these developments was Max Weber. Weber's interest lay less in the field of democratic theory than in organization theory and the theory of competing elites, but his contribution in both of these areas has influenced ideas relating to industrial democracy. His seminal work on bureaucracy is particularly important. Weber's rationale for its growth in capitalist enterprises and his dismissal of decentralization and direct democracy can and have been used as arguments against the adoption of alternative, more democratic systems of management. At the same time, *criticisms* of Weber's ideal type of bureaucracy have been used to support arguments in favour of the replacement of hierarchical systems of authority in industry on the grounds that they are unresponsive, inefficient, lacking in creativity and conducive to inequalities both within the enterprise and in society as a whole (see Christopher Pollitt's chapter for a summary of some of these arguments).

Weber's views on competing elites are also relevant to industrial democracy, mainly because of their influence on the development of pluralist theory. In his view, bureaucracy produces a passive, non-participatory electorate. Democratic politics therefore becomes the province of political parties, the main functions of which are the recruitment and training of elites, the articulation of competing ideas and interests, and the management of the electoral process. This reduction of democracy to a mechanism for legitimizing the authority of a political elite is elevated to a central element of Schumpeter's democratic theory. Here the advance of technology requires government by experts, and 'Democracy means only that the people have the opportunity of accepting or refusing the men who are to rule them' (Schumpeter, 1942, p. 284). This theory provides one of the rationales for regarding industrial democracy as being concerned with the representation of workers' interests by technically qualified individuals or union leaders rather than by direct participation. Such a view is reinforced by the pluralist model of liberal democracy which develops Weber's ideas on the existence of a number of different sources of power in opposition to Marx's insistence on the primacy of economic power in determining political outcomes.

In the pluralist model of society individuals are represented in a variety of capacities through their membership of a multiplicity of different groups. All compete for influence over the decision-making process, and since economic power is considered to have no determining role, its representation is thought to be no more important than any other. Inside the workplace pluralists see different groups of workers and managers as competing on equal terms within a set of democratically agreed industrial relations institutions. Outside the workplace trade unions are seen as performing the function of an industrial opposition party, using their power base among employees to negotiate agreements with employers, holding them accountable for their decisions, representing workers' interests at national level, and legitimating the decision-making process by their participation in the industrial relations system and by their compliance with its results.

Weber, Schumpeter and pluralists such as Dahl (in his early writing) draw on the 'protective' aspects of the liberal democratic tradition. They see liberal democracy as a means of protecting individual liberty from the power of the state, and competitive political parties and open elections as the best way of holding the state accountable for its actions, restraining the power of capital and controlling the activities of public and private bureaucracies. The level of individual participation thought to be necessary to ensure the effective operation of such a system is low. 'Democracy' is defined primarily as a *mechanism* giving the electorate a periodic veto over the abuse of power by a governing elite, and the opportunity to compete with others for influence over the decisions made by that elite.

A similar argument is deployed by members of what is often called the 'new right', for whom democracy is merely a formal device to safeguard the liberty of the individual – a liberty which embraces certain inalienable property rights. According to Chiplin and Coyne, it is 'the continual attenuation of the property rights of resource owners, particularly those entitled to the residual reward who might be deemed those with the strongest incentives' that has weakened industry, worsened industrial relations and reduced the ability to adapt to change and meet the requirements of a modern industrial society (Chiplin and Coyne, 1977, p. 26). Attempts to extend democracy by further attenuating property rights are therefore to be resisted.

In contrast to this approach are those latter-day supporters of developmental democracy such as Pateman and Macpherson, and neo-pluralists such as Lindblom and the 'born-again' Dahl. Whereas Dahl in his previous, archetypically pluralist analysis describes power as being non-cumulative and widely distributed throughout society by the process of competition and negotiation between interest groups, in his more recent work he has accepted that the role of corporate capital within Western industrialized society is such as to give it a completely disproportionate influence (Lindblom, 1977; Dahl, 1985).

Lindblom makes no recommendation as to how this situation might be remedied, but Dahl proposes the establishment of new, non-corporate forms of ownership, such as co-operatives. Dahl argues that if democracy is justified in governing the state, then it must also be justified in governing economic enterprises. It is important to note, however, that although he believes there is a strong justification for the extension of democracy to industry as an end in itself, the main motive for this proposal is not the extension of democratic participation *per se*. He continues to adhere to the idea of a protective liberal democracy and merely seeks to iron out some imperfections in the model.

Difficulties in extending democracy are acknowledged by Pateman, who accepts that politics at the national level may necessarily conform more to a competitive pluralist than a participatory model. Nevertheless, she argues, following Mill, that democracy cannot work properly until people are educated in the process of decision-making and given the opportunity for effective participation in it. For her, democracy in the workplace is important not only because it constrains the power of corporate capital, but also because it gives employees experience of participation in the political process at an immediate level and develops skills which they can use in the operation of the wider democratic system outside.

It is for this reason that Pateman in particular has been concerned not only to advocate industrial democracy but also to consider the implications of the different *forms* that might be adopted.

## 2.3   What is industrial democracy?

It is difficult to decide what criteria should be used to determine the notion of industrial democracy, given an industrial context which, superficially at least, is far removed from the political context in which we are more accustomed to making such judgements. Analogies can, however, be found. As Dahl points out, like the state, 'a firm can also be viewed as a political system in which relations of power exist between governments and the governed' (Dahl, 1985, p. 115). In many ways the government of industry can be likened to the government of Britain before the Reform Acts, when wealth and political power remained in the hands of a few, the majority were denied any role in decision-making, and the population was effectively divided into rulers and ruled. In industry today a similar situation prevails. Employers and employees stand on either side of a power relationship in which the employer's right to the monopoly of decision-making is legitimized either by the ownership of capital or by the administrative powers of the state. How, then, can such a situation be democratized? The answer to this question depends on the different definitions of democracy employed, and involves many of the same arguments used in the debate about political democracy.

*Definitions*
Definitions may be divided into those which emphasize participation by employees in the taking of decisions in the workplace within a framework of *joint control*, and those which emphasize *workers' control*. Within each of these categories there are, however, a number of different definitions of what is meant by participation and what is meant by workers' control.

Coates has suggested that the term 'workers' control' is commonly used to cover two quite distinct concepts, one referring to socialized industries and signifying the management of the industries by the workers, the other, in the context of capitalist industry, referring to a situation in which 'militant Trade Unions have been able to wrest some, or most, of the prerogatives of management from the unilateral disposition of managers' (Coates, 1968). The term has also been used to describe a variety of different organizations, including co-operatives with individual share ownership, trade union-run enterprises such as those operated by the Histadrut in Israel, and various kinds of state-owned industry.

Most definitions of workers' control have their roots in socialism, but there is also a stream of thought which springs from liberal democracy. One of the earliest definitions of industrial democracy in the British context was given by Mill, who proposed 'the association of the labourers themselves on terms of equality, collectively owning the capital with which they carry on their operations and working under managers elected and removable by themselves', a method of production which Mill believed would realize 'the best aspiration of the democratic spirit' (Mill, 1910). This definition accords both with a liberal democratic view of democracy, based on individual property rights, and with Mill's own emphasis on a developmental participatory democracy.

Historically, however, the concept of workers' control has been linked most closely with syndicalism, which has its origins in French nineteenth-century socialism and in the work of Georges Sorel and Tom Mann. Syndicalists believe that the kind of industrial democracy advocated by Mill cannot entail true workers' control since it does nothing to change the system of 'wage slavery' on which economic and political domination is based. Workers' control is defined as the overthrow of capitalism by means of revolutionary economic action by industrially organized trade unions and its replacement by a system in which workers become the owners of the means of production and 'citizens of the industry in which they are employed rather than the subjects of the state in which they reside' (*The Industrial Syndicalist*, 1974). Syndicalists reject proposals for joint control by management and trade unions as being a means of weakening the working-class struggle for democratic control, but they also oppose *state* ownership as being a means of buttressing the interests of the ruling class against those of employees. This philosophy had a significant impact on the organization of the shop stewards' movement during the First World War and on the ideas of G. D. H. Cole and the Guild Socialists, who espoused and experimented with non-revolutionary means of bringing about workers' control by both political and economic routes. It continues to exercise an influence over the British labour movement today. Of far greater influence, however, has been the strongly centralist tendency which is most clearly represented in the writing of Sidney and Beatrice Webb.

For the Webbs, democracy was not an instrument of revolt against an alien regime but the embodiment of the sovereign power of the people already achieved in parliamentary form. They believed it to be both unnecessary and undemocratic for managers to be responsible to, or elected by, 'those whose functions involve obedience' and that 'democracies of producers cannot be trusted with the ownership of the instruments of production of their own vocations' (Webb and Webb, 1920). Given this legacy, it is not surprising that for many in the trade unions and the Labour Party, as well as on the management side of industry, industrial democracy is defined not as workers' control but as *joint* control by capital and labour.

For a great many of those involved the essence of industrial democracy appears to be the *participation* of workers in the taking of decisions in the workplace. But 'participation' means different things to different people, and different parties may also be operating with different definitions of *democracy*. In judging employee participation as evidence of the existence of industrial democracy we must therefore ask some supplementary questions about the kind of democracy that is being aimed at, the degree and scope of participation, the area of decision-making concerned, and whether participation is *de facto*, *de jure*, or both.

First of all, *who* is it that participates in joint decision-making? Is it individual workers, groups of workers delineated by task or occupation, trade union or other elected representatives? Is it men or women, blue- or white-collar employees, skilled or unskilled, full or part-time, native or immigrant workers? Secondly, *where* does the participation take place, i.e. at what level in the decision-making structure? Is it at shop-floor, plant or industry level? Do workers participate only through the formal structures of an enterprise or are they represented in the informal decision-making process? And are there any ways in which workers may participate at a national or an international level? Thirdly, *what* decisions are jointly determined? Are employees involved in the making of executive policy decisions of the kind previously regarded as the prerogative of management alone, or only in the application of such decisions or in day-to-day issues such as job redesign? Finally, and most important of all, what degree of *power* do employees have to ensure that their participation will be effective?

A number of definitions make this a central question. Emery and Thorsrud (1969), for example, define industrial democracy as 'a distribution of the social power in industry so that it tends to be shared out among all who are engaged in the work rather than concentrated in the hands of a minority'. According to this argument, the ability of employees to participate effectively depends on the amount of power they are able to command. Thus Pateman has distinguished between (a) 'pseudo' participation, in which employees are manipulated to accept decisions that have already been taken by management, (b) 'partial' participation, in which they can influence decisions but management retains the ultimate power, and (c) 'full' participation, in which employers and employees have *equal* power to determine the outcome. Much depends, however, on how power is conceptualized and on the perceived relationship between power and control.

As Poole (1978) points out, many advocates of employee participation appear to have a concept of *manifest* power which is based on the institutional pattern of control within organizations and the range of issues over which the different parties have a formal influence. For them participation is itself an expression of power and therefore a major means of augmenting employee control over work. This view, however, ignores the equal importance of the *latent* power of the parties involved, i.e. the economic and ideological resources at their disposal which determine their ability to achieve given ends.

Control within organizations may be based on either a 'unitarist-mechanistic' system, which emphasizes hierarchical control, or on a 'pluralist-organic' model which emphasizes the community of interests of employers and employees. In the first of these the ability of employers to control decision-making rests on the ownership of the means of production and on an ideology which legitimates individual property rights. Employees frequently share this ideology, and although other interests are recognized,

> certain interests are taken for granted and therefore given a practical priority; other interests have to be more explicitly struggled for and contested and, because they are not taken for granted, are more obtrusive and open to question. This reality is expressed through that hierarchical element of organization and the uneven distribution of power in the enterprise which that expresses. (Cressey *et al.*, 1985, p. 128)

The pluralist-organic model of organization, on the other hand, claims to reflect the democratic norms that have ostensibly been accepted in *political* life, seeking to bring about a mutually advantageous consensus by the extension of participation to employees in the decision-making process. In recognition of the split that has taken place between ownership and control and the increase in the extent of public employment, managers lay claim to a legitimate authority which is based on professionalism and technocratic skills rather than on property rights; control is exercised through consent rather than coercion.

Thurley (1984) has suggested that each type of control system may be associated with a different kind of participation arrangement, with unitary authoritarian systems tending towards consultation or bargaining arrangements with employees, and pluralist systems resulting in project team co-operation, in which consultation and participation are part of the normal decision-making process around the solution of particular issues. This categorization is useful but it ignores both the complexity of real-life organizations and the sources of the power on which control is based. In real life, things are not so clear cut: few organizations fall neatly into either control category. As a result, different forms of industrial democracy may mean different things in different circumstances.

*Alternative models*
Alternative models may be divided into those which emphasize:
(a) democratization of the terms of employment,
(b) democratization of ownership,
(c) democratization of the government of work, and
(d) democratization of the process of management (see Walker, 1970).
These are not exclusive categories and, as we shall see, a number of models combine one or more of these elements. Nevertheless, it is useful to identify the main differences in this way before comparing the models' strengths and weaknesses and their claims to be a new form of democracy.

*Democratization of terms of employment.*
One way of achieving greater control by employees is through the extension of workers' *rights*, either by collective bargaining or by means of legislation. Collective bargaining, either of the traditional variety, which concentrates on the negotiation of wages, or of the extended kind, which takes in issues of control, is usually *contrasted* with industrial democracy. Industrial democracy is seen by some as a means of fostering co-operation and unity of purpose, whereas collective bargaining is seen as being based on conflicts of interest. Others, however, see collective bargaining either as a form of industrial democracy or as an important means of achieving it. One such argument is that put forward by Hugh Clegg, whose definition of industrial democracy by his own acknowledgement owes much to the traditions of liberal thought.

According to Clegg, 'the political and industrial institutions of the stable democracies already approach the best that can be realized'. Therefore proposals for workers' control would only undermine the *existing* institutions of industrial democracy already developed under capitalism (Clegg, 1960). Clegg's view of democracy is based on the principle of *opposition*, which ensures the existence of checks on those in power, in industry as well as politics. In political life it is the existence of parties that ensures the continuation of democracy; in industry it is the existence of an independent trade union movement. For this reason, industrial democracy cannot mean co-operation or consensus between trade unions and management.

At the same time, he argues, like the Webbs, that the trade unions do not (and, by implication, cannot) have the technical and administrative expertise necessary to run large-scale industry. Their role is not to manage or to govern but to prevent abuses of power by those who do. For this reason public ownership will make no difference as far as industrial democracy is concerned. In the same way that political opposition is necessary under both capitalism and socialism, if democracy is to be retained, trade union opposition is necessary whatever the form of ownership might be.

This argument has come in for considerable criticism (see Blumberg, 1968). In the first place, it has been pointed out that the definition of democracy in terms of opposition is somewhat naive since, as many former pluralists are now coming to realize, it is necessary for an opposition to be *effective* if democracy is to be guaranteed. The effectiveness of an opposition can be measured by its ability to influence those in power, and to hold them accountable for their actions by facilitating their removal and replacement by alternative leaders. Trade unions do exert some influence over employers and do succeed in modifying management behaviour, although the extent to which they are able to do so is extremely variable. What they cannot do, however, is to hold employers *accountable* for their actions in any meaningful way, largely because, unlike political parties, they are unable to replace them and assume power themselves.

Furthermore, in a political democracy the authority of government derives its legitimacy from the consent of its citizens as expressed through the electoral process, whereas in industry control is considered to be a *prerogative* of employers conferred by ownership. In Clegg's model, unions are expected to be 'an opposition which can never become a government'. The elected trade union representatives of employees are *excluded* from power, which is monopolized by a self selected elite – hardly a democracy by any definition.

Yet another criticism has been made by critics on the left. These argue that although collective bargaining makes the disjunction of interests between capital and labour clear, Clegg's dichotomy between collective bargaining and co-determination is false, since both perform a similar integrative function. Thus the real function of the routinization of industrial conflict is not to challenge management control but 'to institutionalize inequalities between manager and managed' (Eldridge, 1973, p. 161; Herding, 1972).

So trade unions are not an opposition to the capitalist government of industry but a part of it (Clarke, 1977).

This interpretation of the role of trade unions has itself been disputed. Coates and Topham (1974) argue that both Clegg's account of a trade union 'opposition' and Clarke's characterization of trade unions as simply a tool of a management control strategy distort the democratic function of the labour movement. They point out that trade unions have for many years provided the basis on which the working class has entered into parliamentary democracy to achieve social and economic reforms and to alter the power relations that exist in society. The role of trade unions is to increase democratic influences in *both* government and industry, bargaining to extend employees' control over a whole range of new issues, while at the same time attempting to use political democracy to introduce an egalitarian system of ownership to replace capitalism.

To the extent that trade unions seek to establish control over areas previously considered 'management's', it is argued that 'the germs of workers' control exist, in greater or lesser degree, wherever strong independent trade union and shop-floor powers act to restrain employers in the exercise of their so-called "prerogatives"' (Coates and Topham, 1974). Until the question of ownership is solved, this kind of workers' control must always exist in conflict with management. It varies in degree according to the relative strength of different groups of workers, 'and is at the best only a partial and limited form of democratic restraint against authoritarianism'. Nevertheless, for Coates and Topham, it is on this form of day-to-day trade union activity that any conscious movement for workers' control must be based.

*Legislation.* One way in which employees have tried to extend their employment rights and to supplement collective bargaining is by the use of the law. Legislation may be basically *protective*, curbing the excessive use of power by employers without essentially changing the employment relationship; it may be designed to extend *positive* new rights to employees; or it may be used to buttress the power of employers and to reduce that of employees.

In the United Kingdom legislation has, until recently, performed a primarily protective and regulating function, although its scope has been progressively extended. Historically British labour regulation is founded on 'masters and servants' legislation. It was trade union agitation that led to the eventual repeal of this legislation and to the introduction of the concept of a reciprocal contract between employer and employee, but the law has continued to consider the relationship in terms of *individual* contracts of employment. The extension of rights that has taken place under such legislation as the Employment Protection Acts of 1975 and 1978 and the 1970 Equal Pay Act is an extension of individual rights. It uses the power of the law to make employers legally accountable in certain areas but it is still essentially protective and does little to extend employees' control over decisions in the workplace. The contract remains primarily 'a relation between a bearer of power and one who is not a bearer of power' (Kahn-Freund, 1977 p. 6).

There is as yet no equivalent in the United Kingdom to the *positive* trade union freedoms that are guaranteed by legislation or by constitution elsewhere in Europe. This is largely because trade union organization and extra-parliamentary struggle preceded the granting of democratic political rights to working people. The historical development of trade union legislation has meant the gradual repeal of laws expressly concerned to suppress trade unions and the establishment of a series of statutory immunities from prosecution without which the unions could not lawfully have fulfilled their basic functions (Lewis, 1983). The result of this process has been a voluntary system of collective bargaining in which legal intervention has played a secondary role.

According to one view, this principle of industrial self-government with minimal state regulation can be seen as part of a wider pluralist democracy. However, without legal guarantees of their basic democratic rights trade unions are vulnerable to changes in judicial interpretation of the law and must rely on their industrial strength or on the goodwill of employers. In times of economic growth they may be able to extend their control, but there is a danger that this will be lost again in times of recession. Moreover, the lack of positive democratic rights tends to mean that whereas employers' property rights are recognized, trade union activity is perceived as being essentially *illegitimate*. It has also been easier for governments to introduce new legislation which effectively weakens the power of trade unions whether indirectly, by boosting the individual rights of members at the expense of the organizational strength of unions, or directly, like the 1971 Industrial Relations Act and subsequent Conservative legislation, by creating new civil liabilities. Such legislation, by insisting on the individual character of the employment contracts, restricts the ability of unions to equalize their power with that of employers.

Other European countries differ greatly from the United Kingdom. For example, it is a feature of the West German system of codetermination that both the institutional form and the content of relations in the workplace are laid down by law. However, as Marsden (1978) has noted, this tends to disguise the fact that the interplay of interests is much the same as in any other country and that legislation not only provides a framework but is the *result* of such struggles.

Codetermination (*Mitbestimmung*) was first established in the German coal and steel industry in 1947 as a result of trade union pressure, and was only guaranteed by law in 1951. Thereafter its modification and extension to other industries has been accompanied by debate and disagreement at every stage, as has the manner of its operation. The legislation is notable for the way in which it distinguishes three quite separate varieties of democratic right, each embodied in a different institution and relating to a particular set of issues. Negotiating rights, including the right to strike, are accorded to trade unions and employers' associations which determine national wage rates and conditions of employment. At the level of the firm, the institutions concerned are the works council, the management board, the supervisory board and the economic committee. Unions are excluded from both the works councils, which consist of employee representatives who have rights of 'codecision' with the employer (represented by the management board) over certain specified issues, and (in most cases) from the supervisory board, on which employee-elected directors have co-operative joint decision-making rights to participate in strategic planning and oversee the activities of the management board.

In Sweden, too, legislation is the result of economic and political action by employees, but different circumstances have led to a different emphasis. There the tradition of partnership between trade unions and Social Democratic governments has resulted in unions playing a more central role. A series of laws during the 1970s, including the 1976 Work Environment Act and the Joint Regulation of Working Life and the Public Employment Acts of 1977, regularized the long-standing participation agreements between unions and employers and strengthened the position of trade unions in a number of respects. These included board representation, codetermination and the status of shop stewards at workplaces and the abolition of the legal recognition of management's sole prerogative in areas of work organization, hiring and firing.

Among members of the EEC, Britain is the odd one out in terms of industrial democracy legislation. Despite a number of EEC initiatives on the issue, there has been little attempt by the Thatcher government to come into line. However, legislation alone cannot guarantee effective democratic participation. It will inevitably reflect the relative power balance of the respective parties at the time of its enactment, and its operation will be affected both by the values of the constituent organizations and by changes which may take place in the external environment.

## Democratization of ownership

Models which emphasize the democratization of *ownership* rest on the belief that economic and political power are based on, and legitimated by, the ownership of capital. All such models seek to transfer a share of ownership to employees, but the extent to which this takes place and the method whereby it is brought about differ considerably and are based on contrasting models of democracy. As Carnoy and Shearer (1980) point out, 'within capitalist societies there are at least two general forms of employee ownership. The first is management initiated and the second worker initiated'. To this can be added a third which is politically initiated.

*Management initiatives.* Management-initiated forms include: (a) profit sharing; (b) individual shareholding schemes in which shares (or the option to purchase shares) are offered as part of the remuneration of employees; (c) employee buy-outs, in which employees, together with management or members of the local community, raise the loan capital to buy out their employers; and (d) common ownership trusts or partnerships, set up by philanthropic employers, in which ownership usually resides not in individuals but in the working community as a group.

Employee share ownership and in particular employee buy-outs have been suggested as a strategy that not only smooths the readjustment of the economy at minimal cost in times of change but also breaks the pattern of poor industrial relations and helps to establish industrial consensus (Bradley and Gelb, 1983). Such schemes are popular with politicians who see them as a way of increasing employees' commitment to their firms and of restraining 'unreasonable' wage demands. In the USA, legislation has been used to encourage the setting up of Employee Stock Ownership Plans (ESOPs). In the UK the Conservative Party has encouraged share ownership by means of tax incentives. Less predictably, perhaps, the Labour Party has also announced that employee share ownership is 'wholly consistent with the aims of socialism' and 'in the interests of economic success and social cohesion' (the *Observer*, 16 March 1986).

So far, however, the democratization of ownership via shareholding has been slow. Although a number of large firms with household names such as ICI, Sainsbury and Cadbury-Schweppes operate share ownership schemes, by 1986 fewer than 15 per cent of British companies had introduced schemes covering all workers, and only a handful (among them the denationalized National Freight Consortium and the John Lewis Partnership) had majority employee share ownership, partnership or common ownership arrangements. The round of Conservative 'privatization' of publicly owned industries in the 1980s gave rise to a number of attempts by management and employees to raise sufficient capital to take over a variety of different organizations including British Leyland, British Airways, the Devonport Dockyard and Vickers Shipbuilding. In none of these was the proposed employee stake anything like the 80 per cent achieved in the successful National Freight buy-out in 1982. At Vickers the transfer of ownership entailed only 20 per cent of shares guaranteed for local people (including employees), while the (unsuccessful) BA bid initially included executives only and was only extended to employees when the original proposal failed to raise enough money.

This highlights the fact that in many such management-initiated schemes the motivation for the proposals is not the democratization of control but the encouragement of co-operation or the raising of funds. The effect of ownership arrangements on *decision-making* is highly variable, and management in firms with a minority or majority employee shareholding may well be as bureaucratic and hierarchical as in any others.

*Worker initiatives.* Worker-initiated schemes to democratize ownership include public ownership, trade union-owned enterprises and co-operatives. Despite their relatively long history, co-operatives are still decidedly rare. In 1985 Britain had some 1000 workers' co-operatives, employing from between two or three to almost five hundred people, a total of some 8000, which, even if the rapid growth rate of the last ten years continues, would rise to only around 25 000 by the next decade (the *Guardian*, 26 November 1985). Not all co-operatives are directly worker-initiated. Some are of the 'endowed' variety already listed under management-initiated schemes. Some, like those sponsored by the Greater London Enterprise Board, may be municipally supported, while others, particularly in underdeveloped countries, have been the result of political initiatives. Those which are worker-initiated may either be 'rescues' of failing firms (often after worker sit-ins), or 'fresh start' co-operatives, the motive for which may or may not be to initiate a democratically owned and controlled enterprise. There is a variety of possible financial arrangements, some emphasizing individual contributions and some collective ownership, some linking voting rights to the size of financial holdings, and some giving equal rights to all members of the workforce.

The scope for the extension of co-operative ownership as an alternative to private and state capitalism is a matter for debate. Despite the support of the then Industry Secretary, Anthony Wedgwood Benn, for the 'rescue' co-operatives at Triumph Meriden, Kirkby Manufacturing and Engineering and the Scottish Daily News in the mid-1970s, the majority of the trade union movement and the Labour Party has shown little interest in extending co-operative ownership. This lack of enthusiasm is echoed in the Conservative Party. Some resources are available to workers' co-operatives through the Co-operative Development Agency and the Industrial Common Ownership Movement, but growth is restricted by present legal and financial structures and by the operation of the market itself. Company law currently makes it difficult for employees to turn private companies into worker co-operatives, and banks are reluctant to provide the necessary long-term capital to organizations with anything other than strictly commercial objectives.

Were it not for the existence of the flourishing group of co-operatives at Mondragon in the Basque region of Spain, one would be tempted to write off the possibility of any substantial growth in the co-operative sector without a radical change in government philosophy. But the expansion at Mondragon from an initial co-operative of five members in 1956 to a group of over eighty, employing some 18 000 members, in 1980 demonstrates that spontaneous growth *is* possible, given the right circumstances.

It is, perhaps, somewhat surprising that British trade unions have not involved themselves more in extending employee influence through their ownership of shares. Not all trade unions are rich but, as the sequestration of union funds in 1985–6 demonstrated, some trade unions *may* control very large funds indeed, sometimes accompanied by considerable influence over pension funds. Despite this there has been little or no attempt by trade unions to involve themselves actively as a partner in management- or worker-initiated employee ownership schemes. Even the setting up of a 'trade union' investment bank (the Unity Trust) in 1984 seems to have made little difference. This bank exists to provide employment and to regenerate industry in depressed areas but, at the time of writing, there is little sign that this power will also be used to set up trade union-*controlled* enterprises or ones that are more democratically run.

This is not the case with all trade union movements. There is a number of examples of trade unions in other countries which run their own enter- prises. For trade union movements such as the Histadrut in Israel the operation of trade union enterprises is an important aspect of their activities. The Histadrut operates agricultural, industrial and consumer co-operatives as well as a large number of non-co-operative 'administered' enterprises and some partnerships with private concerns aimed at setting up new enterprises and creating jobs. Initially such companies were organized on traditional hierarchical lines, but since 1966 workers' representatives have been elected to nearly all central managements and there has been an attempt to introduce joint management boards wherever possible (Ben Aaron, 1974). There are, however, still strong prejudices against such schemes in Britain, not least from those within the labour movement who see a basic contradiction in trade unions becoming employers.

According to Marx and many of his followers, state ownership of the means of production is the only means of genuinely democratizing work. However, the experience of the operation of a state-owned economy in the Soviet Union and other Eastern European countries has cast doubt on the extent to which systems of this kind are necessarily democratic in practice. *Theoretically*, the transfer of ownership from private hands to the state removes the differences of class interest between owners and workers, and gives everybody an equal share and therefore an equal say in the operation of the economy. But as Lewis (1986) suggests, it is difficult to judge the effectiveness of participation at the local level. Until the death of Stalin, 'scientific management' was the paramount system of work organization in the Soviet Union and the other planned economies of Eastern Europe (see Haraszti, 1985). In addition, centralization and bureaucratization of the economy meant that even management had very little autonomy. Since then there has been a degree of economic reform throughout Eastern Europe, and 'self-management' has even been given the imprimatur of the new Soviet Party Programme (Dyker, 1986), but history has taught us enough to know that public ownership does not automatically equal democratic control.

Lest we get complacent about this situation and attribute it solely to the failings of the communist system, let it be said that much the same applies to public ownership in the UK. Clause 4 of the consititution of the Labour Party proposes the 'common ownership' of industry in order to secure for employees control over their own work. Despite pressure from workers in the industries involved, however, the nationalizations by the 1945 Labour government explicitly rejected employee *control* over their industries and substituted instead systems of joint consultation which were to a large extent ineffective.

Those experiments which have taken place in the nationalized sector, such as the appointment of worker directors to the Post Office Board and the subsidiary boards of the British Steel Corporation, have proved less than completely successful. Meanwhile, the policy of the Conservative Party has been to return as much of the public sector to private ownership (including employee share ownership) as it can.

An alternative to large-scale nationalization as a form of public ownership is posed by proposals such as the 'Meidner Plan' for wage-earner funds which have been put forward in Denmark and Sweden. These schemes operate in a variety of ways, being based on either voluntary or compulsory contributions from employers and wage-earners at industry, regional or national level. A major function of such funds is to provide capital for invest-ment, and they are perfectly compatible with the retention of a capitalist market economy. At their most radical, they provide a means of transferring ownership and control to employees and other members of the community (see Öhman, 1983). However, no such radical schemes have so far been adopted. In a major policy statement issued in 1986 the Labour Party took a fresh look at its constitutional commitment to common ownership and came up with a package of proposals for what it now calls 'social ownership', which showed the influence of such ideas. This included full public owner-ship of some industries, a major government stake in others and support for worker co-ops and 'democratic employee share ownership plans'. Mention was made of industrial democracy and consumer involvement in socially owned industries, but the emphasis is on forms of ownership (including the retention of individual share ownership) rather than on the details of what is meant by democratic control and how this might be achieved.

Whether or not state ownership is democratic depends on the form of control that is exercised and on the definition of democracy that is used. For many liberal democrats, wholesale state ownership is the *negation* of democracy, since it denies individual liberty and the right to the enjoyment of property. For others, the question of whether ownership is public or private is irrelevant to the issue, either because, like Schumpeter, they define democracy purely in terms of institutions and mechanisms, or because, like Mill and other 'developmental' democrats, they define democracy in terms of the level of individual participation in decision-making. On the whole, however, the examples of public ownership in the Soviet Union and the UK appear to show that, whether or not Marx was right to suggest that public ownership is a *necessary* condition before work (or society) can be effectively democratized, it certainly is not *sufficient*. Only when public ownership is combined with explicitly democratic mechanisms for representing employees' interests, whether through the political system or in the workplace, or both, can it have the effect of democratizing the control of industry.

## Democratization of the government of work

In this section we shall be looking at forms of industrial democracy which are based on democratization of the government of work. First, though, it is necessary to define what this means. The easiest way of doing so is to return to the political analogy.

In the political sphere it is the government that decides policies, makes the rules and administers their implementation. The government of an enterprise performs the same function for that enterprise. It determines policy and oversees the implementation of that policy, but it is not involved in the day-to-day management of the firm. As in the political sphere, it operates within a broad legislative framework and, as in the political sphere, there is usually a number of different levels of government (branch, industry, national subsidiary, multinational headquarters) which have both a formal and an informal relationship to each other.

It is generally agreed that the main condition for a government to be considered democratic is that it must pass a minimum test of accountability: that is, it must be subject to regular ratification and to replacement by those who are subject to its authority. There are, however, other conditions which may be attached according to one's definition of democracy. In the economic sphere the same main condition applies. That is, for the government of an enterprise to be considered democratic it must *at the very least* be accountable to the workforce of that enterprise in the same way that, in the political sphere, a government is accountable to its citizens; the workforce must participate, either directly or indirectly, in the making of decisions and management must be subordinate to the overall control of the employees.

Various suggestions for the democratization of the government of industry have been made, some of which have already been mentioned. Co-operatives and employee shareholding are discussed below. Public ownership without any intervening democratic mechanisms cannot, however, be accepted as a means of democratizing the government of work since it provides no means of making the governments of *particular* enterprises accountable to their employees. A process whereby the management of enterprises is accountable to the state and the state is accountable to its citizens is in reality too remote to qualify for the use of the term.

(Public or social ownership, combined with intermediate levels of democratic control, is a different matter and will be discussed under the headings of worker directors and self-management.)

*Worker directors.* One of the most common proposals for the democratization of the government of work is the appointment of worker directors to the governing boards of companies. Such proposals are based on two similar but, in reality, quite different arguments. On the one hand it is argued that neither change of ownership nor schemes for participation at lower levels can be effective in bringing about democratic control unless workers are represented on the chief policy-making bodies of institutions. Alternatively, the case is made that only by involving employees in the government structure of each work community can their compliance with its rules be ensured and their commitment guaranteed. The first is an egalitarian argument, the second is not. This said, it is striking that very few of the actual proposals for worker directors involve any suggestion that employees should choose all, or even the majority, of those who govern them.

Much attention has been focused on West Germany, where employee representatives on the supervisory boards of large companies have long formed the pinnacle of the system of codetermination, and on the operation of schemes in Sweden, Norway and other European countries. It is not surprising therefore that, following the publication by the European Community in 1972 of draft proposals for employee representation on the supervisory boards of companies in the Community and the decision to issue an EEC Green Paper in 1975, the British Labour Government itself set up a committee of inquiry (the Bullock Committee).

The motives for setting up the Committee were largely managerial. Its terms of reference accepted 'the need for a radical extension of industrial democracy in the control of companies by means of representation on boards of directors' and 'the essential role of trade union organizations in this process'. The Committee recommended the introduction of re-constituted boards of directors for companies, which would consist of equal numbers of shareholders' and employees' representatives, plus a smaller number of co-opted board members to be chosen with the agreement of both sides (the $2X + Y$ formula). Employee representatives were to be nominated by workplace unions acting together in a Joint Representation Committee.

It is clear from the context in which the Bullock Committee was appointed that one of the main reasons for setting up the inquiry, and for the particular terms of reference it was given, was the inflationary impact on the British economy of the then increase in shopfloor bargaining and the passing on to consumers of consequent wage rises.

In order to curb this tendency government was prepared to replace a spontaneous form of industrial democracy based on collective bargaining by shop stewards in the workplace by board level representation which would involve the whole workforce 'in sharing responsibility for the success and profitability of the enterprise'. The TUC, in turn, was concerned to re-establish the control exercised by the official trade union hierarchy over 'unofficial' elements who were making demands for an increasing role in decision-making within their own workplaces. At least two clear features are discernible in the majority Report: a preference for *indirect* representative democracy, as opposed to a direct participative model, and a collectivist, as opposed to an individualist, conception of representation.

One of the major issues highlighted in the Bullock Report was that of minority versus parity representation on the board. Where representatives were in the minority, as in Sweden, it was noted that experience had shown that the ability of employees to influence decision-making was restricted by their representatives' lack of control over the composition of committees of the board and their inability to gain access to the information they needed.

Other evidence specially commissioned by the Committee suggested that even when there was an equal number of employee representatives on the board, as in parts of West German industry, 'the worker director is used both directly and indirectly as a lever in the hands of management', and that although worker directors were expected to take joint responsibility for decisions, they rarely had a significant say in them (Batstone and Davies, 1976).

What is noticeable about *all* these schemes, including Bullock's proposal, is that none of them could ever lead to a democratically accountable government of industry, since in none of them are employee representatives in the majority on the board. As Clarke (1977) points out, the fundamental weakness of Bullock was that it legitimated and sustained *capitalist* control of industry. Two political analogies for what was proposed spring to mind. The first is those colonial legislatures of the British Empire in which a small number of native representatives sat surrounded by seats reserved for official nominees of the colonial state and members of the economically dominant white minority. The second is the pre-reform parliaments of the nineteenth and early twentieth centuries in which representation was based on the ownership of property and on economic interests rather than on any concept of universal suffrage.

The Bullock Report was concerned solely with the private sector. At the time of the Report, however, there was already in existence a scheme for worker directors within the nationalized British Steel Corporation. This involved a minority of part-time worker directors on divisional boards or management committees (but not the main board). Opinions differ as to the success of the scheme. Brannen (Brannen *et al.*, 1976; Brannen, 1983) argues that because management had the monopoly of power and 'because the board was not really the place where it occurred the worker directors had no effect on the decision making process'. Bank and Jones (1977) disagree, citing the view of the employee directors themselves that, despite the shortcomings of their situation, they did exercise considerable influence on decisions, and with greater union interest and backing would have been able to do much more.

In 1978 a fresh experiment was introduced in the Post Office. This employed the $2X + Y$ formula recommended by Bullock with representatives nominated by the unions, although appointed by the Minister. According to Batstone *et al*. (1983), the Post Office union nominees did not adopt a managerial approach like their BSC counterparts, but tried to manipulate boardroom norms, and to challenge management assumptions. On the other hand, the extent to which they influenced union and worker attitudes was 'remarkably limited', and they had 'relatively little impact upon the outcome of board discussions'. The fundamental differences in union and management rationales concerning industrial democracy were reflected in the boardroom, and there was little indication of the formation of a consensus view on policy. With the change of government and the subsequent change to a more market-oriented approach in the Post Office in 1979, the scheme was discontinued.

In considering the impact of worker directors on the democratization of the government of work it is necessary to consider the nature and role of the board (which may vary between companies), the organizational form and the nature of the production process, and the influence of individuals and powerful interest groups. But as Batstone *et al*. suggest, 'Schemes that are sufficiently strong to minimize the risk of worker "incorporation" are likely to be opposed by management, and hence are likely to occur on any large scale only in a political climate favourable to the extension of worker and union power'.

*A shareholding democracy?* What effect does employee shareholding have on democracy? In the case of minority shareholding the answer must be 'very little' and even for majority shareholding 'not much'. It is part of the ideology of capitalism that shareholding confers on the shareholder the right to a democratic say in the policy-making of the enterprise which legitimates the decisions made. In practice, of course, shareholders' democracy is largely a myth. Quite apart from the fact that not all shares carry voting rights, virtually the only chance for individual shareholders to participate in any way is at the Annual General Meeting or in specially held ballots on issues such as a takeover bid. On such occasions a formal democratic *procedure* is adhered to, but since voting depends on the number of shares held, there is not even any formal equality between shareholders. The pattern of shareholding in Britain at the time of writing in the mid-1980s is such that 60 per cent are held by institutional shareholders (other companies, banks, pension funds, insurance societies, etc.) and only 40 per cent by individuals. The *areas* of decision-making with which shareholders are directly concerned are also strictly limited. Policy is made not at the AGM but by the board of directors or its sub-committees; furthermore, although some directors may be elected, others are appointed and accountable to shareholders only in the broadest sense. Most shareholders are satisfied as long as the firm is making a profit, and many do not consider themselves to be in any real sense the owners of companies.

It can be said in favour of employee share ownership that at least it makes available to employees the kind of financial information that is given to shareholders, but this in itself may convey little. Individual employee shareholders can exercise very little influence compared to that wielded by institutional shareholders – particularly if they represent interests which are in conflict with the profit motive. Evidence, however, points to the conclusion that, placed in the context of an existing capitalist institution, most accept the values and assumptions associated with that institution. In 1985, faced with the choice of allowing non-shareholding employees a say in decisions, the majority of the 60 per cent plus of National Freight Consortium employees who did own shares said 'no' and at the same AGM accepted the 'economic necessity' for closures and redundancies within their organization. Shareholding is more likely to divide workers than to unite them.

It has been claimed, by the Chairman of the NFC among others, that in firms with a large measure of employee share ownership, directors are genuinely more responsive to the needs of employees. However, evidence from case studies in other English-speaking countries such as Australia and the USA, as well as from the UK, suggests that this is by no means necessarily so (see AMFSU; Zwerdling, 1980). In a survey of the impact of ESOPs on employee attitudes, Kruse (1984) found that motivation was not significantly increased and job satisfaction was significantly *lower* than in a national sample of all firms. This can be explained by the gap that exists between employees' expectations of the rights entailed by ownership and their actual ability to influence decisions.

In most firms, although employees may possess 'passive' ownership rights, they are unable to exercise 'active' rights either because of the strength of existing institutional arrangements or because of the requirements of the ownership arrangements (Perry and Davis, 1985). The greater the extent of employee ownership, the more likely it is that employees will be able to exercise active rights. Some employee-owned organizations, such as the Scott-Bader commonwealth (based near Wellingborough) and the John Lewis Partnership, have extensive representational systems associated with employee ownership, but others, like the NFC, rely on the conventional system of shareholders' meetings. On the whole it can be said that as far as management-initiated schemes are concerned there appears to be no necessary or uniform connection between employee ownership and democratic control.

*Self-management.* For those who define democracy as being essentially participative and developmental, the only true form of industrial democracy is self-management. In self-managed organizations:

> Workers – either directly, as in small enterprises, or through their delegates, as in larger enterprises – decide on economic plans, determine salaries...make investment and development decisions, distribute the organization's income and other benefits...select their top administrators, and resolve internal dilemmas and conflicts. (Baumgartner, Burns and Sekulić, 1979, pp. 81–2)

Perhaps a more appropriate term for this process would be *self-government*, since although self-managed enterprises may operate without the services of a professional management, this is not necessarily or even normally the case. The essential feature of self-management is that it is the workforce that is the sovereign body to which the elected executive is accountable and the appointed management of the enterprise is constitutionally subordinate (Oakeshott, 1978). It has been argued that without some form of supportive institutional or ideological framework it is difficult for such enterprises to succeed where capitalism is the dominant form of economic organization.

As Spear and Thomas (1986) point out, although co-operative workers own their means of production and therefore, *in principle*, control their own work organization, '*in practice* the exercise of this control is not straightforward'. The ability of the whole workforce to exercise control depends on a number of factors, including market constraints, size, differential levels of skill within the enterprise and the circumstances in which the co-operative has been set up. Particularly where existing firms have been 'handed over' or bought up by the workforce, there is a tendency for the policy-making to be left to managers who are only nominally accountable to the worker owners. In these circumstances, previous divisions and attitudes are often retained and, despite formal equality between employees in terms of ownership or representative decision-making structures, control over decisions may become separated from ownership and differentially distributed.

Spear and Thomas have identified the four major constraints on workers' control in co-operatives as being expert power, imported rationalities and expectations, external financing, and market relations. All co-operatives are influenced by the last of these and most by the first three, to varying degrees. As Eccles (1976 and 1979) found in his study of the Kirkby Manufacturing and Engineering Co-operative, even if there are formal democratic structures, 'the fact that ownership has been democratized does not ensure that the government of the enterprise has been similarly democratized'. The duality of power between workers and management which is a feature of capitalist production has often been internalized by both and does not disappear when the organization is self-owned and controlled. In a follow-up study of KME, Thomas and Tynan (1985) concluded that there is often a clash of attitudes between, on the one hand, orientations to work derived from previous work experience (including apathy and instrumentality), and on the other idealistic expectations thrown up by the promise of 'co-operation'. Especially in the case of takeovers or 'endowed' co-operatives, rules, roles and procedures within work organizations are not neutral but permeated by the values, goals and priorities of a larger system of domination (Batstone, 1979).

Horvat (1979, p. 76) suggests that self-management is 'behaviourally incompatible with private or collective ownership' and requires social ownership of the means of production as in Yugoslavia, where self-management began to replace central planning following the break with the Soviet Union in 1948. The precise mechanisms for institutionalizing self-management, however, have undergone a number of changes in response to particular difficulties that have arisen in putting this policy into practice. The overall result has been to give progressively more power to the workers' councils.

In essence, the Yugoslav system as codified in the 1974 Constitution and the 1976 Law on Associated Labour is now based on what are called Basic Organizations of Associated Labour (BOALs) which, in combination with other BOALs, form work organizations. Decisions may be made by *assemblies* or *referenda* of all workers (in the case of amalgamations, amending the statutes of the organization or changing the principles of income distribution), by *workers' councils*, elected on a delegate (as opposed to a representative) principle in all BOALs with over 30 employees, by the *executive organ* of the workers' council, which is elected by the latter from among its members, or by the *management organ* (usually a single director appointed by the works council) (Miller, 1978).

As Miller points out, the assumptions and procedures associated with Yugoslav self-management have a distinctly Rousseauean flavour: 'As in *The Social Contract*, Yugoslav workers in their production units are required to declare themselves and to give their assent to any act which binds them to a certain course of policy or action.' In so doing they are expected to take account not only of individual interests and those of the enterprise, but also of the 'general will', as indicated by the policy guidelines emanating from higher authorities and from other outside organizations. In practice there is some evidence that the decision-making process is controlled by management rather than workers. Studies by Rus (1978 and 1979) indicate that management and technical personnel exercise greater influence than workers. Nevertheless, Tannenbaum (1974) and Rus (1984) argue that although Yugoslav workers do not have as much absolute power as managers, they still have more influence than their counterparts in capitalist countries.

It is difficult to judge self-management from the Yugoslav example in which, although early growth was respectable by international standards, the low level of industrialization and literacy, lack of internal integration, and state intervention in the factor and product markets make it difficult to distinguish the effects of self-management from those of general underdevelopment, market imperfections and government regulation (Estrin and Bartlett, 1982). Moreover, as Dyker (1986) points out, the Yugoslavs have found that under the pressure of market forces, in particular the phenomenon of debt, self-managed enterprises may be effectively stripped of operational independence and self-management reduced to a cipher. Whether or not the disastrous economic performance of Yugoslavia during the 1980s is the result of self-management, as some observers would claim, or of other external factors, is more or less impossible to judge in the absence of other examples with which it can be compared.

## Democratization of management

Whereas democratization of the government of work refers to the determination of overall policy and the exercise of control over day-to-day management, democratization of the management of work requires the introduction of democratic practices into the process of work itself and a consequent democratization of the relationships involved – between workers, workers and managers, and between different levels of management. This may involve either direct democracy on the shopfloor or indirect representative democracy at higher levels. The scope of the democratic process may be similarly varied. Much depends on the overall ideology behind such innovations and on whether the initiative is taken by management or by workers.

*Direct participation.* Direct participation in the day-to-day management of work may take place at the initiative of either management or workers. In the case of management initiatives it may take a variety of forms, ranging from suggestion schemes, job enlargement, job rotation and job enrichment to autonomous work groups. Worker initiatives may include control by craft groups over hours and conditions of work, demarcation and control over job rights, work group practices and direct participation in worker co-operatives (Poole, 1978).

Studies have shown that the motivation behind management schemes to increase employee participation is mainly to decrease alienation and increase commitment and productivity. As far as work humanization is concerned, such schemes may indeed be successful. But to what extent are they *democratic*? Management-initiated schemes for direct participation such as autonomous work groups or quality circles are based on consensus decision-making. Unions generally play no part, the emphasis being on individual participation. At first sight this may appear to be something very close to Rousseau's ideal of direct democracy, but there are some very important differences.

First, the scope of such schemes is strictly limited. Whereas Rousseau envisaged citizens who would participate in making all the major decisions that affected their lives, a major criticism of the schemes of shopfloor democracy initiated by management is that participation is restricted to relatively minor decisions and that these are usually concerned either with the implementation of policies *already* determined elsewhere, or with merely advising on decisions to be made at a later date. In Pateman's terms, it is at worst 'pseudo' and at best only 'partial' participation.

The second difference relates to the relative power of the individuals involved. As Rousseau appreciated, democratic methods cannot be expected to operate effectively when differences in the power of the actors concerned are great. Most schemes for participation are introduced within an avowedly pluralist perspective which emphasizes the diversity of interests within industry and promotes the participation of individual employees or groups of employees as a means of reconciling such differences in pursuit of common ends. There are, however, differences in the latent power available to management and workers in terms of their relative skills and strategic position. Through participation management seeks to integrate employees and to legitimate its own authority within the enterprise. If this fails and employees continue to identify their own interests as being different to those of the organization, the manipulative nature of this kind of participation is revealed and the exercise of power may change from legitimated authority to outright coercion (Cressey *et al.*, 1985).

Rousseau viewed such differences in power in terms of the ownership of property and was of the opinion that, without economic equality, democracy could not work. In modern industrial societies, in which ownership has become both fragmented and separated from individual control, the relationship between individual and corporate shareholders, professional managers and shopfloor employees has become blurred. Nevertheless, it is still true that management can lay claim not only to greater status and financial rewards but also to a legitimacy based on so-called ownership rights which is taken for granted by workers as well as by management itself. In such circumstances both the vision of a pluralist democracy, in which competition between different ideas and interests result in a democratic consensus, and the vision of a direct participative democracy are marred by the manifest inequality of the parties involved.

Employee-owned companies and co-operatives are in a somewhat different position since, nominally at least, employees control the government of the workplace. The degree of participation that does take place depends to some extent on such factors as the nature of the work, the size of the enterprise and the skill level of employees. There are also considerable differences in the operational definition of democracy employed in different enterprises, some being satisfied with representative democratic mechanisms and intermittent control, others insisting on the need for full participation at all levels if expert power and imported organizational rationalities are to be overcome. As might be expected, those employee-owned companies which retain a conventional share structure have tended to retain a conventional business view of the need for line management. However, the same is also true of some co-operatives (including the Mondragon co-operatives) which might be expected to adopt a more egalitarian participative definition of democratic rights.

Outside self-owned enterprises the main means by which employees may extend their direct participation in the management process is through informal work groups and trade union activity. Traditionally the approach of trade unions has been not to rely on reforms initiated by management or by government, but to build on the power that workers already possess. Whereas individually employees may have few resources, collectively they may have strategic bargaining power. Historically this has meant not only the formal negotiation of wages and conditions of employment, but also the exercise of such informal controls as craft restrictions on training and entry, and controls over custom and practice on the job – what are frequently referred to as 'restrictive practices'. The extent to which workers are able to develop such controls depends on the prevailing technology, the organization of work, and employees' own values and perceptions of democracy.

The degree to which employees are able to exercise control over their own work is at best fragmented and variable. Certain groups of workers may, by virtue of their possession of special skills or by their strategic position in the production process, command sufficient latent power to enable them to develop a degree of autonomy. It is also the case that, in times of full employment, employees have been able to use such methods as shopfloor productivity bargaining not only to increase earnings but also to extend employee influence into new areas of decision-making. There are, however, considerable constraints on such opportunities. Employees are vulnerable to changes in technology and management and to changes in the external economic situation. At the same time, whether or not workers actually use the latent power available to them depends on the ideological orientation of the employees concerned.

Frequently, there is a gap between the exercise of negative controls in reaction to management initiatives and the will for greater positive control. Many employees take a purely instrumental attitude towards trade unionism and see it primarily as a means of increasing material rewards. When control issues do arise, as in the case of craft controls over particular aspects of work, they have often tended to be considered within extremely narrow limits, and the question of higher-level decision-making is rarely considered.

Such ideological orientations are not fixed, however, and may be affected by a number of different factors. The changes in material circumstances or involvement in trade union struggles may, as Coates (1971) suggests, stimulate the latent power of working people and the development of socialist democratic ideals. Alternatively, participation in decision-making may itself affect the values of those taking part.

*Indirect participation.* The main kind of indirect participation in decision-making in Britain since the First World War has been joint consultation. This has taken a number of different institutional forms, including joint production committees, joint industrial councils, Whitley Councils and national advisory committees. The powers of these various bodies and the kind of personnel involved have also varied quite widely, but the principles involved have remained the same, namely an acceptance of management's right to a monopoly of control coupled with the use of representative mechanisms as a channel of communication and a means of ratifying decisions.

The most common criticisms of joint consultation as a form of industrial democracy relate to the issues of scope and level. Although mechanisms for consultation at national and industry level are not unknown, the most common levels at which such participation occurs are department and plant levels, i.e. below the level at which policy-making takes place but above the level of direct involvement in task-oriented decisions. The scope of consultation is also restricted by policy decisions on the part of both management and trade unions. Management is reluctant to allow such committees to deal with matters which it considers to be management's prerogative, and trade unions will not allow them to deal with issues which they consider to be matters for negotiation.

It has been noted by a number of writers that joint consultation has most often been used as a way of placating employees' demands at times when trade union power is strong or during periods of political or economic crisis, such as wartime, when workers' co-operation is essential. As Clarke (1977) puts it, joint consultation machinery is primarily a response to a perceived threat to management control, the aim of which is 'to restrict conflict by containing it within joint regulatory institutions which blur the divergent interests of management and workers, erode the basis of independent worker organization, and thereby inhibit the capacity of the workers to take defensive action'. The frame of reference being used is once again that of a pluralist democracy.

The same criticism has also been made of more extensive schemes of participation such as the German system of codetermination. If democracy is defined in terms of manifest power, it would appear that codetermination does indeed extend democracy into the workplace. The election of worker directors gives employees a role in the determination of overall policy, while, as an indirect form of participation in the management process, the works council, on paper at least, has much more influence than the kind of joint consultative committee that is common in Britain. Legislation enshrines not only the right to representation and the right to go to arbitration in cases of disagreement with management, but also the right to be involved in decisions on a number of important questions, including the translation of rates into earnings, job evaluation, redundancies and dismissals as well as the health, welfare and social issues which predominate in the British sytem.

If democracy is defined in terms of *latent* power, however, it can be argued that although the institutional structure of codetermination is democratic in *form*, 'its reality is more concerned with the stabilization of the existing distribution of control between employers and employees and in particular with the binding of trade union strength so that it operates outside rather than inside the workplace' (Marsden, 1978). Leaving aside the constraints on the efficacy of worker directors, it is the exclusion of trade unions from the workplace which most limits the ability of employees to exercise a decisive influence on management. This should not be exaggerated, as Kahn-Freund (1983) points out; unionists *do* participate on works councils and as worker directors are an 'extended arm' of the trade union movement. Nevertheless, the absence of institutionally represented and recognized trade unions and the 'peace obligation' entailed in compulsory arbitration make it difficult for employees to organize collectively to defend their interests. Particular groups such as women and immigrants, who are the most underrepresented in the institutional structure, are unable to improve their position relative to other workers (Herding and Kohler, 1979).

## 2.4  Constraints on participation and prospects for democracy

A number of analysts have pointed out the importance of environment, including both structural and ideological factors, in placing limits on greater participation. Walker (1974), for example, lists the autonomy of the enterprise concerned, the technology and production process, the size of the firm and the organizational structure as important 'situational' variables, and workers' and managers' attitudes and capacities as the most significant 'human' factors influencing both potential and propensity to participate. Marchington and Loveridge (1983) concur that employee involvement may be constrained by the external environment. They use evidence from two different kinds of firm to illustrate how contextual factors may mean that decisions are often made without reference even to specialist managers, let alone the shopfloor. At the same time, however, they agree with Child (1973) that structural elements do not predetermine intra-organizational features: hence the element of choice always exists. In these studies, management frequently rationalized the non-involvement of the shopfloor by reference to the external environment or employees' lack of scientific or financial expertise, but it appeared that it was management's *perception* of the environment and of their own professional skills that was probably the most critical variable.

Cressey *et al.* (1985), in a study of six firms which introduced various forms of employee participation, also suggest that both management ideology and organizational structure play an important role in determining the degree of democratic decision-making. On the one hand there are pre-existing structures of hierarchical authority, legitimized by concepts of bureaucratic rationality, which ensure that when employees enter employment they do so according to existing rules within a managerially established framework. On the other hand there is the fact that managerial control rests on economic power – not the economic power of individual ownership, but the power of organized capital within society as a whole.

These factors inevitably influence perceptions about the possibility of making industry more democratic. As Chiplin and Coyne (1977) point out, any debate about industrial democracy involves the idea of rights, whether this is the right of workers to participate or the rights of property owners. The different formulations of industrial democracy, with capitalist schemes at one pole and Yugoslav self-management at the other, embody opposite formulations of rights. The debate on industrial democracy is concerned with the choice of a position somewhere between the two.

Many writers in the field of industrial democracy see it as a logical and indeed inevitable extension of democracy (however defined) from the political to the economic sphere. Even those writing from a managerial perspective speak as if it is only a matter of time before all reasonable managers and trade unionists acknowledge that democratic participation and consensus decision-making must replace hierarchical authority and conflict as the principal mode of decision-making at work.

This belief is naive. It is based on misconceptions about both the difficulties entailed in the democratization of work and the revolutionary impact which overcoming those difficulties would have. It assumes that full democracy has already been achieved elsewhere in society and that industrial democracy merely requires the transfer into the workplace of the kind of democratic institutions which already exist elsewhere. In reality, however, society is rife with inequalities of class, status, race, gender and power. Often unrecognized, these permeate political institutions and the educational system as well as the organization of work. Merely introducing democratic mechanisms cannot alter these inequalities or the fundamentally undemocratic ideology that underlies them. This is why, even when democratic schemes are adopted, they frequently become distorted and continue to reflect the very inequalities which they might be expected to overcome.

On the other hand, the very centrality of work in our society means that once democratic values are introduced into the workplace, decisions made at work can no longer be divorced from their impact on the community. Those individuals who are relegated by the division of labour into the one-dimensional category of employee have many other dimensions and fill many other roles in the community (including that of consumer) which are potentially in conflict with their role as producer. The democratization of work entails not just the reconciliation of the interests of employers and employees, but also the reconciliation of producers and consumers – the re-integration of work with the rest of society and a reformulation of the democratic polity as a whole.

On the whole it must be said that managerially initiated schemes, whether inspired by government or business, are the least likely to introduce genuinely democratic decision-making. Together, the institutionalized power of capital and the dominant ideology of managerialism are sufficient to ensure that, even in the minority of cases which appear to extend a measure of joint control, ultimate control remains with capital rather than labour and the community at large.

The form of industrial democracy which most nearly approaches the democratic ideal is self-management, which combines democratic owner-ship, government and, frequently, day-to-day management. But in the context of capitalist societies it is difficult enough to maintain this element of democracy, let alone expand it to cover other work organizations. As Thornley (1981) points out, nineteenth-century workers' co-operatives developed initially as a protest against the conditions imposed by industrial capitalism. By downgrading the profit motive and giving priority to democratic decision-making and social and welfare benefits, they chal-lenged capitalist methods of production and provided a vision of a new social order. In practice, however, co-operatives have tended to develop outside the political arena and to represent a retreat *from* rather than a challenge *to* the undemocratic aspects of economic and political organization.

Even in countries like Yugoslavia, where reforms have taken place and there is official ideological and institutional support for self-management, it has been difficult to overcome the problems of poor worker education, adverse economic environment, and tendencies towards oligarchy and the growth of elites. On the face of it the prospects seem gloomy, but there are still some grounds for optimism. It would be surprising indeed if the Yugoslav government had got things right first time. In view of the inauspicious beginnings of the policy, in reaction against Soviet hegemony, and Yugoslavia's underdeveloped condition, it is surprising that the experiment survived at all.

It is true that the level of active participation in Yugoslav self-management is relatively low, but it is also true that those who do participate express a desire for greater, more effective participation in other areas, thus bearing out both Rousseau's and Mill's predictions. The difference between Yugoslavia and other countries is that the opportunities to extend democratic control, although circumscribed by a variety of factors, do exist and are legitimated by the national Constitution. Elsewhere, the necessary democratic institutions exist only in embryonic form. Nevertheless, it is still possible for employees to push forward the frontiers of control and claim further territory for themselves. This requires a combination of political and economic activity on the part of the workers themselves.

A number of authors, including Abell (1985) and Horvat (1983) have taken a cumulative, evolutionary view of this process, arguing that ownership relations can be changed and democracy achieved through the use of codetermination institutions and the progressive socialization of productive capital. In opposition to this view Hunnius (1979) sees codetermination and social welfare legislation as a means of incorporating trade unions which creates an elite within the workforce and reinforces an ideological consensus based on a flawed liberal democratic theory of democracy.

Such a view is unduly pessimistic. Nobody would deny that power is unequally distributed within society, but it needs only a glance at history to see that it is a good deal less unequal under a liberal democratic political system now than it was previously. To assume that the potential for democracy is now exhausted is to ignore the role played by political and economic activity in winning the democratic rights we now possess. Without parallel political moves to remove inequalities and redress the imbalance of power between capital and labour, between the races, between the sexes and between different social classes, industrial democracy will be a sham. But without action to extend democracy within the workplace political democracy will always be incomplete.

## References

ABELL, P. (1985) 'Some theory of industrial and economic democracy', in *Economic and Industrial Democracy*, Vol. 6, No. 4, pp. 435–60.

AMFSU (Amalgamated Metals, Foundry and Shipwrights' Union), video V287, 'Not just a number', Part 3, 'Is it a con?'.

BANK, J. and JONES, K. (eds) (1977) *Worker Directors Speak*, Farnborough, Gower Press.

BATSTONE, E. (1979) 'Systems of domination, accommodation and industrial democracy', in T. BURNS *et al.*, *Work and Power*, pp. 249–74, London, Sage.

BATSTONE, E. and DAVIES, P. L. (1976) *Industrial Democracy: European Experience*, London, HMSO.

BATSTONE, E., FERNER, A. and TERRY, M. (1983) *Unions on the Board*, Oxford, Blackwell.

BAUMGARTNER, T., BURNS, T. and SEKULIĆ D. (1979) 'Self management, market and political institutions in conflict: Yugoslav development patterns and dialectics', in T. BURNS *et al.*, *Work and Power*, pp. 81–140, London, Sage.

BEN AARON, I. (1974) 'Israel', in C. LEVINSON (ed.), *Industry's Democratic Revolution*, pp. 187–98, London, Allen and Unwin.

BLUMBERG, P. (1968) *Industrial Democracy, the Sociology of Participation*, London, Constable.

BRADLEY, K. and GELB, A. (1983) *Cooperation at Work: the Mondragon Experience*, London, Heinemann Educational.

BRANNEN, P. (1983) 'Worker directors: an approach to analysis. The case of the British Steel Corporation', in C. CROUCH and F. HELLER (eds) *International Yearbook of Organizational Democracy*, Vol. I, Chichester, Wiley.

BRANNEN, P., BATSTONE, E., FATCHETT, D. and WHITE, P. (1976) *The Worker Directors, a Sociology of Participation*, London, Hutchinson.

BULLOCK COMMITTEE (1977) *Report of the Committee of Inquiry on Industrial Democracy*, Cmnd 6706, London, HMSO.

BURNS, T., KARLSSON, L. E. and RUS, V. (1979) *Work and Power*, London, Sage.

CARNOY, M. and SHEARER, D. (1980) *Economic Democracy: the Challenge of the 1980s*, New York, Sharpe.

CHILD, J. (1973) *Man and Organization*, London, Allen and Unwin.

CHIPLIN, B. and COYNE, J. (1977) 'Property rights and industrial democracy', in B. CHIPLIN, J. COYNE and L. SIRC, *Can Workers Manage?*, pp. 13–48, London, Institute of Economic Affairs, Hobart Papers.

CLARKE, T. (1977) 'Industrial democracy: the institutionalised suppression of industrial conflict?', in T. CLARKE and L. CLEMENTS (eds) *Trade Unions under Capitalism*, pp. 351–82, Glasgow, Fontana/Collins.

CLEGG, H. A. (1960) *A New Approach to Industrial Democracy*, Oxford, Blackwell.

COATES, K. (1968) *Can the Workers Run Industry?*, London, Sphere.

COATES, K. (1971) *Essays on Industrial Democracy*, Nottingham, Spokesman Books.

COATES, K. and TOPHAM, T. (1974) *The New Unionism: the Case for Workers' Control*, Harmondsworth, Penguin.

CONFEDERATION OF BRITISH INDUSTRY (1977) *In Place of Bullock*, London, CBI.

CRESSEY, P., ELDRIDGE, J. and MACINNES, J. (1985) *'Just Managing': Authority and Democracy in Industry*, Milton Keynes, Open University Press.

DAHL, R. (1985) *A Preface to Economic Democracy*, Cambridge, Polity Press.

DYKER, D. (1986) Paper 11 of D308 *Democratic Government and Politics*, Milton Keynes, Open University Press.

ECCLES, T. (1976) 'Kirkby Manufacturing and Engineering', in K. COATES (ed.) *The New Worker Cooperatives*, pp. 141–72, Nottingham, Spokesman Books.

ECCLES, T. (1979) 'Control in the democratised enterprise: the case of KME', in J. PURCELL and R. SMITH (eds) *The Control of Work*, London, Macmillan.

ELDRIDGE, J. E. T. (1973) 'Industrial conflict', in J. CHILD, *Man and Organisation*, London, Allen and Unwin.

EMERY, F. E. and THORSRUD, E. (1969) *Form and Content in Industrial Democracy*, London, Tavistock.

ESTRIN, S. and BARTLETT, W. (1982) 'The effects of enterprise self management in Yugoslavia: an empirical survey', in D. C. JONES and J. SVESNAR, *Participatory and Self Managed Firms*, Massachusetts, Lexington Books.

GUEST, D. and KNIGHT, K. (1979) *Putting Participation into Practice*, Farnborough, Gower Press.

HANSON, C. and RATHKEY, P. (1984) 'Industrial democracy: a post-Bullock shopfloor view', in *British Journal of Industrial Relations*, Vol. xxii, No. 2, July, pp. 154–68.

HARASZTI, M. (1985), 'A worker in a workers' state', in C. LITTLER, *The Experience of Work*, London, Gower.

HELD, D. (1987) *Models of Democracy*, Cambridge, Polity Press.

HELLER, F., WILDERS, M., ABELL, P. and WARNER, M. (1979) *What Do the British Want from Participation and Industrial Democracy?*, London, Anglo-German Foundation for the Study of Industrial Society.

HEPPLE, B. (1983) 'Individual labour law', in G. BAIN (ed.), *Industrial Relations in Britain*, Oxford, Blackwell.

HERDING, R. (1972) *Job Control and Union Structure*, Rotterdam University Press.

HERDING, R. and KOHLER, C. (1979) 'Codetermination and control', in J. PURCELL and R. SMITH, *The Control of Work*, London, Macmillan.

INDUSTRIAL SYNDICALIST, THE (1974), reprinted by Spokesman Books, Nottingham, with an Introduction by Geoff Brown.

HORVAT, B. (1979) 'Paths of transition to workers' self-management in the developed capitalist countries', in T. BURNS *et al.*, *Work and Power*, pp. 49–80, London, Sage.

HORVAT, B. (1983) *The Political Economy of Socialism: a Marxist Social Theory*, New York, Sharpe.

HUNNIUS, G. (1979) 'On the nature of capitalist initiated innovations in the workplace', in T. BURNS *et al.*, *Work and Power*, pp. 275–312, London, Sage.

KAHN-FREUND, O. (1977) *Labour and the Law*, second edition, London, Stevens.

KAHN-FREUND, O. (1983) 'Labour law and industrial relations in Great Britain and West Germany', in WEDDERBURN, LEWIS and CLARK (eds) *Labour Law and Industrial Relations: Building on Kahn-Freund*, pp. 1–13, Oxford, Clarendon Press.

KRUSE, D. (1984) *Employee Ownership and Employee Attitudes: Two Case Studies*, Pennsylvania, Norwood Editions.

LEWIS, P. (1986) Paper 10 in D308 *Democratic Government and Politics*, Milton Keynes, Open University Press.

LEWIS, R. (1983) 'Collective labour law', in G. BAIN (ed.) *Industrial Relations in Britain*, pp. 361–92, Oxford, Blackwell.

LIKERT, R. (1961) *New Patterns of Management*, New York, McGraw-Hill.

LINDBLOM, C. E. (1977) *Politics and Markets*, New York, Basic Books.

MARCHINGTON, M. and LOVERIDGE, R. (1983) 'Management decision making and shop floor participation', in K. THURLEY and S. WOOD (eds) *Industrial Relations and Management Strategy*, pp. 73–82, Cambridge University Press.

MARSDEN, D. (1978) *Industrial Democracy and Industrial Control in West Germany, France and Great Britain*, research paper No. 4, London, Department of Employment.

MASLOW, A. H. (1954) *Motivation and Personality*, New York, Harper and Row.

MILL, J. S. (1910) 'Probable future of the labouring classes', in *The Principles of Political Economy*, Block iv, Chapter vii, London, Longman.

MILLER, R. F. (1978) 'Worker self-management in Yugoslavia: the current state of play', in *Journal of Industrial Relations*, Vol. 20, No. 3, September, pp. 264–85.

MILLS, C. W. (1959) *The Sociological Imagination*, New York, Oxford University Press.

OAKESHOTT, R. (1978) *The Case for Workers' Co-ops*, London, Routledge and Kegan Paul.

ÖHMAN, B. (1983) 'The debate on wage-earner funds in Scandinavia', in C. CROUCH and F. HELLER (eds) *International Yearbook of Organisational Democracy*, Chichester, Wiley.

PATEMAN, C. (1970) *Participation and Democratic Theory*, Cambridge University Press.

PERRY, S. E. and DAVIS, H. C. (1985) 'The worker-owned firm: the idea and its conceptual limits', in *Economic and Industrial Democracy*, Vol. 6, No. 3, pp. 275–98.

POOLE, M. (1978) *Workers' Participation in Industry*, London, Routledge and Kegan Paul.

RADICE, G. (1978) *The Industrial Democrats*, London, Allen and Unwin.

RUS, V. (1978) 'Enterprise power structure', in J. OBRADOVIC and W. N. DUNN (eds) *Workers' Self-management and Organization Power in Yugoslavia*, University of Pittsburgh Centre for International Studies.

RUS, V. (1979) 'Limited effects of workers' participation and political counter power', in T. BURNS *et al.*, *Work and Power*, pp. 223–48, London, Sage.

RUS, V. (1984) 'Yugoslav self-management – 30 years later', in B. WILPERT and A. SORGE (eds) *International Yearbook of Organizational Democracy*, Vol. II, Chichester, Wiley.

SCHUMPETER, J. A. (1942) *Capitalism, Socialism and Democracy*, London, Allen and Unwin.

SPEAR, R. and THOMAS, A. (1986) *Can Workers in Cooperatives Control Their Own Jobs?*, Milton Keynes, Open University Cooperatives Research Unit.

TANNENBAUM, A. (1974) *Hierarchy in Organizations*, San Francisco, Jossey-Bass.

THOMAS, A. and TYNAN, E. (1985) *KME: Working in a Large Cooperative*, Milton Keynes, monograph 6, Open University Cooperatives Research Unit.

THORNLEY, J. (1981) *Workers' Cooperatives, Jobs and Dreams*, London, Heinemann Educational.

THURLEY, K. (1984) 'Comparative studies of industrial democracy in an organisation perspective', in B. WILPERT and A. SORGE (eds) *International Yearbook of Organisational Democracy*, Vol. II, Chichester, Wiley.

WALKER, K. (1970) 'Industrial democracy: fantasy, fiction or fact?', Times Management Lecture.

WALKER, K. F. (1974) 'Forms and processes of labour/management cooperation', in *Prospects for Labour/Management Cooperation in the Enterprise*, Report of the Regional Joint Seminar, Paris, 24–27 October, 1972, Paris, Organisation for Economic Cooperation and Development.

WEBB, S. and WEBB, B. (1968) 'Democracies of producers', reprinted in K. COATES and T. TOPHAM (eds) *Industrial Democracy in Great Britain*, London, MacGibbon and Kee.

ZWERDLING, D. (1980) *Workplace Democracy*, New York, Harper and Row.

# 3 Community Politics and Democracy
*Allan Cochrane*

## 3.1 Introduction

It has almost become a commonplace of modern political thought that the democratic process needs to be opened up to involve wider sections of the population more directly in decision-making. Yet moves in this direction, whether by the initiative of government or that of ordinary people, remain tentative and unsure. Elsewhere in this book consideration is given to the possibilities of industrial democracy and to ideas that have come out of the women's movement. In this chapter I shall be looking at attempts to generate political change and involvement at a local level based on some shared community of interest. In other words, I shall be examining some of the claims of community politics.

I do not intend to involve myself too deeply in debates about the precise meaning of 'community', which is a particularly elusive and value-laden concept (see, for example, the ninety-four definitions of the term identified by Hillery, 1955; also Abrams, 1978, pp. 10–14; Cockburn, 1977, Ch. 6; and Gusfield, 1975). Despite its frequent use in political discussion, problems remain. As Dennis pointed out perceptively as early as 1958, 'It is one of those terms which . . . are uttered with solemnity, and as soon as they are pronounced an expression of respect is visible on every countenance and all heads are bowed' (Dennis, 1958, p. 74). Today governments seem to use 'community' as if it were an aerosol can, to be sprayed on to any social programme, giving it a more progressive and sympathetic cachet; thus we have community policing, community care, community relations, community development, community architecture and the community programme among others.

In the academic study of local politics the word is often used in yet another way. There is a strong, mainly American, tradition of undertaking what are called 'community power studies'. These generally define the 'community' in terms of local government boundaries. 'Local authority area' (although not authorities as such) and 'community' tend to be used interchangeably. Within these areas researchers attempt to identify those influential individuals and groups which have power in them in order to identify a 'community' power structure (see, for example, Crenson, 1971; Dahl, 1961; Domhoff, 1978; Hunter, 1953; and in Britain, Hampton, 1970; Newton, 1974 and Saunders, 1979, Chs 5–8). The focus of these studies is rather different from the one developed in this chapter, although it should be clear that existing 'community' power structures help to determine the content within which other local political developments take place.

This chapter starts from the other end, not trying to identify current sources of political power but instead trying to see how that power may be challenged or diffused by the development of more democratic processes. I want to explore the extent to which a more locally based politics can be developed, to ask whether individuals and groups will have greater access to it than to national politics and whether they are more likely to participate as a result. Community politics is usually concerned with the collective provision of services to a particular area or group. It typically involves locally (area) based groups in generating demands and either setting out to meet them themselves or putting pressure on state agencies to do so.

This form of politics is important for an exploration of new forms of democracy for two main reasons. First, because it is based on local areas – sometimes quite small neighbourhoods – it suggests the possibility of the direct involvement of people in collective decision-making and so offers the prospect of an active democratic politics more extensive than that offered by traditional forms of representative democracy. Second, in principle, community politics might be expected to allow and even encourage the growth of an independent or autonomous sector of politics outside formal state structures. Some (see, for example, Castells, 1978) would argue that area-based coalitions organized around the provision of public services such as housing, education and transport have the potential to generate a local politics which can move beyond straightforward class divisions mobilizing wider sections of society to challenge the normal priorities of capitalism.

Great claims have been made for community politics by those involved in it, and it has been seen, from a wide range of political perspectives, as a means of moving beyond the limitations of simple electoral politics. Castells, from a Marxist tradition, has made almost mystical claims for it in his analysis of urban movements. He says that they

> produce new historical meaning – in the twilight zone of pretending to build within the walls of a local community a new society they know to be un-attainable. And they do so by nurturing the embryos of tomorrow's social movements within the local utopias that urban movements have constructed in order never to surrender to barbarism. (Castells, 1983, p. 331)

Without going so far, in principle it looks as if community politics might be the answer to some of the central dilemmas of democratic theory identified by Held (1987, Chapter 9). It appears to offer the prospect of transcending the divisions between state and civil society and to a lesser extent between the public and the private spheres. It begins to redefine politics as a process which stretches from the daily experience of ordinary life to wider decisions about resource allocation. It implicitly challenges the notion that certain areas can be defined out of political discussion and that other areas of decision-making, namely government, have to be left to political experts, whether bureaucrats or party politicians.

Community politics can be (and has been) seen as a potential source of fundamental challenge, or at any rate as a living example of the ways in which society might be organized in the future (the term 'prefigurative' is often used to express this). But it has also been supported by others as a means of adjusting to new demands *without* directly challenging existing political and social structures. A third interpretation of community politics would stress still more modest aims, in particular the need to control the excesses of state bureaucracy to restrict its expansion and to encourage rational decision-making. Quite what the various forms of 'community politics' mean for democratic practice can best be judged with the help of examples presented from within these various interpretations.

## 3.2 Challenge from below

Community politics has frequently been associated with radicalism: with organizing the poor, whether fundamentally to challenge existing political and economic structures or to fight for a fairer deal within them. Often, too, radical approaches have made claims to greater democracy because they claim to involve those who have previously been excluded from decision-making, and even from consideration by those who make the decisions. Not only have they sought to identify particular communities whose views might otherwise be lost in the aggregate voting patterns of representative democracy, but they have also stressed the importance of active involvement.

The radical approach has traditionally been strongest in the USA, both in practive and in its more programmatic justification. The work of Saul Alinsky, in particular, has been used as a guide to community action, not only in America but also in Britain (see, for example, Cowley, 1977, p. 239). Alinsky himself was an activist as much as a theorist, and he presents his arguments as rallying calls to action (Alinsky, 1947, 1969 and 1970). He explicitly eschews a commitment to any political ideology, stressing instead that he wants communities to make their own decisions and choose their own directions. As Castells (1983, p. 62) explains, Alinsky's contribution is directly rooted in the American populist tradition with its emphasis on local self-reliance, and is presented as an alternative to socialist or communist initiatives as well as to the problems faced by the poor in contemporary society. 'Community organisation' for Alinsky 'was first of all a political tool and a new form of government complementary to the representative institutions of liberal democracy' (Castells, 1983, p. 61).

Despite his populist orientation, Alinsky's guidelines for action are well developed and prescriptive. They depend, first, on the involvement of a (paid) community organizer brought in from the outside by the community itself (rather like Yul Brynner in 'The Magnificent Seven'). Alinsky ran a foundation which offered such organizers to the poor, and this provided a model for many other community workers. The Alinskyite organizer has the task of helping to build up a genuine local active political community, which s/he can then leave as soon as it is well established with its own leaders.

In order to do this the organizer needs to weld the community together in a series of campaigns which are capable of mobilizing the people on the basis of real, achievable demands directed against clearly identified enemies. For Alinsky, the specific aims of these campaigns become almost secondary. Clearly it is important to win them, but it is the mobilization itself and the new organizational structures that arise from them which matter most. If all goes well they will become self-sustaining, and the previously unorganized and marginalized will be able to make their voices heard. What is needed is continuous struggle and the continued ability to show supporters that success is possible. Lipsky and Levi (1972, p. 188) stress that Alinsky has 'a militant interest in goals *per se* and a militant concern for developing community power so that the group can develop its own goals'.

Alinsky's model for building a new democracy, despite its initial attractiveness as a shortcut to success, does not stand up very well to closer examination. The role of the community organizers themselves seems problematic and hardly consistent with democratic organization. It is difficult to see how they can always avoid becoming directly involved in more political campaigning and offering political leadership to those they are purporting to represent. In some cases the organizers (or professional advocates) may feel strongly that the direction being taken by 'their' territorially based organization is mistaken (and even dangerous); for example, if problems in predominantly white neighbourhoods become defined in terms of pressures from black areas. In other cases, the organizers may simply feel that alternative political programmes need to be presented to give coherence and lead to longer-term change (see, for example, Hartman, 1970; Rosen, 1970).

The experience of the Community Development Projects (CDPs) in Britain points in a similar direction. These projects were set up in the early 1970s on the initiative of the Home Office; at the height of the programme there were twelve of them. They were located in particular 'deprived' – mainly urban inner-city – areas, including Saltley (Birmingham), Canning Town (London), Benwell (Newcastle), Batley and North Tyneside. The initial hope within the Home Office was that groups within local communities could be mobilized (with the help of professional organizers) jointly to tackle their multiple social problems. Many of those employed within the projects were rather more radical than this. They often had ideas close to those of Alinsky, although not necessarily directly influenced by him. It was hoped, both by the Home Office and the radical professionals, that solutions – albeit very different ones – would be generated by the people of the deprived areas.

The organizers of the CDPs came to challenge these initial assumptions following their experience of community work in practice. In part their criticism was that it was impossible to deal with structural problems of economic and social inequality at the local level. The inner cities, they argued, were not aberrations which could be corrected if there was sufficient will within the local community. They were the product of wider economic pressures, left over and marginalized in the process of economic and social restructuring (see, for example, CDP, 1977a). But the Projects also increasingly turned to local and national political campaigning to get their message across. It was not enough, they felt, merely to reflect and service the demands of local communities; political lessons had to be drawn, learned and fed back to those communities (see, for example, CDP, 1977b; Higgins *et al.*, 1983, Ch. 2; Lees and Mayo, 1984, pp. 22–24 and 24–37; Loney, 1983).

The constant search for new campaigns in which victory is possible and the target is clear is unlikely to be successful in the long run. And the evidence from the 1960s, when Alinsky-inspired community initiatives were at their height in US cities, suggests that they were not generally very successful in winning their main demands and 'were totally incapable of altering the logic of delivery of services' (Castells, 1983, p. 64). In Britain, the evidence suggests that the rules of the political game serve 'to protect established policies *and* the easy access of those groups and interests advantaged by them, at the same time as groups urging changes' are 'ruled out of course by a whole series of exclusion devices' (Dearlove and Saunders, 1984, p. 70). Even where pressure groups succeed in winning concessions, they are on relatively trivial issues at significant cost in time and effort. Victory tends to help legitimate the already powerful instead of transferring resources to the disadvantaged. Saunders describes the unusual success of one group (the Crystal Palace Triangle Association) in Croydon in winning a day nursery, but stresses that the success was on a narrow issue, did not affect overall nursery provision in the borough, and may have effectively diminished provision elsewhere in the borough. The success relied largely on the skills of the campaign's leaders in staying within the rules of the game while mounting criticism of the council, which suggests that leadership remains more important than democratic involvement. 'At best,' says Saunders, 'participation succeeds in securing limited objectives, but. . .at worst it results merely in the symbolic legitimation of the system without securing any fundamental concessions. Far from representing a challenge to the prevailing pattern of resource allocation, they have strengthened the pattern of distribution by competing for the crumbs while resolutely ignoring the cake' (Saunders, 1979, p. 288).

There is also an inherent danger in this sort of campaigning that instead of focusing attention on the real causes of problems it may divert attention elsewhere. It may encourage a shift away from 'top dogs' towards easier targets – the 'middle dogs' – who can more readily be identified at the local level. Repo argues that the attempts of community organizers to organize the 'poor' frequently result in an implicit (or even explicit) attack on the working class who, it is said, exclude the 'poor' from their own relative security (Repo, 1977, pp. 65–90). In some cases, on the other hand, community organization may be directed against pressures coming from other (weaker) groups: several Alinsky–supported community organizations ended up defending predominantly white working-class areas against black or Hispanic incursion (Castells, 1983, p. 63).

Community politics of this sort, however, faces still more insidious pressures. As indicated above, it is predicated on the ability to get results, to deliver the goods. Yet, at the same time, the groups being organized are among the weakest in society, and the likelihood of long-term effective mobilization over a range of issues is slight. Any offers of institutional co-operation from above, therefore, tend to be accepted relatively easily. From radical voices of urban protest, community organizations risk becoming little more than channels for the effective (targeted) delivery of funds and services. They are in danger of becoming part of the delivery system rather than an alternative to it. There is, of course, nothing necessarily wrong with that, but it fits rather better with the theories of community management discussed below (in Section 3.3) than with the development of a radical new democratic involvement. Local leaders tend to be sucked into official structures and, since community activism occurs in bursts on particular issues rather than in encouraging a constant involvement, they may end up valuing those long-term links and feeling threatened by pressure from below. Community 'leaders' are notorious for being marginalized by explosive events such as urban riots.

Community organizations will find it difficult to refuse apparent concessions and additional responsibility, but accepting them may also undermine their long-term viability. Lipsky and Levi illustrate this with the official response to rent strikes in St. Louis public housing:

> With maintenance costs increasing, repair costs accelerating in older buildings, federal public housing subsidies frozen and vacancy rates rising, the Public Housing Authority in St. Louis vested authority in a tenant's board. Yet it is uncertain whether the economics of public housing permit successful operation at current inadequate levels of government subsidy, particularly where deterioration of projects has been permitted to advance markedly. (Lipsky and Levi, 1972, p. 189)

'Victory for community organisations', they stress, 'may prove hollow when symbolic or substantive victories are not accompanied by sufficient resources to permit realization of success over time' (Lipsky and Levi, 1972, p. 190).

Despite these problems, demands for community control have remained an important part of the US radical tradition. But there has been less emphasis on the 'poor' as an organizing category and more on particular ethnic groups, above all black people, Puerto Ricans and Mexican Americans. It was when Alinsky-style initiatives were taken over by black militants that they gained some life. In the 1960s, 'the semi-autonomous large urban ghettos' were used

> as a form of social organization and institution – building for the new militant community. Although the riots were the most open declaration of the state of insurgency against racist institutions, most of the daily work of the community organizations in the inner cities was also part of a black-related mobilization against the living conditions imposed by racial discrimination and economic over-exploitation of the ethnic minorities that were concentrated into those areas by urban segregation. (Castells, 1983, pp. 65–6)

Demands for community control became demands by particular groups to control their 'own' areas and became principally associated with the demands of black radicals. In many ways they learned from Alinsky, stressing the need to show immediate results. The Black Panther Party in the late 1960s, for example, even launched a Free Breakfast for Children Program, both as a means of putting pressure on local businesses for support and as a sign of their ability literally to 'deliver the goods'. Organizations such as the Black Muslims and others have undertaken similar initiatives, going further to stress the need for a separate economic structure, owned and controlled by black people. The Black Panther Party called for community control of the police based on neighbourhood councils.

> The people throughout the city will control the police rather than the power structure, the avaricious businessmen and demagogic politicians who presently control them. The point of community control of police is that those people living in these neighbourhoods will actually do the hiring and firing of the policemen who patrol that area, and those policemen will be people from those neighbourhoods – black police for a black neighbourhood, Chinese for a Chinese neighbourhood, white for a white neighbourhood, etc.' (Seale, 1970, p. 465)

In practice, the radicalism of such demands was dissipated by the experience of the 1970s.

Some political liberals took up the demand (see, for example, Altshuler, 1969), stressing the values of decentralization and arguing that it would allow greater citizen participation. It would, they felt, both encourage material reform, making it easier to tackle poverty, and more securely integrate the previously marginalized into the political system. More important perhaps, the 'white flight' to the suburbs in many of America's large cities means that black politicians have increasingly been able – albeit still not in overwhelming numbers – to achieve power in urban governments. Many urban cores now have local governments with black mayors and executives, while, of course, almost all suburban governments remain dominated by the white middle classes.

This shift in the personnel of political control in some of the USA's older cities has not been accompanied by a major shift in power relations or a marked improvement in material conditions. Amir Baraka (previously Leroi Jones) was a leading campaigner in the 1960s to elect a black mayor and black leadership in Newark (New Jersey). He argued that 'Our aim is to bring about black self-government in Newark by 1970' (quoted in Allen, 1970, p. 244). By 1975 this had been achieved. But in an interview, Baraka explained that the economic and political situation in the mid-1970s meant that massive cuts in spending were being imposed, particularly on education:

> Now, the mayor, he comes to us and he's going to take the role of the enforcer. He's going to come to the people and tell them 'Yeah, that's all you going to get, and there ain't no need of you making no noise about it, because that's all you going to get'.
> Now that's a perfect stooge a perfect lacky [sic]. Your child now goes to school and they come home saying 'we ain't going to have no more library' and now this man comes up to you and justifies that and see he can justify it with a little more authority than the white man, because Ken Gibson grew up on the streets too, so he can come and get tough with you too. (Baraka, 1975, p. 27)

In other words, argues Baraka, the product of community-based black radicalism is also likely to be double-edged. Symbolic victories may, in practice, make little difference and may even make it more difficult for communities to challenge external constraints. Similar conclusions can be drawn from a more sympathetic analysis of Detroit in the 1980s. There General Motors was able to demand increased concessions in terms of tax abatements, subsidies and infrastructural investment if it was to construct a new plant. Trachte and Ross contrast Detroit's (black) mayor with his immediate predecessor (Jerome Cavanaugh), noting that despite a greater commitment to social reform the practice appeared *less* reformist, making more concessions to General Motors:

> Our understanding of this contrast does not presume that Young was in some sense less favourable to working-class or poor people's interests than Cavanaugh. Rather, Young came to municipal power at a moment when capital had become less tolerant of the welfare state, more demanding of national and local government, because, finally, it had been forced to free itself of any commitment to any given locale within the worldwide mosaic of choice. (Trachte and Ross, 1985, pp. 212–13).

One of the problems associated with community politics is that, as generally defined, it is based on shared notions of locality. Yet few of the political or economic forces and agencies that it confronts have any similar commitment to particular areas. On the contrary, they view regions, nations and even the globe as suitable arenas within which to decide locations. There is a particularly sharp mismatch between communities and the decision-making processes of large, often multinational firms.

Decisions made by their directors on perfectly rational and reasonable economic criteria may have dramatic effects on small areas which are unlikely to be taken into account. New communities may be created and old ones destroyed on the basis of such decisions (see, for example, CDP, 1977a; Massey, 1984, Chs 4 and 5). If it is to be an option for the future, radical community politics needs to fit into a wider political framework, in which issues of production can also be considered.

### 3.3 Reform from above

The radical promise of community politics has been difficult to sustain in practice, but it has also been approached from another direction, with rather different aims. Community politics has become part of a package of reform from above, presented as a way of altering the *status quo* without fundamentally challenging it – as an alternative to socialist and anti-capitalist strategies. In some ways there is thus an echo of Alinsky but without the fire. The aim is to involve people in decision-making to commit them to decisions and to generate independent activity which is not threatening but supportive and – ultimately – subordinate rather than complementary.

These ideas are not particularly new. Leggett (1968, Ch. 8) describes the organization of block clubs in Detroit in the 1950s when an attempt was made by the City Planning Commission to 'prevent central city neighbourhoods from becoming slums' (p. 131). They sought out local activists and tried to organize local groups at block level, based initially on home buyers and owners, who were felt to have a greater commitment to maintaining and improving the neighbourhood than those living in rented property. Once the club was set up, however, all block residents could join on the payment of the appropriate dues. Active membership usually settled down at no more than 10–20 per cent of residents. An early emphasis of the clubs was on cleaning up their areas, and recreational activity focused on children tended to draw people together. There was also joint activity in which skills were shared, so that one resident might help with carpentry and another with house-painting, and so on. The results, according to Leggett (p. 134) 'were visible improvements in the neighbourhood and greater cohesion among families, who could take pride in their collective achievements'.

Various other joint activities were developed to draw people into activity or support, and links were made with city and other authorities over crime and issues such as the extension of leisure facilities.

The block clubs, according to Leggett at least, succeeded in encouraging a process of collective problem-solving. But they also soon developed in directions far away from those hoped for by their original proponents within local government. They began to raise more obviously political questions, challenging the policies of the municipal governments which spawned them. Over half of Detroit's block clubs become involved in at least one of the following issues: 'zoning (i.e. planning policy), urban renewal, policy protection, school boundary gerrymandering' (Leggett, 1968, p. 135). As well as campaigning on particular issues, at election times many of the block clubs organized discussions with candidates and even endorsed particular candidates.

> Many city politicians reacted negatively to what they considered annoying block-club demands. These politicians finally abolished that section of the planning commission that had organized and maintained the clubs. The city had created a problem-solving agent which it could not control. In fact, the block clubs sometimes opposed the proposals of the city planning commission. Moreover, because they fought pressure groups such as organized real estate interests, which traditionally worked closely with the planning commission, the city council and powerful economic interests, the clubs invited opposition. Yet, to the amazement of many, hundreds of block clubs continued to flourish without the support of the city planning commission. (Leggett, 1968, pp. 135–6)

In practice many of the block clubs became a focus of political militancy, particularly for those with a large black membership. (The nature of Detroit's central areas was such that a large number of the block clubs were in neighbourhoods in which there was a high proportion of black people – mainly members of the working class.) The search for collective solutions to neighbourhood problems in the end led to a growth in political militancy which went beyond local participation to challenge other elements of the political hierarchy.

Community politics is a set of processes, not a finished and neatly rounded activity. It cannot easily be controlled from above, and the paths it takes are often unpredictable. Once people are involved in active debate about their neighbourhoods it is not possible to lay down clear boundaries beyond which those debates may go, whatever politicians and officers may want to see. This is also confirmed in more recent US experience, particularly that of the Model Cities Program (part of the War on Poverty) in the late 1960s and early 1970s. The Model Cities Program channelled federal funds through local authorities to community-based projects which rarely accepted the bureaucratic rules of the game set by the funder. It had the reputation of losing funds to organizations racked with internal dissension whose survival was doubtful and, worse, which were liable to use the money to mount continuing campaigns against the donors. In 1974 the Program (and the War on Poverty) were brought to an abrupt end by President Nixon.

In Britain, too, state-inspired community politics has had rather contradictory results for those who initiated it. Cynthia Cockburn (1977) vividly charts the experience of Lambeth Borough Council in the early 1970s. Lambeth is only one example of a wider movement in the management of local government which developed in Britain at the end of the 1970s. An attempt was being made from the centre to transform local government from a traditional administrative backwater into a modern and efficient system based not only on the provision of the usual services, but on the perceived needs of the local area. In the present period of political hostility to the wider claims of local government, it may be difficult to believe that these developments were encouraged not only by the writings of academics such as those associated with the Institute of Local Government Studies at the University of Birmingham (see, for example, Stewart, 1974; Leach and Stewart, 1984) but also, and more important, from the centre (for example in reports such as that of the Study Group on Local Authority Management Structures, 1972 – the Bains Report – and its Scottish equivalent, Scottish Development Department, 1973 – the Paterson Report).

The changes being proposed had two main, but clearly connected, elements. First, it was argued that a new approach to management was required which did not start from existing departmental boundaries but encouraged the development of an overview, allowing an authority-wide policy to be developed. This approach – known as corporate management or corporate planning – was usually associated with the appointment of a policy-oriented Chief Executive (to replace the old legally oriented Town Clerk) and with the development of interdepartmental policy groups to cover programme areas previously divided arbitrarily between service departments. Secondly, this corporate approach, it was felt, required a rather different structure of democratic or community involvement. If an overall view of a local authority area was to be developed, it seemed unlikely that the existing system of electoral democracy would assist either in the identification of genuine demands or the active involvement of people outside the council.

Some authors (such as Benington, 1976) saw the development of these policies as a means of officers' avoiding democratic control. They argued that setting up wider means of consultation, often based on particular local areas or communities, was in practice a means of avoiding supervision by those with political power. Cockburn makes similar points about the Lambeth experience, stressing the extent to which and the ways in which corporate planning borrowed its rationality from that of business management. But she goes beyond this to consider the experience of the neighbourhood councils that were set up to act as links between the new corporate council and the local population.

In 1971 six of these councils were established, and by 1974, when the Borough sub-committee to which they had direct access was wound up, there were ten of them covering different parts of the Borough. Each was intended to provide a channel of communication to and from the Borough Council, to encourage a partnership which would make it easier to tackle problems of poverty and deprivation, and to encourage political participation and support for local councillors. It was hoped that ultimately all parts of the Borough would be covered by neighbourhood councils, but this aim was never achieved, and once Borough Council patronage was withdrawn they gradually lost their strength.

There were important differences between the ways in which the neighbourhood councils operated and the extent to which they were able to involve a wide range of people from their local communities. Some were largely inactive, others acted in what was seen as a responsible way – working closely with sitting (Labour) councillors – and some came into open conflict with the council, largely over issues connected with housing redevelopment and campaigns over squatting. Councillors were unable effectively to manage some of these political challenges and, as in Leggett's Detroit, they chose to cut off the institutional contact which was felt to give them their power – in this case a sub-committee which, uniquely, gave the neighbourhood councils direct access to the Borough Council machinery without having to pass through the usual screening mechanism operated by officers. In fact one set of local authority officers who were involved (the community workers) appear to have 'gone native', supporting the neighbourhood councils against their employers and, perhaps more important, against their formal superiors in the officer hierarchy. According to Cockburn, senior officers were even more concerned than the councillors to remove the neighbourhood councils' special legitimacy because it challenged their normal role more than that of the politicians.

The lessons of Lambeth for community politics are fairly mixed ones. Some of the neighbourhood councils could not be controlled by the Borough Council and soon went beyond the aims originally set out. In other words, it was not possible to manipulate community politics in quite the way Cockburn claims the Borough Council and its officers wanted. But nor were the neighbourhood councils able to develop a full and powerful autonomy in the absence of political legitimacy endorsed from above. This makes one a little sceptical about Leggett's claims in Detroit, too. I suspect that the block clubs also lost their strength (slowly perhaps) when their special relationship with the Planning Commission was dissolved. Community politics initiated from above is difficult to control because it begins to generate demands based on neighbourhood local issues which develop a life of their own and may point to unacceptable solutions for the councillor and officer hierarchy. But it also seems to be a rather weak challenge in the end because it continues to rely on a special relationship with those whom they challenge. As I argued in Section 3.2, it is only this relationship that enables community politics to 'deliver the goods' to those who participate in it; without it, a crucial pillar of support disappears.

*Towards a better social democracy*

The tension between community politics and orthodox political and bureaucratic structures, however, is precisely their strength for those who see them as a means of encouraging social change and democratic change without the need for total upheaval. The problem for the existing state is one of positively managing the demands from below, rather than stifling them or allowing them to be dissipated in negative criticism. The aims of community politics initiated from above were and are to affect 'the course of social change through forming social relationships with different groups to bring about the desirable change . . . helping to relate the activities of service agencies more closely to the needs of the people they serve . . . facilitating citizen participation to give "life to social democracy" ' (quoted in Lees and Mayo, 1984, p. 3). There is a mix between arguments for better targeting – more efficient management in Cockburn's terms – and increased involvement by local residents. At its most modest, this was expressed in proposals for area management, which was to:

a. analyse problems, formulate policies, and monitor their effects in a corporate way at an area level;
b. operate services more sensitively to local needs by better evaluating their performance;
c. provide a convenient channel of communication between the council and neighbourhood councils, residents' associations and other groups and individuals;
d. provide a framework in which elected members can relate council policies to local case-work and vice-versa.

(Department of the Environment press release, September 1974, quoted in Community Development Project, 1977b, p. 16)

Of course, this careful articulation between existing hierarchy and previously excluded groups – the attempt to create pluralist pressure groups where none existed before – has, as the cases of Detroit and Lambeth illustrate, not always had the results its supporters hoped for. A long list of failed urban or community initiatives, at least from the policy-makers' point of view, could readily be presented for Britain and the USA. The Community Development Projects in Britain and the Model Cities Program in the USA from the late 1960s and 1970s are only the best known of these. In each, official control and even effective monitoring of projects was lost early on while funded agencies appeared to turn to bite the hands which fed them.

But these experiences have only brought an end to particular experiments. The overall aims have remained important, and in more modest initiatives, learning from the lessons of past failures, there has been a greater emphasis on piecemeal reform to achieve them. In Britain, Hadley and Hatch have identified and enthusiastically supported shifts to more decentralized service provision in the social policy area. They consider a series of apparently unrelated initiatives in government departments, local authorities, health authorities and the voluntary sector among others, and build on them to present more generalized proposals for alternative structures of decision-making and government (Hadley and Hatch, 1981).

Hadley and Hatch reject what, following Macpherson (1977), they call pluralist elitist models of democracy reflected in existing forms of representative democracy. They are particularly critical of the past failures of the social democratic state in bureaucratically handing down welfare from above. Instead they argue for participatory democracy which they say rests 'upon more positive beliefs in the ability of ordinary citizens to define issues, decide and act for themselves and in so doing to achieve a measure of self-realisation and fulfilment' (Hadley and Hatch, 1981, p. 105).

In order to illustrate what they mean by this, they discuss a wide range of particular, and relatively small-scale, projects which combine the provision of services with the involvement of local people or of people who would in more traditional models be defined as 'clients' or passive consumers. Some of the examples they consider might not usually be seen as relevant to discussions of democracy or democratic government, but Hadley and Hatch put a greater emphasis on participation, on involvement in the operation of policy, than on the counting of individual votes. Their cases include community centres and neighbourhood councils which encourage the active participation of local residents in policy-making, the delivery of services and the development of projects (such as pensioners' lunch clubs, holiday play schemes, English classes for ethnic minorities, and self-help groups). Less familiar structures include patients' committees organized by general practitioners, to encourage dialogue (sometimes critical) with doctors and encourage the development of community health care campaigns, such as helping with transport, self-help groups (e.g. on smoking) and other preventive medicine. Attempts to achieve more democratic structures of ward organization in hospitals, involving all grades of nursing staff and patients, and the extension of democracy in schools (particularly involving pupils) are also discussed. But an important element in the argument is that direct involvement, too, involves an increase in democracy. Thus, for example, an increase in the use of volunteers in service provision – instead of centralized professional organization – is in itself seen as a move towards democratization. Hadley and Hatch cite instances of 'good neighbour' schemes to monitor the position of the 'frail elderly' (p. 124), and schemes of volunteer home nursing and care for the dying. 'We are relying on the sensitivity, the common sense, and the ability to learn of well balanced people' (Baker, 1978a, quoted in Hadley and Hatch, 1981, p. 125). 'There is an enormous reservoir of untrained but skilful people in the community who can do this work [i.e. the care of the dying]. . .the failure of this society is that when it sees a need it thinks immediately in terms of bricks and mortar, and not of people. . .[but]

nearly everyone has a bed in his/her own home and that is the proper place to die' (Baker, 1978b, quoted in Hadley and Hatch, 1981, p. 126).

For Hadley and Hatch, the orientation towards bricks and mortar is also, almost axiomatically, an orientation towards centralized, professionalized, bureaucratic and inherently undemocratic practice. Conversely, the shift of provision out of the buildings of the state and the hands of the professionals and into that of volunteers (as an accepted part of civil society) is, almost equally axiomatically, also a shift towards participatory democracy. Even the move from residential care to paid fostering placements for difficult adolescents is presented as an extension of democracy, particularly where existing foster parents, as well as professional social workers, have a role in the selection of new ones. 'While the general directions of social policy', say Hadley and Hatch (p. 147) 'are still determined by the elected members of central and local government, the ways in which the policies are developed and applied are open to discussion and amendment by both social services staff and clients, for their involvement is regarded as indispensable if available resources are to be maximised and variations in need/demand are to be recognised'.

Hadley and Hatch present a new model of democracy within social policy which could, presumably, be extended to other aspects of government and society. They argue against an expansion of existing statutory services, suggesting instead that what is needed is an extension of 'community based initiatives'. The development of several sources of service provision ('plural provision') is crucial to their argument. But, secondly, they want existing state-run services to be decentralized and oriented more towards the communities they deal with and away from existing hierarchies. This would also involve a shift towards greater direct participation of consumers, employees and other agents involved. Committees in local government might involve representatives of these groups as well as those directly elected to the council. This, it is suggested, would increase democratic involvement.

Finally, Hadley and Hatch seek to avoid the problems of lack of co-ordination and the danger of inadequate levels or partisan direction of provision by particular autonomous groups by calling for a 'stronger monitoring and inspection role' for the state. Accountability would be through contracts rather than officer hierarchies (Hadley and Hatch, pp. 166–7).

Much of the language of Hadley and Hatch is radical and seems directed towards undermining the apparently monolithic edifice of the British welfare state, constructed so painstakingly since the Second World War. They go so far as to place themselves within the revolutionary tradition of William Morris and the guild socialists led by G. D. H. Cole, in contrast to the Fabian socialist tradition initiated by Sidney and Beatrice Webb, which they identify, a little unfairly, as the theoretical basis of all the centralization and professionalism which they reject so comprehensively. In practice, however, their own arguments seem rather disingenuous in the current context.

There is an underlying, if only implicit, concern throughout their work with the costs of service provision, as well as the desire for greater democracy. The use of volunteer labour is, of course, also a way of reducing costs to the state (and replacing professional employment). It is by no means clear that the use of volunteers in the social policy area will necessarily reduce the problems of distance between providers and 'clients' which Hadley and Hatch identify. On the contrary, in so far as the growth of the voluntary sector implies an increase in the ethos of charitable provision, it may actually reduce the sense in which 'clients' view services as something to which they have a right and increase their feeling of subordination. It is easy to hate a social worker, but do we have the right to hate a volunteer who keeps trying to encourage us to participate?

In any assessment of democratization it is necessary to question simple equations betweeen the growth of the voluntary sector and democracy. Since voluntary organizations are, by definition, self-selecting, it is hardly possible to generalize about their democratic value. One of the reasons for the Webbs' arguments at the turn of the century was precisely that the decision-making of charitable organizations was often arbitrary and reflected the prejudices of the volunteers more than the needs of the clients. That was why they argued both for greater control by elected local authorities and an increased level of professionalization (see, for example, Webb and Webb, 1910). One does not have to agree with all the consequences of Fabianism or all the arguments of the Webbs to recognize their strength here.

For our purposes, however, it is more important to consider the nature of the community politics implied by the Hadley and Hatch model. They have managed to escape from some of the consequences of community politics discussed earlier, but only at the expense of genuine political involvement – that is, only by removing community 'politics' from any serious access to power. They do this in two main ways, first by their broadening of the definition of democracy to include non-professional (voluntary) involvement in service provision, and secondly by introducing the notion of contractual negotiation between state and community organization. We have already briefly considered the first of these, but the second is significant, too. It means that any community group must be dependent on external funding not, usually, on the basis of its overall budget, but on a piecemeal basis. Grants will come for particular activities, for short periods, and not for, say, the whole activity of a community centre or residential home. This is liable to encourage not democratic involvement but the construction of funding proposals which fit in best with the current obsessions of the funding agencies, rather than local needs.

It is more appropriate to the growing market sector in social policy than genuine (autonomous) community-based organizations. It is likely to fragment them into small groups with special interests instead of bringing them together with some wider notion of community or neighbourhood.

Another aspect of the contractual approach is a committment to increased monitoring and inspection. Hadley and Hatch stress the need for a more extensive and critical process of inspection for the voluntary sector, like that currently undertaken in the education field by HM Inspectors. Arguably this could be used to improve standards across the board and avoid incompetence, but it could also be a means of ensuring that some demands which arise from community organizations are kept under control. Otherwise funding will be at risk. Instead of encouraging community politics, such an approach may in practice constrain them severely, because of its seductive offer of extra resources (or just *some* resources) if the game is played according to the rules.

Whether the Hadley and Hatch model can fully escape from the threats of radical community action posed by Cockburn remains open to question, but certainly it is increasingly being put forward as a way out of the dead end which social democracy appeared to have reached at the end of the 1970s. A properly managed community politics of this sort may offer increased commitment from those involved without necessarily generating more fundamental challenges. It is less clear that it really does mean greater democratic involvement, although that is what it is supposed to offer. Instead it seems likely to tie local activists still more closely to the priorities of councils, provide new means of control over them, and useful channels of information from them to council officers. (This is discussed further by Christopher Pollitt in Chapter 7; see also Smith, 1985.) It may be a better management system and provide greater democratic legitimation, but it is hardly more democratic in itself.

### 3.4 Community politics as a control system

Many of the normative arguments for pluralism as the most appropriate form of political organization in liberal democracies can also be seen as arguments for a form of community politics. As a description of the political process in countries such as the USA and Britain, pluralism has lost its force, but it retains significant power as an alternative model. In particular, the theory's stress on the importance of interest groups competing openly on political issues and with good access to government opens up important arguments about the nature of democracy. It does so in two main ways: first, it challenges the notion that the election of a particular party to government even by an absolute majority is the end of the political process, since that continues through the activity of interest groups mobilized on sectional issues; secondly, it challenges the idea that a majority decision is necessarily more democratic than one which allows those minorities most affected by or concerned about a decision to have a greater say than those for whom the issue is fairly marginal. In other words, 'differential preference intensities' need to be taken into account, and can be if interest groups as well as political parties are an accepted part of the political process.

Clearly, not all of pluralism's hoped-for myriad, competing interest groups will be based on local communities. They may, instead, be based on particular issues of authority-wide relevance or arise from class or corporate interests, such as trade unions or local industry. But the concerns arising from particular areas do seem likely to provide an important base for pluralist interest groups. Obvious examples might include campaigns against plans for new urban motorways, or campaigns organized by tenant groups. Even wider campaigns are likely to be based on local support. In his study of Birmingham, Newton (1974, Ch. 9) presents a case study of a city-wide campaign based on educational issues, but it is clear that its main bases of support and action are in particular wards of the city.

Within this model, however, the role of community politics is essentially one of balance, of countervailing power against detrimental change, rather than a clear channel for any effective or positive alternatives. Indeed, in its most strongly argued form (see, for example, Wildavsky, 1964 and 1975), the diffusion of political decision-making in this way is presented as a necessary justification for a process of incrementalism. The only way in which community groups and others can be involved, it is argued, is if they are presented with a series of small changes relevant to their particular areas of interest. The presentation of some overall plan or programme for approval *in toto* will simply ensure that groups objecting to this or that part of it are overwhelmed by the demands of the greater – allegedly societal or authority-wide – good.

For Wildavsky, whose fears echo some of those put forward by Niskanen (discussed in Chapter 7) – the involvement of interest groups offers one way of controlling the self-aggrandizing empire building and lack of financial control which he suggests characterize most public sector bureaucracies. He stresses the extent to which spending programmes begin to generate a life of their own which appears to have little connection with initial proposals. In one particularly forceful book, Pressman and Wildavsky chart the ways in which competing professional approaches and demands effectively undermined federal attempts at urban renewal. The sub-title of the book says it all: *How great expectations in Washington are dashed in Oakland: or, why it's amazing that federal programs work at all, this being a saga of the Economic Development Administration as told by two sympathetic observers who seek to build morals on a foundation of ruined hopes* (Pressman and Wildavsky, 1979). Elsewhere, Wildavsky has criticized British government departments for the extent to which the main concerns of budget-holders have been professional and departmental rivalry within Whitehall (the policy community) rather than any external priorities (Heclo and Wildavsky, 1981).

Incremental decision-making plus an openness to pressures from interest groups are felt to be one way of controlling these tendencies, at local government level at least, and many of the interest groups are likely to be based on local communities. This is essentially a 'conservative' view of community politics with particular resonance in the USA. There the pluralist tradition is strongest and appears, superficially at least, most strongly to reflect the realities of a decentralized urban politics.

The existing structure of local government in the USA is based on smaller geographical units than in the UK, and on a multitude of functional divisions, including, for example, separate school boards. This is reflected in the great number of local government units in the country (over 90 000 including 2000 countries, 18 000 municipalities, 17 000 towns and townships, 50 000 school districts, and 15 000 special districts). In proportion to its population, the USA has about thirty-five times as many units of local government as Great Britain. The importance of this is particularly clear in the great metropolitan areas. The New York Metropolitan Region is made up of 1500 units of local government, each with its own powers to tax and spend; Chicago has five counties with a total of 1172 units; and even the St. Louis metropolitan area (with a population of 2.4m and 600 local governments) has more units than the whole of Britain. Because there is little consistency in size or boundaries between these local governments with their different functions, local government in the USA is like a complex patchwork in which different units of government overlap, compete and conflict with each other.

In other words, there is not, as in the UK, a concentration of power in major local authorities. Partly as a result of this, community politics has an accepted place within the American political tradition which it has not yet achieved in the British context. Political power already appears to be diffused, within a wider community. But this also reflects the remarkable extent (by British standards, at least) to which there is differentiation between neighbourhoods not only on the basis of class, but also race, ethnicity, culture and even sexual preference (see, for example, the development of gay areas in San Francisco discussed in Castells and Murphy, 1982, and Castells, 1983, Ch. 14). The emphasis of pluralist writers on the role of broadly based interest groups in local politics has always seemed more convincing in the American context than it has in Britain. Even Newton's pluralist analysis of Birmingham, which identified some 4000 active interest groups, served to highlight the absence of effective pressure groups rather than their importance.

In America, too, the limited extent to which weaker groups can be expected to influence policy has been widely recognized. For example,

Bachrach and Baratz, in their study of the Poverty Program in Baltimore, highlight the exclusion of the poor from decision-making. Indeed, they suggest that powerful political actors effectively remove any consideration of their demands from the agenda of government so that they do not even emerge as recognized problems or issues. They call this process 'non decision-making' and argue that it is at least as important as formal decision-making within government (Bachrach and Baratz, 1970, Ch. 7).

More important, perhaps, is that such is the degree of social and ethnic concentration and segregation within American cities that community control at the level of local governments can be effectively used by some groups to exclude others who may threaten the services they supply, in particular to defend middle-class white children from 'busing' to black schools (or even the arrival of black and poor children to white schools in the suburbs). Authors such as Banfield (1970 and 1974) argue that attempts to educate the poor in middle-class schools will at best be wasteful and at worst may raise expectations which cannot be met, increasing the likelihood of rioting in poorer areas.

It would hardly be justified in these cases, however, to suggest that calls for community control are, in fact, calls for an extension of democracy. On the contrary, they clearly offer means of *excluding* certain groups from political power. Instead of extending democracy, they are intended to limit it.

But some activists on the American new right have been confident enough to go beyond these essentially conservative demands, and to make positive demands for change, based on community organization of a sort. They have, in particular, been prepared to mobilize taxpayers and ratepayers at a local and state level in campaigns such as that for Proposition 13, which was carried in a referendum in California in the early 1980s. In line with the wider ideology of economic liberalism, this Proposition was intended to lay down clear rules limiting state budgets and tax revenues which could not then be ignored by governments. In other words, there was no demand for continued and continuing participation. Nevertheless, as a campaign, it succeeded in mobilizing a wider movement than most left radical ones. It became a model for other citizens' movements across the country, although few were as successful. It certainly succeeded in making politics a part of ordinary people's lives for a time in a way that normal electoral politics rarely succeeds in doing. As a model it offers a reserve power to the citizen rather than the prospect of permanent mobilization. Indeed it is premissed on the hope that by such action the state will cease to impinge on individual freedom (and, as far as possible, income), allowing citizens to act without interference or extensive involvement in decision-making in the longer term. The government is seen as 'rule maker and umpire' (Friedman, 1962, p. 25) and not a part of everyday life.

In this respect it differs substantially from the pluralist approaches discussed earlier. They may have had similar aims – namely to restrict the power of the state and state officials – but they assume a wider and continuing involvement in politics, broadly defined, rather than a sharper, neo-liberal division between state and civil society, in which the state's role is explicitly and deliberately narrowly defined. For the pluralists, community politics may be seen as an ongoing process of control over and involvement in the decision-making process. For the neo-liberals it is more a reserve power to be mobilized as required to keep the state and its agencies in line.

In Britain, neither of these forms of community politics has been espoused with any great enthusiasm on the right of the political spectrum. In general, arguments for increased democratic control have been in other areas such as the election of trade union officials and the increased use of ballots in trade union affairs, where there has arguably been an extension of representative democracy, rather than a development of more participative or direct democracy. Only in schools has an extension of what might be called community control been encouraged in the early 1980s, since there has been an increase in the number of directly elected parent governors and a decrease in those appointed by other agencies. The likely impact of these reforms (and even their purpose) are not entirely clear, although they seem to owe less to a vision of increased democracy and more to a desire to encourage schools to maintain high (and traditional) educational standards free from the interference of those professionals who are more influenced by 'progressive' educational ideas. In this one can begin to see arguments close to those of Wildavsky, although one might also expect this form of decentralization to encourage demands for even more resources than those presented by the professionals. More recently, neighbourhood watch schemes have been developed as a means of bringing people together to watch out for criminal behaviour in their localities, but they have been clearly tied and subordinate to local police rather than attempts to extend democratic control. Indeed, in many cases they have been presented as alternatives to more 'democratic' control of the police through council committees.

Elsewhere, the main emphasis has generally been on the widening of *choice* for individuals rather than their increased involvement in decision-making. Writers such as Johnson (1977) have stressed the need for constitutional reform, through which legal guarantees would restrict the power of politicians and officials to act irresponsibly or limit the freedom of individuals (and companies) to act as they wished. The vision of ratepayers as a political force – expressed, for example, in a government-sponsored local government bill which made provision for referendums on rate increases but was later dropped in favour of central control – brought a slight echo of other approaches, but even that has not been taken further in recent years. The aim may be the same as that of US neo-liberals, but there seems neither to have been the need nor the political culture to encourage mobilization of the sort developed in America. The British centralist tradition has instead reinforced the view that rights can be guaranteed more effectively by national rules and national government than by the factional self-interest of particular groups within local government.

## 3.5   Community politics and democratic transformation

Despite the problems associated with the notion in its many incarnations, community politics continues to have a resonance in contemporary debates about democracy. It remains an expression of the possible, showing how one might begin to square the circle of representative government and direct or participative democracy. The failures of community politics should not surprise us. Instead we should, perhaps, be surprised that examples are continually being thrown up which confirm the continued force of such ideas.

The weakness of the movements for community control in the face of massive external constraints should not make us write it off altogether. Even if it is difficult to imagine community politics on its own providing the basis for long-term political organization, it may provide fragmentary insights about future possibilities and may also, despite its acknowledged weaknesses, allow for campaign action on issues of common concern. In themselves such campaigns, by involving the previously uninvolved for however short a time, may increase democratic activity. Not all neighbourhoods at all times will allow for the development of an active community politics, but the combination of social demands and neighbourhood organization may in some circumstances be a powerful force, able to mobilize large numbers of people. The search for a universalizable community politics may be a chimera, but the analysis of the politics of particular communities is still worthwhile in illuminating democratic possibilities for the future. They help to show that some of those usually excluded from political decision-making are quite capable of presenting coherent alternatives to the plans of the decision-makers.

In Britain the development of community politics as a radical alternative has come from developments and debates within and around the state. The argument has been that politics of that sort needs to be consciously developed rather than arising spontaneously from the poor, ethnic minorities or other groups. This has echoes of Alinsky about it, but the arguments are more explicitly political and finally have little in common with his. A well developed community politics is almost seen as a necessity if a socialist alternative is to be generated. But an explicit socialist or, sometimes, feminist orientation is also frequently said to be essential if community politics is to survive and be effective. Lees and Mayo argue, for example: 'What is being proposed is neither to expect socialist policies to emerge automatically from any such democratization process, nor to revert to former ways of ignoring the inputs from community groups; but rather to engage them in a systematic process of critical dialogue' (Lees and Mayo, 1984, p. 192).

From a feminist perspective community politics is an ambiguous arena within which there are both potential and constraints. Cockburn (1977) argues strongly that it offers the possibility of involving women in political conflict over issues of reproduction (not only in its most obvious biological sense, but also in the wider sociological sense of maintaining the existing workforce and the future workforce, and sustaining those without paid employment). Women, she argues, become involved because these issues affect them directly. But her case-study evidence from Lambeth suggests that on its own such involvement will be difficult to sustain. A focus on local, community politics may also leave women trapped in a political backwater, unable to generalize more widely and ultimately trapped in the rules of the game handed down from above. The need to link politics developed 'from the bottom up' in the course of individual campaigns to a wider national political framework was stressed centrally in the arguments of a book called *Beyond the Fragments* (Rowbotham, Segal and Wainwright, 1979). This started from an analysis which saw the failure of centrally organized national politics to generate support for any process of social change and stressed, as an alternative, the vitality and viability of fragmented initiatives in workplaces, communities and in the women's movement. The task they identified was the need to bring the fragments together to build a more unified political approach.

In their analysis Rowbotham *et al.* identify a crucial problem of community politics, but their own solution is not entirely convincing. They stress the need for joint campaigns on particular issues, but that seems to suffer from similar problems of fragmentation and, incidentally, dangers of further fragmentation and dissipation as campaigns grind to a halt. Community politics is confronted by a major dilemma. It arises out of grassroots mobilization on particular issues, but the difficulty of sustaining such activity is widely recognized. Castells (1983) suggests that when it becomes widely supported, it tends to be absorbed by the main political parties, as activists move from local issues to more general ones. Radical demands tend to be diluted in the process. Conversely, it is sometimes argued (e.g. Cowley, 1977; Castells, 1978; and Lees and Mayo, 1984) that community initiatives will only be able to sustain themselves if they take on and commit themselves to more developed political programmes. In either case, the initial strengths associated with community politics as a separate or autonomous area seem condemned to disappear.

Recently, attempts have been made to bring state-sponsored initiatives and community politics together through local government. At its most extreme this has found its expression in the work of Seabrook, who calls for local authority intervention to recreate a self-confident working class (Seabrook, 1984). Socialist local authorities, argues Seabrook, through the use of neighbourhood offices, should begin to rebuild working-class communities which would be capable of then developing their own politics and developing new support networks. Underlying Seabrook's analysis is the vision of a revitalized and independent community politics. He partly blames the growth of centralized but insensitive welfare provision and partly the development of capitalist materialism for what he sees as the decline of working-class community. This double concern was expressed against the background of political defeat which was partly blamed on the experience of an overcentralized and bureaucratic state which excluded most people from decision-making and was associated with the traditional policies of Labour (see, for example, Hodgson, 1984).

Another response to this has been a series of initiatives by left Labour local authorities, such as the Greater London Council (now abolished), Sheffield and a number of London borough councils, which have also stressed the importance of decentralized decision-making and the involvement of local communities. For the GLC this included support to a wide range of community groups, including the development of a People's Plan for Docklands as an alternative to the undemocratic London Docklands Development Corporation (Newham Docklands Forum, 1983). The GLC's employment work survives in a reduced form in the Greater London Enterprise Board. Blunkett and Green (1983) argue that the general structure of policy-making needs to be changed. Instead of flowing from the top down it needs to flow from the bottom up. Communities need to be involved, although councils can be expected to retain ultimate power. This, they say, is what they have tried to achieve in Sheffield.

These initiatives have sought to deal with another central problem of community politics by attempting to bring together issues of production, as well as those of 'community', more narrowly defined. They have recognized the need for a secure economic base if local neighbourhoods are to be given any long-term stability. They have also recognized the need to link industrial democracy (discussed by Margaret Kiloh in Chapter 2) with the demands of community-based democracy, but have learnt from the experience of the Mondragon experiment in Spain, where the growth of co-operative production has drawn in a local community around it. Debates link questions of what should be produced and how to the interests of the locality (see, for example, Campbell *et al.*, 1977). External constraints remain strong, however, even for Mondragon. For the local authorities there is still a long way to go and the aims are mixed: greater democratization, increased opportunities for women and ethnic minorities, and, above all, more secure jobs. They are not always consistent, and the scale of intervention remains small. There is little chance of directly influencing major employers. The need to defend jobs often becomes dominant and more social aims sometimes take second place (for further discussion see, for example, Cochrane, 1986). The principle remains important even if the reality is a bit more difficult to achieve.

The success of these initiatives remains difficult to judge. Some of the claims made seem justified more by rhetoric than experience. But for our purposes here two points are clear: first, the authorities are seen to have a major role in actually encouraging a community response; and secondly, there is an underlying assumption that in any case local provision and decision-making must somehow be more democratic and community-based. The problem with the first point (even more than with Alinsky) is that if the community initiatives get out of hand they are likely to challenge the very authorities which created them. If and when they become embarrassing, then – just as Cockburn describes in Lambeth and just as the experience of the Community Development Projects from the 1970s suggest – we can expect them to be dismissed as unrepresentative and (probably) closed down. The second claim is highly problematic. For many of those dependent on local authority services, they continue to appear remarkably undemocratic even in those places where the left is in control and decentralization has begun. The main measure of democracy for clients would be for their demands to be met quickly. Financial constraints in the past five years have made that less, not more, likely, so the points made by Trachte and Ross about Mayor Coleman in Detroit are likely to be valid here, too.

The utopian hopes of many proponents of community politics and urban social movements have not been realized and are probably not realizable. At best, as Lowe argues, in Britain at any rate, these movements 'are locked into a party-dominated political system, as seeds of the new politics in the womb of the old politics' (Lowe, 1986, p. 202). Past experience suggests that germination may be some time off, but even the existence of the seeds suggests that the search for new forms of democracy is not just an academic preoccupation.

# References

ABRAMS, P. (1978) 'From analysis to facts: the problem of community', in ABRAMS, P., *Work, Urbanism and Inequality*, London, Weidenfeld and Nicolson.

ALINSKY, S. (1947) *Reveille for Radicals*, Chicago, University of Chicago Press.

ALINSKY, S. (1969) *Rules for Radicals*, New York, Random House.

ALINSKY, S. (1970) *The Professional Radical*, New York, Harper and Row.

ALLEN, R. (1970) 'The politics of black power', pp. 237–52 in SLATE, W. (ed.) *Power to the People!*, New York, Tower.

ALTSHULER, A. (1969) *Community Control. The Black Demand for Participation in Large American Cities*, Indianapolis/New York, Pegasus.

BACHRACH, P. and BARATZ, M. (1970) *Power and Poverty*, New York, Oxford University Press.

BAKER, J. W. (1978a) 'How a village helps the dying to cope at home', the *Guardian*, 3 March.

BAKER, J. W. (1978b) 'Care unlimited', unpublished.

BANFIELD, E. C. (1970) *The Unheavenly City*, Boston, Little Brown.

BANFIELD, E. C. (1974) *The Unheavenly City Revisited*, Boston, Little Brown.

BARAKA, A. (1975) 'We see ourselves revolutionary nationalists still', *Muhammad Speaks*, Vol. 14, No. 48, 8 August.

BENINGTON, J. (1976) *Local Government Becomes Big Business*, London, Community Development Project Information and Intelligence Unit.

BLUNKETT, D. and GREEN, G. (1983) *Building from the Bottom. The Sheffield Experience*, Fabian Tract No. X91, Fabian Society.

CAMPBELL, A., KEEN, C., NORMAN, G. and OAKESHOTT, R. (1977) *Worker-Owners: The Mondragon Achievement*, Anglo-German Foundation for the Study of Industrial Society.

CASTELLS, M. (1978) *City, Class and Power*, London, Macmillan.

CASTELLS, M. (1983) *The City and the Grass-roots. A Cross-cultural Theory of Urban Social Movements*, London, Arnold.

CASTELLS, M. and MURPHY, K. (1982) 'Cultural identity and urban structure: the spatial organisation of San Francisco's gay community', in FAINSTEIN, N.I. and FAINSTEIN, S.S. (eds) *Urban Policy under Capitalism*, Beverley Hills/London, Sage.

CDP (1977a) *The Costs of Industrial Change*, London, Community Development Project.

CDP (1977b) *Gilding the Ghetto. The State and the Poverty Experiments*, Community Development Project.

COCHRANE, A. (1986) 'Local employment initiatives: towards a new municipal socialism?', in LAWLESS, P. and RABAN, C. (eds) *The Contemporary British City*, London, Harper and Row.

COCKBURN, C. (1977) *The Local State. The Management of Cities and People*, London, Pluto Press.

COWLEY, J. (1977) 'The politics of community organising', in COWLEY *et al*.

COWLEY, J., KAY, A., MAYO, M. and THOMPSON, M. (1977) *Community or Class Struggle?*, London, Stage 1.

CRENSON, M. A. (1971) *The Unpolitics of Air Pollution*, Baltimore, Johns Hopkins Press.

DAHL, R. A. (1961) *Who Governs? Democracy and Power in an American City*, New Haven, Yale University Press.

DEARLOVE, J. and SAUNDERS, P. (1984) *Introduction to British Politics. Analysing a Capitalist Democracy*, Cambridge, Polity Press.

DENNIS, N. (1958) 'The popularity of the neighbourhood community idea', *Sociological Review*, Vol. 6, No. 2, reprinted in PAHL, R. (ed.) (1968).

DOMHOFF, G. (1978) *Who Really Rules: New Haven and Community Power Re-examined*, New York, Transaction Books and Good Year Publishing Company.

FRIEDMAN, M. with the assistance of FRIEDMAN, R. (1962) *Capitalism and Freedom*, Chicago, University of Chicago Press.

GUSFIELD, J. R. (1975) *Community: A Critical Response*, Oxford, Blackwell.

HADLEY, R. and HATCH, S. (1981) *Social Welfare and the Failure of the State. Centralised Social Services and Participatory Alternatives*, London, Allen and Unwin.

HAMPTON, W. (1970) *Democracy and Community: a Study of Politics in Sheffield*, London, Oxford University Press.

HARTMANN, C. (1970) 'The advocate planner: from "hired gun" to political partisan', *Social Policy*, July/August.

HECLO, H. and WILDAVSKY, A. (1981) *The Private Government of Public Money*, 2nd edition, London, Macmillan.

HELD, D. (1987) *Models of Democracy*, Cambridge, Polity Press.

HIGGINS, J., DEAKIN, N., EDWARDS, J. and WICKS, M. (1983) *Government and Urban Policy-Making Process*, Oxford, Blackwell.

HILLERY, C. A. (1955) 'Definitions of community: areas of agreement', *Rural Sociology*, No. 20.

HODGSON, G. (1984) *The Democratic Economy. A New Look at Planning, Markets and Power*, Harmondsworth. Penguin.

HUNTER, F. (1953) *Community Power Structure*, Chapel Hill, North Carolina, Chapel Hill Books.

JOHNSON, N. (1977) *In Search of the Constitution. Reflections on State and Society in Britain*, London, Methuen.

LEACH, S. and STEWART, J. (eds) (1984) *Approaches in Public Policy*, London, Allen and Unwin.

LEES, R. and MAYO, M. (1984) *Community Action for Change*, London, Routledge and Kegan Paul.

LEGGETT, J. C. (1968) *Class, Race and Labour. Working Class Consciousness in Detroit*, New York, Oxford University Press.

LIPSKY, M. and LEVI, M. (1972) 'Community organization as a political resource', in HAHN, H. (ed.) *People and Politics in Urban Society*, Urban Affairs Annual Reviews, Vol. 6, Sage.

LONEY, M. (1983) *Community Against Government: British Community Development Project 1968-1978*, London, Heinemann.

LOWE, S. (1986) *Urban Social Movements. The City after Castells*, London, Macmillan.

MACPHERSON, C. B. (1977) *The Life and Times of Liberal Democracy*, London, Oxford University Press.

MASSEY, D. (1984) *Spatial Divisions of Labour: Social Structures and the Geography of Production*, London, Macmillan.

NEWHAM DOCKLANDS FORUM (1983) *The People's Plan for the Royal Docks*, London, Newham Docklands Forum and GLC Popular Planning Unit.

NEWTON, K. (1974) *Second City Politics*, London, Oxford University Press.

PAHL, R. (ed.) (1968) *Readings in Urban Sociology*, Oxford, Pergamon.

PRESSMAN, J. L. and WILDAVSKY, A. (1979) *Implementation*, 2nd edition, Berkeley, University of California.

REPO, M. (1977) 'Organising the poor – against the working class', in COWLEY *et al.* (1977).

ROSEN, S. (1970) 'Comments', *Social Policy*, No. 1, May/June, p. 36.

ROWBOTHAM, S., SEGAL, L. and WAINWRIGHT, H. (1979) *Beyond the Fragments. Feminism and the Making of Socialism*, London, Merlin.

SAUNDERS, P. A. (1979) *Urban Politics: a Sociological Interpretation*, London, Hutchinson.

SCOTTISH DEVELOPMENT DEPARTMENT (1973) *The New Scottish Local Authorities: Organisation and Management Structure*, London, HMSO (the Paterson Report).

SEABROOK, J. (1984) *The Idea of Neighbourhood. What Local Politics Should Be About*, London, Pluto.

SEALE, B. (1970) *Seize the Time. The Story of the Black Panther Party*, London, Arrow.

SMITH, B. (1985) *Decentralisation. The Territorial Dimension of the State*, London, Allen and Unwin.

STEWART, J. D. (1974) *The Responsive Local Authority*, Croydon, Charles Knight.

STUDY GROUP ON LOCAL AUTHORITY MANAGEMENT STRUCTURES (1972) *The New Local Authorities Management and Structure*, London, HMSO (the Bains Report).

TRACHTE, K. and ROSS, R. (1985) 'The crisis in Detroit and the emergence of global capitalism', *International Journal of Urban and Regional Research*, Vol. 9, No. 2.

WEBB, B. and WEBB, S. (1910) *The Minority Report on the Poor Law*, London, Longman (reprinted 1963, London, Cass).

WILDAVSKY, A. (1964) *The Politics of the Budgetary Process*, Boston, Little Brown.

WILDAVSKY, A. (1975) *Budgeting: a Comparative Theory of Budgetary Processes*, Boston, Little Brown.

# 4 Feminism and Democracy
*Sheila Rowbotham*

## 4.1 Historical introduction

It has been a persistent theme of political thought that women and democracy do not go together. Women have been outside the rubric of democracy. 'The Lawes Resolution of Women's Rights', published in 1632, was quite decisive on the matter: 'Women have no voice in Parliament, they make no laws, they consent to none, they abrogate none' (Thompson, 1974, p. 222).

It did not prove to be the resolution, of course. For equally persistent has been the assertion by women of the right to have a say and express their needs as they see them. In the process women have extended the conception of democracy. Invariably when there have been popular upsurges of oppressed people and the claim to power has been made by the unprivileged, women's voices have been heard. This has often involved women in arguments within popular movements as well as with political rulers (see, for example, Rowbotham, 1972). During the Civil War and its aftermath women petitioned and beseiged Parliament. In the Suffolk election for the Long Parliament in 1640 women even tried to vote (Thompson, 1974). Again, in the French Revolution and in the radical and working-class movements of the nineteenth century in Europe, women's claims to democracy were made. Women used the arguments current at the time to justify their inclusion in democratic rule, shifting from religious references to the secular concept of political rights.[1]

The vote was claimed as a right within the concept of free, independent individuals. One person could not be included in the franchise of another, for an individual could not be dependent on the will of another. In seventeenth-century radical theory the individual person was held to be inviolable. It was maintained that everyone had a property in one's own person.

But did this apply to women or not? The issue of women's freedom hinged on whether 'woman' was subsumed in the term 'man'. If the rights of man also meant the rights of woman, even more extensive changes were needed in society. For women were not regarded as free and independent individuals but as attached to fathers or husbands.

Male political theorists divided on whether women could be equal and whether the rights of man included women. The opponents of women's emancipation claimed women could only be dependants. They could not therefore claim to have an equivalent property in their own person and equal political rights. Writers like Mary Wollstonecraft, who in the late eighteenth century sought to vindicate the rights of women, consequently claimed that if society were arranged differently women would show they could be equal to men. She did not claim the vote, however (see Rowbotham, 1972).

In 1869 John Stuart Mill's *On the Subjection of Women* stressed that women's interests could not be included in the interests of the men in their families any more than subjects' interests could be regarded as included in the interests of the King (see Okin, 1980, p. 204).

In the nineteenth century, the discontent of middle-class women in Europe and North America focused on lack of access to education and respectable employment and on political inequality. Democracy and equality thus went together in the suffrage movement, cautiously at first, then, in the early twentieth century in Britain, with greater militancy after the Pankhursts formed the Women's Social and Political Union. The emphasis behind the demand for the franchise was women gaining equality with middle-class men (Rowbotham, 1985, pp. 47–50).

The demand for equal rights assumes a universality. It was used in many contexts with radical consequences. Yet it comes up against social limits. Kumari Jayawardena, in *Feminism and Nationalism in the Third World* (1986), points to the interesting contradictions that appeared when the idea of equal rights was applied to colonial situations. In the nineteenth century progressive Asian male reformers argued for women's right to education. In India and elsewhere schools were set up. This in turn stimulated agitation among the young women who became educated.

> Similar to European women who demanded equal access to higher education, bourgeois women in Asia began to agitate for further educational opportunities that would give them access to new avenues of income-earning opportunities and hopefully greater freedom. The bourgeois males of these countries were faced with the usual liberal dilemma: the democratic rights championed by followers of the Enlightenment in Europe, though ostensibly 'universal', were intended for bourgeois men to the exclusion of the workers, colonial peoples and women. Similarly the indigenous bourgeoisie, while willing to grant some concessions to women of their own class, had no intention of applying the concepts of natural rights, liberty, equality and self-determination to the masses of women or to the workers of their own countries. (Jayawardena, 1986, p. 17)

For the poor there were evident snags with the demand for equal rights. Democracy based on a theory of individual rights does not secure a means of livelihood. Nor does it allow for the interdependence of human beings in maintaining themselves and their children.

These difficulties were already evident to early nineteenth-century socialist thinkers who argued for economic change. William Thompson's *Appeal of One-Half the Human Race, Women, against the Pretension of the Other Half, Men, to retain them in Political and thence in Civil and Domestic Slavery* (1825) went further because he took on the problems of women's cultural subordination as a sex and the need for a society in which all women could enjoy freedom and equality – including working-class mothers.

In his introduction to the book (dedicated to the socialist feminist Anna Wheeler, who had influenced his thought) Thompson stated the vision of the transformed society which they both shared:

> You look forward to a better aspect of society, where the principle of benevolence shall supersede that of fear, where restless and anxious individual competition shall give place to mutual co-operation and joint possession, where individuals in large numbers, male and female forming voluntary associations, shall become a mutual guarantee to each other for the supply of all useful wants and form an unsalaried and uninsolvent insurance company against all insurable casualties; where perfect freedom of opinion and perfect equality will reign amongst the co-operators. (Thompson, 1825, reprinted 1983, pp. xxv–xxvi)

The idea that the liberation of women required not only political freedom and economic equality but also a community based on mutual co-operation has never completely disappeared. It has been submerged, to be rediscovered whenever movements for the liberation of women have included poor and unprivileged women.

Rosalind Pollack Petchesky points out that there exists a danger, noted by Marx, in the

> concept of 'rights' in general, a concept that is inherently static and abstracted from social conditions. Rights are by definition claims stated within a given order of things. They are demands for access for oneself, or for 'no admittance' to others, but they do not challenge the social structure, the social relations of production and reproduction. (Petchesky, 1984, pp. 7–8)[2]

Petchesky argues that needs, on the other hand, exist in concrete historical circumstances. Thus the liberation of women has to be linked not only to the tradition of equal rights but to the articulation of the needs and wants of women in specific situations.

There was a tension apparent in liberal feminist thinking even while the equal right to the franchise was being asserted. It was apparent that there were needs based on women's different biological and social circumstances which could not be met in terms of equality.

When the campaign for the vote no longer held the women's movement together, this divergence became of greater significance. Feminism did not end with the limited franchise gained in Britain in 1918 for women over 30. In fact, it spread into a wide range of social and political causes, from better conditions for pregnant women to peace. But by the late 1920s a split had occurred between feminists who believed in equality and the 'new feminists' who argued that women had differing needs from men. Demands for protection at work or birth control could not be contained within an egalitarian framework in which individuals were seen as simply equivalent. Equality for this new generation of feminists was not enough (Lewis, 1975; see also Rowbotham, 1977, pp. 19–21).

Recognition that political equality was an insufficient guarantee of emancipation was growing among those middle-class feminists in Europe and America who learned of working-class women's lives. Their investigations of low pay, sweated labour, domestic toil and unwanted child-bearing revealed the inadequacy of conceiving democracy simply in terms of political equality.[3] As working-class women began to take up the arguments for the suffrage they tended to assume that political democracy was the first step to wider economic and social reforms. The vote was thus linked to economic independence, trade union organization, better conditions for maternity, housing, education, and even the reorganization of domestic work (see Liddington, 1984).

There was a series of struggling attempts throughout the nineteenth century to form trade unions in which working-class women often met opposition from men of their own class as well as from employers. For this reason, labour movement women knew not only that political democracy alone was inadequate, but that the right to organize at work was linked to a challenge to their subordination in the family and in society (see Drake, 1984; Lewenhak, 1977). For example, in the 1890s Annie Martin from the Bristol Women's Co-operative Guild condemned both low wages and the low esteem in which husbands held the work of their wives, 'as general servant, cook, nurse, washer-woman, tailoress and mother all at once' (Rubinstein, 1986, p. 149). After the First World War Margaret Bondfield, an active trade unionist and member of the Labour Party, pointed out that the reorganization of women's work had to include domestic activity:

> At a West Country conference the future development of domestic work was being discussed: a trade union comrade arose and impatiently dismissed the subject with, 'why do we waste time discussing domestic service – we workers never have domestic service – we can't afford it!' He was promptly told by the housewives present that he got domestic service all right, but he paid nothing for it. (Bondfield, 1980, p. 86)

Clearly democracy was merely an abstract idea if people were working long hours in unhealthy conditions over which they had no control or toiling in the home caring for large families in poverty. Women took their cue from the trade union attempts to limit the hours of paid employment by law. 'What about women's right to a nine-hour day?' asked a song of 1871 (Henderson *et al.* 1979, pp. 128–9).

A series of strategies attempted to emancipate women from housework, and make socially possible a greater degree of control over domestic activity. In the United States and Britain, utopian communities in the nineteenth century initiated co-operative housekeeping. These experiments provided the incentive for the invention of technology for washing clothes and pots, and serving food. They also pioneered the design of the environment and adventure playgrounds. These schemes were not always welcomed by women. Nor were they necessarily democratic. It was often the case of the male leaders deciding what was good for the women. A general problem faced by the communities and the utopian vision of perfecting all aspects of human relations was that they overemphasized collectivity and disregarded, even denigrated, individual needs. On this conflict many of the communities floundered (see Muncy, 1974; Hayden, 1981).

For this reason American socialist feminists in the early twentieth century turned away from the communities as a solution to housework and childcare. They began to advocate instead collective services to private apartment blocks, providing meals, a laundry service and child-care while both partners worked (see Hill, 1980; Strasser, 1982).

In Britain the Women's Co-operative Guild, formed in 1883, took up the idea of co-operative forms of living as a way of tackling women's confinement in the household and enabling working-class women to play a fuller part in political life. They advocated co-operative laundries, co-operative nurseries and co-operative shops (Gaflin and Thoms, 1983). Sharing housework and child-care more equally between men and women was also mooted. But the middle class had domestic servants, many married working-class women did not go out to work, and male manual work was physically arduous. Working-class housewives did not tend to compare their predicament with men unless they were active in the socialist and feminist movement and in need of time for their politics.

From the late nineteenth century in Britain local government became an important arena for women's demands for social change. Women like Emmeline Pankhurst and Charlotte Despard began to campaign for improved conditions in the treatment of the poor locally before they both became involved in the suffrage movement nationally (Rubinstein, 1986, pp. 165–78). After the First World War there were radical proposals for free municipal electricity, home helps, nurseries, laundries, municipal cinemas. These implied a conception of democracy as integrally connected not only to women's social equality but also presenting a challenge to women's unequal access to the resources controlled by the state. In retrospect, because they were achieved, we take some of their demands for granted: home helps, tea in the parks and welfare centres for mothers and children are familiar elements in the welfare state. But to contemporaries their achievement was no more to be assumed than demands for municipal cinemas, where working-class children would not be debarred from aesthetic sensibility, or free municipal electricity so that working-class women could benefit from municipal vacuum cleaners. They had seen many of the self-help projects that had arisen on the basis of everyday domestic needs, like welfare centres, nurseries and laundries, become part of wider campaigning policies. It seemed likely that democracy could assume new social contours. Nor did they limit themselves to the humdrum: immediately before and after the First World War, women in the labour movement in Britain touched on pleasure, enjoyment, leisure and the creation of a new culture which echoed William Thompson's glimpse of a society 'where the principle of benevolence shall supersede that of fear' (Gaflin and Thoms, 1983).

There was a shift from self-help to local government and then to the hope that the new Labour Party would secure social and economic improvements in women's lives. It seemed evident to Labour women that the state should secure women's welfare. The implication was still that this would free women for greater democratic participation in government (see Rowbotham, 1986).

But there were certain snags in turning towards the state as a means of transforming women's social inequality and extending democratic opportunity. There was more to the advocacy of welfare than the reform of inequality or mutual aid. An important argument was the belief that a welfare capitalism was a more efficient means of maintaining healthy human stock. This assumption was not only to be found among the right-wing advocates of the welfare state; it was also present in some of the socialist arguments. Welfare thus lost its early links with the idea of extending control over social life through co-operative organization. It became a more efficient kind of social engineering.

In the 1920s and 1930s socialist models of welfare were authoritarian and dismissive of individual needs and democratic involvement – as Trotsky noted of the Soviet Union in his *Problems of Life* in 1924. After the First World War Vienna was the first large city in Europe in which a Social Democratic town council was able to realize its programme of community policies. These included improvements and innovations in housing and social welfare. But they contained a strong element of social control. People were scared of the caretakers. Women in the communal washing rooms of the large flats known as the 'Karl Marx Hof' were anxious about how to fit in with the regulations which a male supervisor checked. Anna Sturm recalled: 'I always used to have nightmares about not finishing the washing...I used to get palpitations and stomach-ache and sore throats and everything. For years and years, as long as I went down there' (Sieder, 1985, p. 39).

There was a process akin to the Taylorization of industry apparent in these authoritarian models of welfare. Like some of those nineteenth-century community builders, reformers were concerned to improve human beings according to their specifications rather than develop new communal forms based on the articulation of needs from below. In ways which remain historically unclear, the democratic aspirations both of users and workers were regarded by the dominant forms of socialism as less important than the structuring of welfare. It was perhaps an understandable error in hard times. It was nonetheless an error, the consequences of which still resound. A compromise was struck in which democratic rights were sold for limited gains in social welfare in capitalism. Because women's lives involve them so crucially with welfare provision, this had particularly serious effects on movements for democratic control over everyday life.

It was also the case that many of the demands for the co-operative reorganization of life were overtaken by changes in capitalist society. Communal wash-houses became rather like dinosaurs, as laundrettes, private bathrooms and individual washing machines became more common after the Second World War.

During the Second World War in Britain, the need to increase wartime production meant that the state became involved in many aspects of everyday life. This produced some extraordinary double binds: while one part of the state was exhorting women to go into work in munitions and forget the housework, another was emphasizing women's role in the family. Some of the welfare schemes for which earlier generations had struggled were introduced, not on the basis of democratic human needs but because the state in wartime was concerned to maximize production. Municipal restaurants, canteens at work, school dinners and nurseries were all social gains. But they were also part of a stronger state intervening in everyday life (see Summerfield, 1984).

Feminism did not disappear after the war, but it was somewhat daunted, preserving the old demands in a series of pressure groups. Organizations of working-class women like the Women's Co-operative Guild carried on, but they were ceasing to renew themselves and their membership was growing older. Many of their former preoccupations appeared to be marginalized by the development of the welfare state.

There was, though, in Britain an important movement for economic equality among trade union women in the 1960s. This was stimulated by the struggles against the reversals that had occurred after the Second World War and by the gains that white-collar women had won. In the favourable circumstances of relatively full employment in the late 1950s and 1960s, manual working-class women were gaining in confidence and asserting equal rights again. The 1960s also saw the legalization of abortion and the emergence of voluntary groups, setting up play-groups for example, and self-help organizations like Gingerbread for single parents. Gaps in welfare provision led to the re-emergence of self-help. In squatting, struggles over homelessness and against landlords, working-class women were active. All of these apparently disparate forms of action were to affect the emergence of the women's liberation movement.

## 4.2 Transforming the meaning of democracy?

When the feminist movement reappeared in the late 1960s it seemed as if it was not linked to any previous organizational forms. It appeared to be using political assumptions which were quite unlike either those of liberal feminism or the working-class women's organizations of earlier eras.

After nearly two decades the wheel has turned several circles. The contours of similarity and contrast appear somewhat differently. It is possible to see more clearly the changed social circumstances which brought so many young women in most of the developed capitalist countries to contest their feminine destiny. The expansion of education hurtled a generation beyond the confines of their mothers' world into the male sphere of public affairs and work. Yet these social changes were not accompanied by shifts to greater social provision for children. So young mothers who had been educated for equality found themselves tied to the home when they had children. Geographical mobility cut them off from kinship networks which could have provided some assistance. Housing intensified this isolation. 'The captive wife' was discovered before the women's liberation movement emerged. She might not have anyone to talk to, but she could aspire to a fridge, a washing machine and tranquillizers like Serenid D. The market for domestic goods was flourishing, but there was no equivalent development of social provision to meet women's needs as carers and domestic workers.

The emphasis on consumption also affected the beauty industry. Here again there was an incongruence. While the adverts played on young women's anxieties about desirability, the political message was that equality had been achieved. The existence of a form of contraceptive technology which could be relied upon to be effective – before the health hazards of the pill were widely known – meant that control over fertility was no longer a gamble. Yet even amidst the optimism of the pill there were increasing numbers of young single mothers dependent on the state for welfare. There was moreover a clash in attitudes towards women's sexuality. One morality demanded virginity, another sexual proficiency, imaginative performance and the untroubled achievement of orgasm (Heron, 1985, pp. 1–9).

It is perhaps not surprising that young women facing these contradictory versions of what women should be like, which, with differing emphases were also prevalent in North America and Europe, began to seek their own definitions. It was hard to find a language that carried them into the arena of politics (see Rowbotham, 1973). Their aspirations could not be expressed in terms of political democracy. The vote after all had been won. Nor did they completely coincide with the arguments for economic equality which working-class women in the trade unions were expressing. They were to involve widening the definitions of democracy to include domestic inequality, identity, control over sexuality, challenge to cultural representation, community control over state welfare and more equal access to public resources. Strangely enough this has been a process of looking backwards as well as forwards and discovering many lost trails which had been silted over in women's past struggles. Historical recognition emerged which signposted ways in which feminists had wanted much more of democracy than the vote – not only in the capitalist countries but in the Third World as well (see Jayawardena, 1986).

But the political concepts used by women's liberation were to be found in more recent movements. The new movement drew on ideas current in civil rights, black power, the American new left, the student movement and the May events in France in 1968.

Already in these earlier movements it is possible to find extended meanings of democracy which have come to be associated with feminism. These are the idea that 'the personal is political', which involves challenging the boundaries of concepts of politics, the assumption that democratic control has to be extended not only to the workplace but to the circumstances of everyday life, and the conviction that the *forms* of actions chosen contribute to the result, and should consequently seek to prefigure an alternative (see Breines, 1982; Duchan, 1986).

It is not to diminish women's liberation as a movement to say that it drew on ideas which existed in other social movements as well as rejecting the male domination that was present in these. Feminism developed often as a challenge to the way these movements failed to live up to their own democratic ideals in relation to women. Women turned the men's rhetoric towards their own inequality, both in the public politics of radical movements and in personal life. The recognition of political derivations is in fact a useful corrective to the danger, which is always there in considering feminism, of fostering an artificially contained sphere of thought which is presented as having no dynamic interaction. This, of course, leaves 'politics in general' still a male sphere.

The women's movement put the political concepts of the earlier radical movements to a sustained test in practice. The attempt to understand how they have served us – for well or ill – and where the difficulties have arisen is of relevance not only for feminism but for other political movements. This would be an enormous project if it were to be done in depth. What follows here is a cursory note on influences and the working through of concepts. I believe the innovations in thinking about democracy were creative. They are still of political relevance. This does not mean, of course, that they are sacrosanct. There is sufficient historical evidence now to reflect on their deficiencies. It is evidently wearisome and costly to repeat unnecessary follies, so the effort to disentangle recurring patterns of log-jam and muddle is worthwhile.

In the 1960s the American new left, which arose mainly among students and young people opposing the Vietnam war, asserted that political action must be taken by and for oneself. The political process must be a means to change and the realization of power. They moved beyond the idea of equal rights to a demand for equality of power. Those concerns were reminiscent of C. Wright Mill's preoccupation with power and powerlessness. The student movement saw politics not as an external and formal area of activity but as about creating new relationships in one's own life, prefiguring new forms of communal connection. Democracy must be direct and participatory, there must be no distinction between leaders and led. The origins of these approaches to democracy can be traced back to the civil rights movement of the 1950s and even further back to radical strands of Christianity which were struggling with conflict between a gospel of love and its denial in a racist society.

John Lewis, for example, was a young Baptist who became involved in the civil rights sit-ins and the Freedom Rides against segregation in Nashville. In *They Should have Served that Cup of Coffee*, he reflects on his politicization:

> We talked in terms of our goal, our dream, being the beloved community, the open society, the society that is at peace with itself. You come to the point where you forget about race and color and see people as human beings. And we dealt a great deal with questions of means and ends. If you want to create the beloved community, create an open society, then the means, the methods must be ones of love and peace. And redemptive suffering, if necessary, may in itself help to redeem the larger society. I think we had grown up with these ideas to a certain degree... And I just had the feeling of a holy crusade – with the music and the mass meetings and without anything else, only with a dream, with a daring faith. (Lewis, in Cluster, 1979, p. 7)

These feelings stirred people far beyond Nashville. They brought a renewal of radicalism when socialism was in a crisis over the destructive effect of inhuman and barbaric means (Stalinism), when socialism had abandoned the utopian vision and ceased to inspire with dream or quest. People far beyond America saw the civil rights marches on television, saw photos of black Americans being attacked by police dogs, read about the bravery of people like Rosa Parks, who refused to give up her seat on the white section of a crowded bus in Montgomery, Alabama and started a bus boycott. A generation learned that democracy was not only about voting but involved direct action.

As Bernice Reagon says, 'the Civil Rights Movement borned not just the Black Power or Black revolutionary movements but every progressive struggle that has occurred in this country since that time... the centering, borning essence of the 60's, of the New Left, is the Civil Rights Movement' (Reagon, in Cluster, 1979, pp. 37–8).[4]

### 4.3 'The personal is political'

The assertion in the American black movement that democracy involved issues of identity and culture was taken up by the women's and gay liberation movements. It highlighted the forms of control that persisted even within movements overtly committed to equality and freedom.

Leslie Cagan was involved in the civil rights movement, in the struggle against the Vietnam war, in the early women's liberation groups in the USA and 'came out' as a lesbian. She expresses various aspects of the meaning of 'the personal is political' in her memories of the 1960s in *They Should have Served that Cup of Coffee*. She notes the emphasis on process in these early women's liberation groups. The rejection of hierarchy and the attempt to find a new community in collective living with shared child-care and domestic tasks were important. There was also a probing of the external definitions of equality:

> We weren't all equals in the house. There is a way that men were able to integrate the surface changes like doing dishes and cooking and laundry, but there is another level of what it means to be a man and what it means to be a woman that we still haven't changed. There is a deep psychological kind of thing, and it has to do with where our own identities are centred. (Cagan, in Cluster, 1979, p. 249)

The pursuit of 'deep psychological kinds of things' introduced into the discussion of democracy feelings and aspects of life which has generally been considered to be outside the orbit of politics. The insistence that the personal is political could make comprehensible forms of behaviour in political movements which otherwise seemed irrational. Silence in meetings from women could be accompanied by smouldering resentment outside, for instance. It also challenged the split that many young women noticed between men's public acceptance of formal equality for women and the reversal in private sexual relations in which men assumed women were inferior. Leslie Cagan says: 'We began to see that sex between men and women, for instance, is often the arena where the power relations between the sexes is played out' (Cagan, in Cluster, 1979, p. 253).

Gay liberation and lesbians in the women's movement began to question the cultural assumption that heterosexuality was the norm. The definition of normality was seen to be an expression of political power. Leslie Cagan adds:

> I think we still don't know a lot of what we're talking about when we say that sexuality is a political issue, or how it is used to control people, but whatever sexuality is, people still don't talk about it openly and freely. It's still an area where people are very much afraid to step out of line. It is a kind of repression that makes people afraid to assert their own needs and desires. (Cagan, in Cluster, 1979, p. 253)

The slogan 'the personal is political' opened up the possibility of under-standing aspects of public politics which were disregarded, and extended political argument about democracy in the domestic and sexual life. But the levels of complexity that it has encountered in attempting to democratize these aspects of life have been manifold. Some of these have been so discouraging that often the attempt has tacitly been abandoned in sheer exhaustion. Yet clearly the concept touches on vital elements in subordination. It is worthwhile examining the points where the vision of total democracy wore itself out. For with each new upsurge among women the impulse reappears to personalize democracy, because the social subordination of women is so deeply enmeshed in how we come to identify and value ourselves in personal and intimate ways. Perhaps there is a course to be steered and errors to be avoided.

It became evident that declaring the personal to be political put people under a tremendous moral strain. It was a vision of change premised on an effort of will – always a strong current in American radicalism. This total transformation of life, almost akin to conversion, could carry people in a state of exaltation into action which was inconceivable in their previous lives. But it could become an intolerable burden. For the declaration that the personal is political does not solve the problems of material life, any more than the assertion of equal rights. Nor does it ensure individual happiness.

Tremendous tussles were to ensue between political parts of the personal and individual feeling. The fusion of the personal with politics denied individual differences of experience, knowledge, skill. Combined with the passion for democracy it produced organizational contortions in which people denied capacities which could have been useful to others out of shame in excelling in any area of activity. Moreover, as the consensus of collectivity replaced any procedure for establishing the choice of leaders, a whole series of aberrations of democracy ensued. Thick-skinned and authoritarian characters emerged by default and were presented by the media as the movement's leaders. Or, less noticeably, an internal hidden leadership operated as a network developing a new style of political skills in small groups. Individuals caused havoc by using emotions to block majorities. The problem of how to organize without leaders revealed that leadership had varying forms, some negative and others positive. Understanding did emerge from these painful experiences. For example, the distrust of individual skill was relaxed. Women's conferences adopted a mixture of clearly defined structures with unplanned and more personal forms of organizing. But the problem of how to disagree politically with 'sisters' to whom you were personally connected, the vexation in challenging leaders who were invisible, meant that the distancing of more formal styles of limited democracy was impossible. The political opponents had to be bad people and thus no longer sisters. They had to be made outcasts if the 'beloved community' was to retain its purity.

As for politicizing sexual relations – and democratizing them, too – someday this valiant endeavour will find worthy chroniclers among feminists with the precision of Proust and the ornery passion of Lawrence – perhaps. I confess I am wary of dipping into such deep water and surfacing with oversimplified 'political' pronouncements.

There have been intense conflicts in women's liberation both among lesbians and heterosexual women about the personal/political dimensions of sexual desire. The theory was that by politicizing all aspects of life it would be possible to bring democratic relationships into being. Only when this split was overcome could political participation be 'self-actualizing' and integrate women as whole people.

At times in the history of the women's movement individuals have experienced this integration. But there have been other more tricky manifestations. Joan Nestle, who was involved in early lesbian feminist groups in New York, has pointed to the creation of new boundaries. 'The beloved community' had the danger of closing itself off from the old immoral world, becoming a self-righteous elect with a consensus ethic which can become a new form of repression rather than a means of democratic self-realization:

> I started noticing that there were whole populations of women who had given me strength to survive, women that I had loved in the late 50's and 60's that I did not see any place in this new world. I learned that I had to keep my mouth shut about certain things because it didn't fit in to the required 'pass port' to enter this world and stay in it. I learned that class played a role, but wasn't to be talked about: and certain sexual practices were taboo . . . Now I was living another double life in feminism . . . I knew that something was missing in the world I saw around me; understandings were missing. Just as feminism had given me things, I was also losing something. (quoted in Gottlieb, 1986, p. 23)

It may be that the development of a conscious political commitment to change necessarily involves a certain estrangement, a distinguishing from as well as a desire for union. But it is necessary for a democratic movement to hold the tension open between the impulses. The desire to fuse the personal with the political has attempted to dissolve the tension by will and has constructed new boundaries.

Concealed inequalities of power can be present within the formulation of personal needs, as Joan Nestle observed. In other words, some women are able to define the personal as having a general validity when it is simply their own social conception as persons. This has led to the recognition of much deeper dimensions to the issues of democracy and inequality than would be possible within the scope of an equal rights approach alone. Speaking at a trade union college in the United States a few years ago I said how in the early days of women's liberation the stress on organizational autonomy from men was important because so many of us felt dependent on men emotionally and intellectually. A young black working-class woman remarked that this was not her problem. She would like some of this dependence for a change. Then she could perhaps reject it. The apprehension of personal need is always within a specific set of circumstances. It cannot always be lifted from one situation to another. The difficulty then comes in developing radical demands and policies which do not express only partial and inegalitarian concepts of need.

Another stumbling block has been the incongruence between individual happiness and pleasure and the politicization of personal life. Again individual women have known harmony. There have been glimpses of possibility. But in between the glimpses there has been considerable confusion. Awkwardly sexual desires and emotion do not always go in accordance with the conscious aim to democratize human relations. Against the evident inadequacy of attempting to regulate the erotic by issuing a series of moral imperatives, many feminists have turned to therapy and psychoanalysis. It is not clear where this leaves the effort to understand how aspects of experience, which have tended to be outside politics in its conventional definition, affect our comprehension of democracy (see Barrett, 1980, pp. 42–83).

It is much easier to note what has gone wrong than to produce, like the philosopher's stone, a new synthesis. But I would suggest that while the effort to understand consciously all aspects of our lives is important, it cannot always be equated with individual happiness. Thus while the aim of political action should not be to make us miserable, we cannot guarantee that politics will make us happy. Perhaps, too, it is an oversimplified translation of the democratization of relations to assume that our wants are consistent and our consciousness uncontradictory. For instance, we can want control and loss of control at the same time.

The interconnection between our conscious efforts to extend democracy and erotic exploration of fantasy and play can be both reflective and ambivalent. This can reveal opposition in desires. Such oppositions can serve to illuminate rigidities which appear in those aspects of our conscious politics which we ignore. This does not make for peace of mind or orderly agendas, but it brings a certain dialectic into theories of democracy.

The recognition that there is not an easy 'fit' between different aspects of human experience is not to deny their interaction. Shifts in the culture of sexuality do occur. Sexual relations and people's perception of their sexuality clearly have altered and continue to change. But the process is not one that can be simply equated with a demand for political rights or economic equality. Nor can we assume that they will synchronize historically. The capacity to imagine relations of freedom, 'the beloved community' in opposition to relations we know, will draw on personal psychological experience. But this does not mean that our feelings can be administered even by democratic decree. Democratic political theory is in many ways lumbering and archaic in response to the complex interactions between our personal sense of our wants and desires and their public expression.

However, the slogan 'the personal is political' is apposite even if, like aerosol sprays, it should be used with caution, for it represents a radical recognition that democracy has to fight on the new terrain of subjectivity.

## 4.4  Politics, work and inequality

The connection between the personal and the political has also brought insights about areas of activity already included in the sphere of politics. It indicates the complexity of women's needs in paid employment and the inadequacy of existing male-controlled forms of organizing as a vehicle for their expression.

The effort to tackle women's inequality at work in relation to relationships in the family has led to a wide range of demands to change the nature of work and labour movement politics. In linking control over work to other aspects of control in the home, the community and the state, feminists have been among the radical groups who have argued not only for a 'bigger piece of the pie' but for a qualitatively different economy and for a concept of economics which is not confined either to profit or the redistribution of the fruits of paid labour (see Phillips, 1983).

Existing theories of democracy based on equal rights or workers' control are not adequate to express the double identity women often express of work and home. Women can thus create forms of democratic organization but not see them as 'politics'.

The insight that the personal is political has been a means of illuminating how consciousness at work cannot be detached from other aspects of identity. For example, Anna Pollert, in a study of a Bristol factory in the 1970s, describes how the women tobacco workers lived a split life in which their view of themselves as women did not accord with their actual predicament. They knew that their working lives were to be continuous, yet they still thought that ideally a man should be expected to support them. They were not the same as men workers. They saw themselves as having only secondary rights to work. As one woman said: 'I don't really believe in married women working. Well 'cos there's not much work anyway, and they ought to make room for people what've got to lead their own lives'. Anna Pollert comments: 'What emerge are the fragmentary ideas of unresolved commonsense. . . because it is a partial acceptance and partial rejection of ruling conceptions of the world it is full of contradictions' (Pollert, 1981, p. 232–3).

Judy Wajcman, in her study of the Fakenham co-operative in Norfolk, which was started by women shoe-workers as a response to closure in 1972, shows how the fragmentation of consciousness and identity of the women co-operators expressed both an experience of new relationships of work and conceptions of politics which were in accord with their encounters with unions and parties. The worker-director, Nancy, said she believed in shared decision-making: 'People aren't afraid to talk here. . . when we make a decision it's an overall decision by everybody' (Wajcman, 1983, p. 157). She felt the co-op had enabled them to grow in 'self-confidence'. Despite the economic struggles of the co-op the women enjoyed the changes in work relations in the factory. One told Judy Wajcman, 'It's a home from home' (p. 159).

At the same time the women maintained that they were not interested in 'politics'. Nancy herself said that although the struggle for the co-op took her away from the conservatism which prevailed in Fakenham, it did not make her think she would vote Labour: 'I'm Conservative-minded at heart'. She had grown up in a predominantly conservative area of Ireland and was an active Catholic. The co-op alone was not to counter these roots in conservatism.

There is not an automatic transmission belt from one experience of more democratic and equal relations through to left-wing political organizing. Ultimately, at the Fakenham co-operative enthusiasm was not sufficient to overcome lack of managerial skills and the market. The union was no great help. The Conservatives were the only political party in Fakenham.

The desire for the extension of democracy and equality can thus coexist with an opposing desire to hang on to what we know. Our needs are ambiguous. They are rooted in what we know as well as searching for an alternative expression. Because formal politics often ignores both personal domestic life and personal feeling, these aspects of life are often asserted in opposition to radical change. 'The personal is political' has thus enabled feminists to approach women's attitudes to work and the economy with new understandings.

The effort to understand the basis for desires to conserve can sometimes indicate limits in an apparently radical political formulation. Audrey Wise (no date) tells a story of her experience as an USDAW official, encountering suspicion and opposition from women to the demand for equal pay. When she probed a little deeper she found that these feelings were locked in with fears that equal pay would mean women had to work nights. Their commitment to their families was more important than money. If the criterion of economic bargaining is used, this consciousness is likely to be downgraded. Yet Audrey Wise shows how such feelings also reached towards a more radical vision of what might be. One woman maintained: 'If the economy tells me I have to work nights, I want a different economy'.

The link between the personal and the political has brought the consciousness of domestic life into the sphere of politics and economics. Betty Friedan's *The Feminine Mystique* (1963) pioneered discussion in the early 1960s of a problem without a name, the unhappiness of American middle-class suburban women whose predicament could not be expressed in terms of unequal rights or material exploitation. A search for a solution to the feelings of lack of identity which did not simply swell the profits of the drug corporations was a significant element in the emergence of women's liberation. The first step was the admission of such feelings within the sphere of politics. The form of the small consciousness-raising group served to communicate individual distress in a social context. It was yet another manifestation of the personal as political. It gave rise to a literature of complaint. An early account in Britain was Suzanne Gail's 'The housewife':

> It was never a burden to me to be a woman before I had Carl. Feminists had seemed to me to be tilting at windmills; women who allowed men to rule them did so from their own free choice. I felt that I had proved myself the intellectual equal of men, and maintained my femininity as well. But afterwards I quite lost my sense of identity; for weeks it was an effort to speak. (Gail, 1980, p. 108)

Not content with the repeated expression of dissatisfaction, women sought solutions. They sought to confront the inequality between men and women in the 'personal' sphere of the family, not only in the radical communes or in middle-class homes but among the working class as well. Domestic inequality has been linked to the inequality between men and women in paid employment and to the interconnecting aspects of democracy. One of the best summaries of these arguments is Sandra Kerr's song 'The Maintenance Engineer':

> One Friday night it happened, some years after we were wed,
> When my old man came in from work as usual I said,
> Your tea is on the table, clean clothes are on the rack,
> Your bath'll soon be ready, I'll come and scrub your back,
> He kissed me very tenderly, and said 'I tell you flat,
> The service I give my machine ain't half as good as that'.
> I said, 'I'm not your little woman, your sweetheart or your
>     dear,
> I'm a wage slave without wages, I'm a maintenance
>     engineer'.
> So then we got to talking I told him how I felt,
> How I keep him running just as smooth as some conveyor
>     belt,
> For after all it's I'm the one provides the power supply,
> (He goes like the clappers on my steak and kidney pie),
> His fittings are all shining 'cos I keep them nice and
>     clean,
> And he tells me his machine tool is the best I've ever
>     seen.
> (Kerr, in Henderson *et al.*, 1979, pp. 136–7)

The song goes on to describe the terms of employment of domestic labour and the benefits both to the male worker and his employer. Then there is the woman's part-time job on low wages, from which yet another man profits:

> He looked a little sheepish and he said, 'As from today
> The lads and me will see what we can do on equal pay.

> Would you like a housewives union? Do you think you should
>   be paid?
> As a cook and as a cleaner, as a nurse and as a maid?.
> I said 'Don't jump the gun, love, if you did your share at
>   home,
> Perhaps I'd *have* some time to fight some battles of my
>   own!'

In the last verse she adds:

> I've heard you tell me how you'll pull the bosses down,
> You'll never do it, brother, while you're bossing me
>   around.

The exposure of a neglected inequality has led to arguments about how time is apportioned and activities divided, not only between individual men and women in particular households, but in society as a whole (see Beechey and Whitelegg, 1986; Herzog, 1980; Liff, 1985). The modern women's liberation movement has questioned fundamentally how work and pay is structured, how the economy is conceptualized and planned, and how in our society dependants are cared for, skill is defined and work valued.

Feminists have also challenged the hidden inequalities in the distribution of social resources which is institutionalized in state policy. Women as a sex are responsible for a great deal of unpaid caring and labour in domestic life. Yet the awareness of society's responsibility to contribute resources to make it easier for these activities to be done by either women or men is minimal.

It has become clear, too, that women are underrepresented in the political institutions where decisions about economic life and state policy are taken. The right to the vote has not been a sufficient means of engaging with the inequality that persists in society between men and women.

These issues are so wide-ranging in their implications for fundamental change that it has been difficult to find a strategic focus which could indicate how we could begin. In the tighter circumstances of the 1980s it might appear that the desire to extend democracy over the relations of everyday life would be forced into retreat.

However, the impetus to meet everyday needs has not been lost, despite changing economic circumstance. A significant step towards attempting to meet the neglected needs that women experience in everyday life, both in terms of employment and the home, was taken in London by the Greater London Council in the early 1980s. Here the lack of women's presence in representative democracy was to a degree tackled at the level of local city administration. Interestingly, the experience of attempting to meet unmet needs through representative democratic forms involved new combinations of these with the direct democracy of rank-and-file groups of workers and community organizations.

The issue of more equal forms of distribution was thus linked to changes in the relationship of the local state with people in London. Because some of the Labour councillors believed that elected power was a resource, which people excluded from the democratic process and with unequal access to public funds should be able to utilize more fully, the GLC gave grants to many voluntary groups and trade unionists to tackle the economic and social problems that faced them.

Some public resources began to reach women through this radicalization of local government, in which feminists have played an important role. Attempts to tackle women's low pay and lack of training revealed how employment interconnected with domestic care. The desperate need for nurseries in London, where there are many single mothers and married women with young children who are likely to work, was asserted more immediately. This led to proposals from groups of women not simply for nurseries but for ways of changing the inconveniences of child-care in a big city which is more hospitable to the motor car than the young. There was a need for help with small children at work, in training centres, in meetings, in shops. Apart from setting up crèches and campaigning for training courses to include child-care, the GLC approach also served to enable women to express fears about the lack of safety in the design of council housing, the danger from lorries on busy roads, and the inconvenient design of public transport. Young people themselves proposed plans for their area: water sports on the disused docklands, a sports centre in an enormous empty shed in North Woolwich, for example.

Pensioners who could not afford washing machines argued for a community laundry, Westway in Notting Hill. The laundry did the washing for a neighbouring nursery, and the children's pictures were all round the walls. It served as a social meeting place and informal advice centre where elderly people felt welcomed and safe. The popularity of the laundry suggests that convivial washing places are still needed by the 20 per cent or so of households without machines. If they were widespread and free they could mean that a washing machine was not the only choice.[5]

These innovatory proposals had only a few years to develop. They suggest that there are a whole range of disgruntlements which go unexpressed because people can see no hope of change. The market has been capitalism's means of responding to needs. In certain areas of life it has been a deft and adroit mechanism, though at severe human cost. In the zone of caring for people, which happens to be assigned largely to women, the market is clearly an inadequate means of meeting needs – except by providing private services for the rich.[6] The demonstration in practice that the details of everyday life could be a great deal more pleasant is an important element in strengthening the case for a wider understanding.

**4.5 Needs, demands and processes**

Small groups in the women's liberation movement – originally called consciousness-raising groups – have provided an organizational form which has enabled women to find a way of expressing their needs in political language. Such groups have proved adaptable as a political form to women in very different circumstances; they provide a forum which is one step removed from simply talking with friends.

In Flin Flon in Canada, Meg Luxton interviewed three generations of women in the 1970s. The women began meeting and talked about their responses to women's liberation. One of them said, 'I think the women's movement is any women who try to figure out what happens to women and then try to do something about it to make it better'. Meg Luxton summarizes this process:

> As women become conscious of the conditions of their work, they begin to face the contradictions of their daily lives. Then they decide what their immediate needs are. Once they have determined those needs, they establish a series of demands based on where they decide they want to go. This means that the women's movement is constantly grappling about what kind of life women want to live. (Luxton, 1980, p. 204)

Of course, translating the open discussion into a specific attempt to make change has not always gone so smoothly. Problems have consistently recurred. Once needs turn into demands they tend to become uprooted. Demands travel more easily but they can lose the flexible character of needs. Detached from the contradictory muddle of life they can shed important facets. When demands are lifted from one culture to another what is lost can distort their implications. There has been considerable danger that the feminists of the big, powerful capitalist countries assume that their version of what women need is universal. Feminist demands come from particular social circumstances. Priorities of need vary.

Even within the same society there can be an implicit imperialism of assumption. Needs articulated by more privileged women are assumed to be those of all women. The consensus of the small group can have a hidden form of inequality preserved unchallenged within it. The direct democracy of the small group is not infallible. The articulation of needs is not completely free from a tendency within the concept of rights to 'uproot' needs. Needs can be presented as universal demands – demands which ignore that circumstances vary with the social context in which needs develop. For example, the challenge to the sexual division of labour and the insistence on men and women sharing child-care has been a very strong element in contemporary feminism. But it tends to assume that there is one kind of household.

Beverley Bryan, Stella Dadzie and Suzanne Scafe, in *The Heart of the Race* (1985), point out that families differ. Many black women bring up their children and the children of other relatives on their own. They have been forced to take on this responsibility because the cultural forms of the family from slave times have meant that the men are not always around. They are concerned to recognize that this has contributed to the strength and independence that has developed among the women, without romanticizing the heavy burden of labour as an ideal. This suggests that, for example, the demand to share housework and child-care is not so appropriate: the man has to be there in the first place for this to make sense. When needs become formulated into a means of action in the form of demands they lose their ambiguities. Women can at once resent housework and continuous child-care and find fulfilment by trying to do these well. Arguments for change can be perceived as a denigration of what is done and an assault on identity. These contradictory needs can be expressed in a small group. But it is not always possible then to find ways of acting upon them without reducing their complexity.

The women's movement has not solved the political conundrum of how you divide domestic labour more equitably between the sexes and yet enable the skills and creativity that are present amidst the repetitive toil to be developed and socially valued.

Dissatisfaction with everyday life is not automatically aligned to feminism. In North America there have been grassroots movements of the right which are anti-feminist, seeing feminism as connected to modernizing strands in modern capitalism which threaten values they cherish (see Segal, 1983). These are not arguments *against* the extension of democracy through new political forms into everyday life. The point is the recognition that while the women's movement has opened up new ways of uncovering what people want, this is by no means a facile process. There are many checks to democracy and the creation of 'the beloved community'.

### 4.6 Alternative futures and the state

It is not always possible to travel the journey from need through demand and strategy and glimpse visions of what might be. One woman's vision of the future is, of course, not necessarily another's. Nonetheless, visions of what might be are precious, for they sustain hope and humour: without these qualities democracy becomes far too difficult for most of us to bother with. Visions pop out amidst the politics of needs and strategies in women's liberation writing.

In the mid-1970s, a member of a food co-op on a housing estate in Bow, for example, said:

> I'd like to get out of this house and go into a larger house and live communally . . . because that's the ideal form of how these tower blocks could be if people were really together instead of having 100 kitchens used by the appropriate amount of people so that all the ladies can have time off 'cause they all do the same thing the same way and they're all neurotic as hell all popping their

pills and seeing their doctors twice a week – for what? Because of the agitation of the tower block. But really it would be so cool and nice if they really got together, if they forgot that one has the better possession than the other, because we should all be working for freedom and not just getting tied up with possessions and making money to buy more possessions that will tie us up even more. We'd only need one washing machine between us all. We'd cut the manufacturers' production line because we'd only need a few of the special things. (People's Food Co-op, Lincoln Estate Newsletter)

This particular vision clearly inclines to the Greens. There have been others which draw on socialist and kibbutz models of large communes. A writer in the Socialist Workers' Party's *Womens Voice* in 1976 envisaged the children all 'sleeping in a communal neighbourhood dormitory being looked after by a qualified nurse' (to the horror of the typesetter, who inserted a sarcastic comment in the article). There have been visions of detachment. A woman who organized a demonstration at Fulham Town Hall in 1971 – over conditions in a halfway house – talked of her hopes for a new relationship she had found with a man called Joseph in the London Women's Liberation Workshop Newsletter, *Shrew*:

What would I do? Maybe a bit of gardening, tootle along...Joseph and me'll see each other at weekends. I think it's good for men and women to get away from each other and not be under each other's feet the whole time. Otherwise you just run out of speech. (*Shrew*, September 1971)

In *From Hand to Mouth* Marianne Herzog describes how the women welding fuses in a German factory dream of their loves before marriage, of owning an ice-cream parlour: 'Piecework dreams go back mostly to the past. When they are welding, one fetches them; when the bell goes for a break, they disappear (Herzog, 1980, p. 53).

In 1973 French women workers occupied their clock factory, Lip. Afterwards a participant who was reinstated described her mixed feelings to be back in the old regime of 'conformity and punctuality' and the rush to combine work with housework: 'I would once again become dependent on a society which doesn't give us the time to think' (Herzog, 1980, p. 140). She said she would miss the 'fraternal freedom, a freedom of expression, a form of culture' acquired in the occupation. Yet she felt strength from their victory and things were not quite the same as before: 'the great friendship which arose during the struggle is still alive' (Herzog, p. 140).

The radical movements of the last two decades which have so tantalizingly yearned for 'the beloved community' or 'the great friendship' have remained puzzled about how it comes about that people move from expressing immediate needs within the society as it is, towards a desire for new ways of living and new relationships. How can such a transition be fostered and the will o' the wisp glimpses garnered to enlighten dark times?

A strong impulse in women's liberation has been the effort to prefigure visions of the new in the effort to transform the old. This has influenced both how strategies of action have been developed and how organization has been approached.

Again, the concept of prefigurative politics was present in the earlier movements of the 1960s. It was particularly influential in the German student movement, where for the first left generation after fascism, the need to create a new culture which was anti-authoritarian and democratic was a passionate endeavour. The German students tried to create new kinds of communal families where children would not be subject to adult authority. They set up 'kindershop' nurseries in empty shop fronts in which they squatted. While the children played, the grown-ups discussed Marxist theory and sexual politics. The French equivalent was the *crèche sauvage* which was stormed by the Paris police in 1969 (see Rowbotham, 1983). Transplanted to Britain, though, this form of prefiguration proved to be a non-starter.

In 1969 Susan Cowley (now O'Sullivan) reported in *Shrew*:

> An essential part of the German kindershop and of our projected group has been the necessity of men and women, parents and non-parents being involved in order to break down the women's role as child-minder and to develop the concept that children are the responsibility of the community...At our first meetings with children and adults we found we had nothing to say. All of us at one time or another had talked articulately about a creche. But there we were with no compelling interest in one another and while the kids were happy we weren't. (Cowley, 1969)

It was not to be a complete damp squib, however, because the ideas that child-care should embody more equal sharing relationships and prefigure a caring community were to persist. In a British context, though, with strong political assumptions of campaigning for state provision as a right, the strategy of setting up your own child-care group on a self-help basis appeared to some women to be an evasion. After all, the state controlled public resources to which people had given their contribution. They had a right to claim these back in the form of social provision. Otherwise they were putting in a double effort, setting up self-help projects and paying the state to provide welfare.

Throughout the 1970s there was a radical attack on the hierarchy within welfare services. It was argued that welfare itself was a means of controlling and manipulating people. It existed only because capitalism needed a healthy workforce to keep up production levels.

These arguments resounded in the women's movement and were one of the reasons why it took so long to develop a child-care campaign. Feminists have never produced a clear position on the state. Intense hostility to the state has appeared in the context of single mothers struggling against social security, black women confronting immigration laws and Irish women's conflicts within prison. At the same time women have made demands on the state for increased benefits (the family allowance campaign and money for carers of dependants) and the abortion campaign has involved the lobbying of Parliament. Moreover, the significance of welfare in women's lives has been clear. In some feminist arguments dependence on the state has even been seen as preferable to dependence on the man in the family. The state has been presented as already prefiguring collectivity.

The contradictory encounters with the state and the need for the resources it controls gave rise to an attempt to make demands upon it without abandoning the effort to change relationships in welfare provision and retain democratic control over services. These approaches were outlined in the late 1970s in the London to Edinburgh Weekend Return Group's *In and Against the State* (1979) and by Rowbotham *et al.* in *Beyond the Fragments* (1979). But they came out of innumerable discussions about specific struggles.

For example, Audrey Wise responded in 1970 to socialist women who were critical of the self-help approach to nurseries in women's liberation. They were arguing that the demand for nurseries was the priority; the issue of control could be sorted out later. She said that community control had to be part of the struggle to get the resources from the state. Democracy was crucial. Here the arguments of workers' control which were being raised in the trade union movement influenced child-care (Wise, 1970). It was an important breakthrough which was hardly observable at the time.

Wise's theoretical connection became a practical possibility early in the 1970s when a group of women in London started the Dartmouth Park Hill nursery. They persuaded Camden Council to buy an old house and they organized the nursery. In other parts of London buildings were squatted and eventually grants were obtained from the council. Over time the voluntary enthusiasm became formalized into paid employment, with the workers being unionized. Community nurseries linked up with other child-care groups, first in boroughs and then on a London-wide basis – a process which was assisted in the mid-1980s by the GLC.

It has been much harder outside London. But the combination of pre-figuration and demands for public resources have appeared in other contexts. In 1975 some women on a Catholic estate in Northern Ireland tried to set up a play-group. They were called 'Catholic bastards' but defiantly they named it 'Saorise' – freedom. They wrote in *Spare Rib*:

> Of course community nurseries are only stop-gap measures in themelves. We are demanding free nursery facilities for all children. But they will only be provided if we involve ourselves in projects such as this and break down some of the structure imposed on us by the system. We hope to create in the nursery an awareness of collectivity and sympathy amongst our children before they enter primary school. (*Spare Rib*, No. 41, November 1975)

Because the community nursery represents very clearly both the democratic aspiration to embody new relationships and the older democratic insistence on the need for a more equitable distribution of resources, the problems that have arisen from practice throw light on the political tensions in the strategy of regarding the state as a terrain of struggle. Direct democracy is not always untroubled.

One recurring problem is what is meant by community. In some places a group like these Irish women can claim with confidence that they are 'the community'. In London and other large English cities, however, 'the community' can often simply be an empty space or in reality innumerable lost souls or competing groups. As black women have pointed out also, 'the community' could well be at loggerheads with one another, a problem which tended to be pushed under the carpet by the people who started community nurseries, who were mainly white. Community control can thus be a complicated extension of democracy. Between competing interests within the community or between workers and users in a community nursery, who decides? Increasingly it tends to be the sovereign body of the local council. It is representative democracy that holds the purse strings.

Moreover, by bringing democratic control into the circumstances of everyday life, the problems that exist with the remote control we have through the franchise are not completely avoided. Not everyone wants to be out every evening prefiguring 'the beloved community' in draughty rooms. After a few years when the zeal dies down the democratic imperative can become a bind not a joy, leaving the nursery's committee stranded until some crisis occurs. There can be as much a problem in getting parents to participate in running a nursery as political parties have in dragging people out to exercise their right to vote.

Community nurseries have also come up against the conflict between the aim to serve the local community democratically, reaching out to everyone rather than a select radical few, and the desire that they will prefigure a democratic future. There is no reason why wanting your child to go to nursery implies you believe in anti-authoritarian and anti-sexist child-rearing. There can be a clash between immediate needs and visions of alternatives. There is no easy democratic answer.

A worker in a Chapeltown nursery in Leeds said in *Spare Rib* in 1976: 'You can't suddenly say to a girl you're wrong to want to be in the kitchen and give a dish-cloth to the lads. You wouldn't do it fast anyway. Because the parents are at home and they're doing it differently' (*Spare Rib*, No. 53, December 1976).

There has been a sustained tussle over the whole issue of centralized state services and grassroots democracy. This has had implications far beyond feminists' concern with democracy. For example, speaking to the Women's Royal Voluntary Service in 1981, Margaret Thatcher said she believed the government should 'help independent voluntary bodies financially, because those bodies can do things which the government can't or they can do them a lot better' (quoted in Ungerson, 1985, p. 217).

The government, 'merely the instrument of the taxpayer', has to help, but not too much or else they might sap the voluntary organisations' 'vitality'. She added: ·

> the willingness of men and women to give service is one of freedom's greatest safeguards – it ensures that caring remains free from political control. It leaves men and women independent enough to meet needs as they see them, and not only as the State provides. And that's why voluntary organizations such as ours can only exist effectively in a free society. (quoted in Ungerson, 1985, p. 217)

It is interesting that the conservative utopian vision expressed here is concerned to preserve freedom as a value which exists already against the centralized parasite of government (with which the speaker curiously has apparently incidental connection). The radical utopian vision sees in existing values and relationships a glimpse of a projected future. Radicals too would argue that the grassroots democracy of voluntary groups is important. But they can do little without resources and they cannot be expected to substitute for all welfare services. The power to decide how much of society's means goes to caring is with the government – sinister parasite that it is. Local government might be seen as a corrective to the overweening pride of the centre. It may be that this form of elected democracy, being another 'instrument of the taxpayer', decides to redistribute some of our livelihood towards more democratic forms of welfare. Curiously this has proved most unattractive in practice to Margaret Thatcher's centralized government. There has been a sustained onslaught on welfare, with untold human suffering as a result. Feminists have thus been involved not only in a persistent search for alternatives in the process of seeking to meet needs; they have also had to defend services against government cuts. Some of the tensions I have described in regard to child-care have appeared in other contexts, for example in housing, education and particularly health. In the 1970s the abortion campaign led outwards to a whole range of demands for information, for less hierarchical relationships, for human-centred technologies, for alternative approaches to health, for control over both treatment and research, and for a recognition of racist assumptions and unequal access to resources. In the 1980s feminists have been forced to change tack.

Lesley Doyal summed up the paradox which socialist feminists faced in these health struggles:

> On the one hand, state services can be a source of oppression as the feminist critique has shown, but on the other hand, they do contain elements of considerable value that need to be defended. This is an obvious dilemma, because in criticising services we can be accused of giving support to those who wish to cut them, and our defence of them can seem contradictory and even hypocritical. The answer, of course, lies in a more sophisticated strategy that involves the defence of services in order to maintain those aspects that we really need, while at the same time campaigning for qualitative changes in those services to meet the real needs of both users and workers. (Doyal, in Ungerson, 1985, pp. 155–6)

The demand for qualitative changes in health care have not disappeared in the 1980s, but there is no doubt that it has grown harder to combine them with the defence of the NHS. For as hospital beds go, cleaning and catering are privatized and our health service disintegrates in crisis, its desperate defence becomes all-consuming. This has placed considerable strain on the prefigurative strategy of struggling within and against the state. It has not demolished it, but it has made the integration of alternatives within the mainstream of the NHS harder.

## 4.7  Sisterhood and conflict

Strains of a rather different kind have appeared in the effort to create organizational forms within the movement of women's liberation itself. Whether feminists insisted that the movement should be autonomous, that is to say independent in defining its own course but prepared to form links and alliances with other organizations, or separatist, detached completely from men who were in this analysis seen as the enemy, it was realized that we were tackling a deep culture of subordination. We sought consciously to overcome the distrust and competition which divided women by the loving discovery of 'sisterhood'. Certainly women's liberation has meant that women have developed capacities which could not have been possible as individuals alone. Also the movement has engendered love and community and 'the great friendship'.

But when political disagreements have occurred, the intensities of these hopes of transcending existing relationships and the passionate personal emotions aroused have also given rise to painful acrimony.

Because the political was fused with the personal and because there were no external structures and formally elected leaders, there were no mechanisms for distancing feelings of hurt, betrayal and anger, and the movement fractured. The timescale has varied from country to country, town to town, but the relatively coherent networks of the 1970s have given way to a much more diffused consciousness.

Sara Evans has described this in relation to the American movement: 'As the women's movement dispersed, splintered, formed and re-formed, its importance lay less and less with the specific groups who initiated it and more with the kinds of responses it made possible' (Evans, 1979, p. 226).

The process has not of course been all one of loss, for the influences have reached wider. But it has made it difficult to maintain continuity of memory, and to examine ideas which are accepted more as articles of faith than strategic implements for transformation. There have been tremendous difficulties in maintaining a balance between the prefigurative desire for new democratic relations and strategic purposes.

Sara Evans says that in the USA, 'a preoccupation with internal process – the effort to live out the revolutionary values of egalitarianism and co-operation within the movement itself – took precedence over progress or effectiveness' (Evans, 1979, pp. 222–3).[7]

In Britain the influence of the 'old left' has been stronger. But the tension has been real. In the mid-1970s the women's group to which I belonged was discussing a question posed in our London Women's Liberation Workshop Newsletter: 'Are we a movement of liberated women or a movement for the liberation of all women?'

The danger of the desire for prefigurative liberation hardening with disappointment into a moralistic and self-righteous sub-culture has been off-set by opposing tendencies. The upsurge of popular movements from below always dissolves the tension; and in the 1980s the peace movement, the women in the mining communities and the radicalization of black women in growing numbers have reasserted a balance and reduced the inclination to turn inwards. Nonetheless it would evidently be better to understand more consciously how this occurs.

The organizational emphasis on prefiguration has faced a similar problem to the strategic preoccupation with means. It can evade challenging the existing structure of politics. This recognition in the 1980s has brought many socialist feminists, black as well as white, into labour movement politics, through trade unions, the Labour Party and local government. The movement towards existing institutions was made with confident hopes of changing these. This moment of confidence was crystallized in the response to *Beyond the Fragments*. Our somewhat tentative exploration of the organizational lessons of the 1970s which we hoped would bring contributions from other groups was transformed by the political needs of the movement into a standard: 'women can do it better.'

Not surprisingly it was not to be so easy. As the political circumstances of the left in the Labour Party grew more fractious and socialist feminists began to question many of the assumptions of the 1970s, women have found themselves stranded.[8] It is not at all clear how the positive aspects in the processes developed in participatory democracy which have involved so many women can combine with the representative structures of a party. Feminism in the Labour Party has tended to be phrased in terms of equal rights rather than the transformation of relationships, which was the concern of women's liberation. This restricts and forecloses the ambiguity within needs which can remain relatively open in a movement. But a party seeks programmes – ideas which cannot be modified in resolutions are simply erased. Political experience in women's liberation does not equip non-aligned socialist feminists to do battle in Labour Party committees. There has been also a paralysis over the issue of power. Did we or did we not want it? It is difficult to be effective in a party when you cannot make up your mind. The women's movement has allowed space for uncertainty – up to a point. But these are not the traditions of socialist politics. The 'not sures' tend to go to the wall – or the pub – not into the higher echelons.

On the other hand, feminists could not ostrich-like pretend with honesty that 'the movement' possessed the democratic answer. There are clearly disadvantages as well as advantages in participatory democracy. Informal leadership arises. The constant reversal of decisions makes it impossible to steer a consistent course. These difficulties apparent in the attempt to prefigure relations and change society have provoked an extreme rejection of any subjective pettifogging on the revolutionary left.

Kate Marshall, for instance, tells us in *Real Freedom*: 'The Feminist party is not concerned about catering for internal needs as such, it's aim is to give a lead in the class struggle. The feminist hostility to leadership stems from its preoccupation with individual fulfilment and with its limited aims' (Marshall, 1982, p. 108).

Behind such clarity there is in fact a hidden personal seduction, the promise of entry into a chosen elect in return for submission to the authority of a sect. There is an act of extraordinary faith in expecting that forms of organizing which require such devout subordination of self are to be the means of making a new society based on freedom. There is, moreover, a grim record of the consequences of disregarding the individual needs for freedom and letting the means take care of themselves in the history of socialism in practice. The tragic consequences have been more seriously destructive of radical possibility than the practical problems of the effort to create new democratic forms.

This history makes the effort of the women's liberation movement in the last two decades to find a better balance between means and ends, process and goal, needs and vision of considerable political significance. The consideration of the question this experience has raised is itself part of a sustained challenge to the denial of democracy to women.

Three hundred years after the Puritan women petitioned Parliament, Lorraine Bowler, a member of Barnsley Women Against Pit Closures, said at the first women's rally:

> We, as women, have not often been encouraged to be involved actively in the trade unions and organisation has always been seen as an area belonging to men. We are seen as the domesticated element of a family. This for many years has been the role expected of us. I have seen a change coming for years and the last few weeks has seen it at its best. (Bowler, 1984, p. 23)[9]

The claim to be included was not resolved in the seventeenth century. Nor has this right of access been the only claim made by women on democracy. In different historical periods, groups of women have also presented proposals for democratic forms which meet their own definition of needs. Because of differing social circumstances these have frequently contested male-defined ideas of what is required of democracy. There are thus two political endeavours which Audrey Wise has summed up as the attempt 'to feminise the general, and generalise feminism'. Women have tried to change the contours of a male-defined concept of democracy *and* assert the struggles for democracy which have been present within women's movements as integral to a democratic body politic.

It is absolutely true that this sustained historical project has not been without disagreement, error and the repetition of mistakes. It has also been resolute, creative and resilient. Its implications for change continue to be fundamental and transformatory. As one of the women at Flin Flon put it,

> What I'd really like to do is to change pretty well everything about the way people get fed, clothed and live. It takes lots of time, lots of work and not just one person to make such big changes. It seems if you don't do something, no-one will, but if one person starts and keeps things going others will. (Luxton, 1980, p. 228)

## Notes

1. See Rowbotham (1972). On Britain see Barbara Taylor (1983) *Eve and the New Jerusalem: Socialism and Feminism in the Nineteenth Century*, London, Virago, 1983; Dorothy Thompson (1984) *The Chartists*, London, Temple Smith, pp. 120–51.
2. See also Juliet Mitchell 'Women and equality', in Juliet Mitchell and Ann Oakley (eds) (1976) *The Rights and Wrongs of Women*, London, Penguin.
3. See Martha Vicinus (1985) *Independent Women, Work and Community for Single Women, 1850–1920*, London, Virago; Sheila Rowbotham (1985) pp. 51–4; David Rubinstein (1986) *Before the Suffragettes*, Brighton, Harvester Press. On America see Meredith Tax (1981) *The Rising of the Women*, New York, Monthly Review Press.
4. On the connections to women's liberation see Sara Evans (1979) *Personal Politics: the Roots of Women's Liberation in the Civil Rights Movement and the New Left*, New York, Knopf.
5. On projects backed by the GLC see *Jobs for a Change*, the newspaper of the Industry and Employment Branch and the publications of the Women's Committee.
6. See 'Domestic work and childcare', *London Industrial Strategy*, London, GLC, 1985.
7. On Britain see Liz Heron, 'Sisterhood re-examined', *New Statesman*, 1 April 1983, pp. 12–13.
8. See Sarah Perrigo (1986) 'Socialist-feminism and the Labour Party, some experiences from Leeds'. *Feminist Review*, No. 23, Summer. On women in relation to existing political structures see Barbara Rogers (1983) *Getting Women's Power Into Politics*, London, The Women's Press.
9. See also Sheila Rowbotham, interview with Jean McCrindle, 'More than just a memory, some political implication of women's involvement in the miners' strike 1984–85', *Feminist Review*, No. 23, Summer 1986.

## References

BARRETT, M. (1980) *Women's Oppression Today*, London, Verso.

BEECHEY, V. and WHITELEGG, E. (1986) *Women in Britain Today*, Milton Keynes, Open University Press.

BONDFIELD, M. (1980) 'Women as domestic workers', in ELLEN MALOS (ed.) *The Politics of Housework*, London, Allison and Busby, p. 86.

BOWLER, L. (1984) in *Barnsley Women Against Pit closures*, Women Against Pit Closures, Barnsley, p. 23.

BREINES, W. (1982) *The Great Refusal: Community and Organisation in the New Left, 1962–1968*, New York, Praeger.

BRYAN, B., DADZIE, S. and SCAFE, S. (1985) *The Heart of the Race*, London, Virago.

CAGAN, L. (1979) in DICK CLUSTER (1979) p. 249.

CLUSTER, D. (1979) *They Should Have Served That Cup of Coffee*, Boston, Southend Press.

COWLEY, S. (1969) 'The Tufnell Park Creche', *Shrew*, Summer.

DOYAL, L. (1985) 'Women and health care policy', in CLARE UNGERSON (ed.) *Women and Social Policy*, pp. 155–6.

DRAKE, B. (1984, first published 1920) *Women in Trade Unions*, London, Virago.

DUCHAN, C. (1986) *Feminism in France from May 1968 to Mitterand*, London, Routledge and Kegan Paul.

EVANS, S. (1979) *Personal Politics: the Roots of Women's Liberation in the Civil Rights Movement and the New Left*, New York, Knopf.

FRIEDAN, B. (1963, reprinted 1974) *The Feminine Mystique*, New York, Norton.

GAFLIN, J. and THOMS, D. (1983) *Caring and Sharing. The Centenary History of the Co-operative Women's Guild*, Manchester Co-operative Union.

GAIL, S. (1980) 'The housewife', in ELLEN MALOS (ed.) *The Politics of Housework*, London, Allison and Busby, p. 108.

GOTTLIEB, A. (1986) 'Interview Joan Nestle', *Cayenne, a Socialist Feminist Bulletin*, Toronto, Vol. 2 No. 1, March.

HAYDEN, D. (1981) *The Grand Domestic Revolution: a History of Feminist Designs for American Homes, Neighbourhoods and Cities*, Cambridge, Mass., MIT Press.

HENDERSON, K. with ARMSTRONG, F. and KERR, S. (1979) *My Song is My Own*, London, Pluto.

HERON, L. (1985) Introduction to HERON (ed.) *Truth, Dare or Promise. Girls Growing Up in the Fifties*, London, Virago.

HERZOG, M. (1980) *From Hand to Mouth, Women and Piecework*, Harmondsworth, Penguin.

HILL, M. A. (1980) *Charlotte Perkins Gilman. The Making of a Radical Feminist 1860–1890*, Philadelphia, Temple University Press.

JAYAWARDENA, K. (1986) *Feminism and Nationalism in the Third World*, London, Zed Books.

KERR, S. (1979) 'The Maintenance Engineer', in HENDERSON *et al.*, *My Song is My Own*, pp. 136–7.

LEWENHAK, S. (1977) *Women and Trade Unions*, London, Ernest Benn.

LEWIS, J. (1975) 'Beyond suffrage. English feminism during the 1920s', *The Maryland Historian*, Vol. VI, Spring.

LEWIS, J. (1979) in DICK CLUSTER, *They Should have Served That Cup of Coffee*, p. 7.

LIDDINGTON, J. (1984) *The Life and Times of a Respectable Rebel, Selina Cooper 1864–1946*, London, Virago.

LIFF, S. (1985) 'Women factory workers, what could socially useful production mean for them?', in Collective Design/Projects (eds) *Very Nice Work If You Can Get It: the Socially Useful Production Debate*, Nottingham, Spokesman.

LONDON TO EDINBURGH WEEKEND RETURN GROUP (1979) *In and Against the State*, London, Pluto.

LONDON WOMEN'S LIBERATION WORKSHOP (1971) 'Once they've got a baby by you, they've got a hold of you', *Shrew*, Vol. 3, No. 8, September, p. 7.

LUXTON, M. (1980) *More than a Labour of Love. Three Generations of Women's Work in the Home*, Toronto, The Women's Press.

MARSHALL, K. (1982) *Real Freedom. Women's Liberation and Socialism*, London, Junius.

MILL, J. S. (1983, first published 1869) *The Subjection of Women*, London, Virago.

MUNCY, R. L. (1974) *Sex and Marriage in Utopian Communities*, Baltimore, Maryland, Penguin.

OKIN, S. MOLLER (1980) *Women in Western Political Thought*, London, Virago.

PETCHESKY, R. P. (1984) *Abortion and Women's Choice: the State, Sexuality and Reproductive Freedom*, New York and London, Longman.

PHILLIPS, A. (1983) *Hidden Hands. Women and Economic Policies*, London, Pluto.

POLLERT, A. (1981) *Girls, Wives and Factory Lives. A Study of Women in a Tobacco Factory*, London, Macmillan.

REAGON, B. (1979) in DICK CLUSTER, *They Should Have Served That Cup of Coffee*, pp. 37–8.

ROWBOTHAM, S. (1972) *Women, Resistance and Revolution*, London, Allen Lane.

ROWBOTHAM, S. (1973) *Women's Consciousness, Man's World*, Harmondsworth, Penguin.

ROWBOTHAM, S. (1977) *A New World for Women: Stella Browne – Socialist Feminist*, London, Pluto.

ROWBOTHAM, S. (1983) *Dreams and Dilemmas*, London, Virago.

ROWBOTHAM, S. (1985) *Hidden from History*, London, Pluto.

ROWBOTHAM, S. (1986) *Friends of Alice Wheeldon*, London, Pluto.

ROWBOTHAM. S., SEGAL, L. and WAINWRIGHT, H. (1979) *Beyond the Fragments. Feminism and the Making of Socialism*, London, Merlin.

RUBINSTEIN, D. (1986) *Before the Suffragettes*, Brighton, Harvester Press.

SEGAL, L. (1983) 'No turning back – Thatcherism, the family and the future' in SEGAL (ed.) *What is to be Done about the Family?*, Harmondsworth, Penguin.

SIEDER, R. (1985) 'Housing policy, social welfare and family life in red Vienna, 1919–34', *Oral History*, Vol. 13, No. 2, p. 39.

STRASSER, S. (1982) *Never Done*, New York, Panthean.

SUMMERFIELD, P. (1984) *Women Workers in the Second World War*, Beckenham, Kent.

THOMPSON, R. (1974) *Women in Stuart England and America*, London, Routledge and Kegan Paul.

THOMPSON, W. (1983, first published 1825) *Appeal of One-Half the Human Race, Women, against the Pretension of the Other Half, Men, to retain them in Political and thence Civil and Domestic Slavery*, London, Virago.

UNGERSON, C. (ed.) (1985) *Women and Social Policy*, London, Macmillan.

WAJCMAN, J. (1983) *Women in Control. Dilemmas of a Workers' Co-operative*, Open University Press.

WISE, A. (1970) 'Community control', *Socialist Woman*, November–December, Vol. 2, No. 5.

WISE, A. (no date) *Women and Workers' Control*, Nottingham, Spokesman.

# 5 Political Parties
*Alan Ware*

## 5.1 Introduction

The relevance of political parties to the promotion of democracy has long been controversial. It was not until the states of Western Europe granted manhood suffrage, at the end of the nineteenth century and in the early twentieth century, that it became argued widely that parties were essential for the operation of democracy in a nation state. In Britain, for example, discussion about the role of parties was largely absent from the debates about the extensions of the franchise in the early 1830s and in the mid-1860s. (An exception is Park, 1832.) There were two reasons why the link between parties and the growth of liberal democracy in Britain should have attracted so little attention.

First, very little was known about political parties. The re-emergence of party-based divisions in Parliament in the years before the Great Reform Act of 1832 was short-lived; by the mid-1840s the Tory Party was split, and for more than twenty years British parliamentary politics was dominated by a system of loose coalitions, rather than by parties. Within the twenty years following the passage of the second Reform Act of 1867, the pattern of British politics had changed radically: relatively cohesive party divisions had emerged in Parliament, extra-parliamentary party organizations had developed, and manhood suffrage had been granted (1885). In other words, the transformation from party-less elite politics to mass democracy involving parties happened very rapidly.

Secondly, the one country where, in the early to mid-nineteenth century parties were organizing mass electorates, the United States, did not provide a good example for those who would argue that the advantages of democratic government were best developed by parties.[1] British Tories in the 1820s used the American experience of corrupt electoral practices to discredit the reform movement; with the rise of urban political machines in the late 1840s, even 'British moderates [were] seriously alarmed by American trends' (Crook, 1965, p. 134). For much of the nineteenth century the venality of American party politicians served as a warning both as to the dangers of democracy and to the limitations of parties in furthering the democratic objective.

However, the nineteenth-century American exemplar was not the only force militating against acceptance of the link between democratization and political parties. For conservatives, organization of the masses was always dangerous: it increased the likelihood that the economically deprived would be able to seize the resources of the privileged. Fear of democracy was fear of the ability to make numerical superiority count, and it was believed that it *would* count when the masses were organized. Yet, while true conservatives cautioned against any extension of the franchise, a more subtle approach to the 'problem of democracy' had been outlined in the late eighteenth century by James Madison. In 1787, defending the US Constitution, which he had helped to draft, against its critics, Madison had drawn attention to the impossibility of removing 'factions' from society (*Federalist No. 10*; see Rossiter, 1961). Like all the Founding Fathers, Madison had been worried by the threat to the social order posed by mass participation in the polity, but he argued that the effects of faction could be controlled under certain conditions. These conditions included a large (rather than small) state, the fragmentation of power to a number of political institutions in that state, and the use of indirect mechanisms of popular control. Faction would be contained by an appropriate institutional framework. This 'republican', rather than democratic, form of government would force factions to operate in conditions where it was difficult for majorities, even well organized ones, to take over the state. The limited, quasi-democracy established in the United States was never designed to give anything more than a limited role to factions (or parties); excessive power for such groupings was seen as the antithesis of republican government.

Moreover, among radical democrats there was one tradition which was also hostile to organized power, and hence to parties. Rousseau had argued for the importance of the individual, rather than the group, in the ideal state. It was individual participation that would facilitate the translation of individual preferences into a General Will, which all members of the state could accept. Organization of individuals into groups would be destructive of this process. Even more so than Madisonianism, this tradition of the direct participation of citizens in government was opposed to party politics. Party government was the enemy of self-government.

We can see, therefore, one important difference between the situation of industrial democracy in the 1980s and that of 'party democracy' at the beginning of this century.[2] Over the years there have been a number of experiments in industrial democracy which have been used by democratic theorists both to explain how further democratization in this area might be achieved, and also to assess the importance of industry as a forum for democracy (see, for example, Pateman, 1970). Theory and practice have been well integrated, although the extent of industrial democracy has been fairly limited. In contrast, parties emerged as major participants in the liberal democracies of Western Europe within a very short period and without any comprehensive theory of their contribution to democracy having been developed in advance. While they seemed essential to the functioning of mass democracy by the early twentieth century, there was no theory of 'party democracy', nor were they generally viewed as much more than necessary instruments for the conduct of democratic government. Socialists had most readily come to accept their value – after all, electoral mobilization promised the possibility of seizing power for the working class, a goal which economic organizing had been slow to realize. Of course, this was to prove a chimera: it took years for socialists to control governments, and even then their ability to effect major policy changes was rather limited. Yet even in the early stages, organizing for political power also meant modifying a number of socialist ideals. Bourgeois liberals too found that parties had significant advantages: they could out-organize the landowning classes and gain full control of the state for themselves. Not surprisingly, conservatives believed they had least to gain from the advent of mass party politics, but their survival also depended on their organizing around parties.

Once parties were established as a cornerstone of liberal democracy, democratic theorists began to construct new theories of democracy. Some, like those of British constitutionalists, merely incorporated parties into their analysis of the British Constitution. This was not too difficult a task, since parties based on parliamentary elites had been periodically active since the late seventeenth century. Others, like the American, E. E. Schattschneider, provided a normative theory of democracy, in which internally democratic and cohesive parties were the central element (Schattschneider, 1942, 1948 and 1960; see also Committee on Political Parties, 1950). Yet another approach was exemplified in the arguments of Joseph Schumpeter (1943, Chaps 21 and 22). In his view, the advent of competitive parties fighting for the votes of mass electorates prompted a rejection of what he termed the 'classical doctrine of democracy' and its substitution by a more realistic account. This process of accommodating parties to democracy was an important feature of much of the writing on Western European politics during the first fifty or sixty years of this century. Yet during all this time and with some important exceptions there was very little consideration of what today would be considered two crucial questions: how could the internal organization of political parties best promote the democratic ideal, and how could the mechanism of party competition make it possible for citizens to have control over the government of themselves? In the early 1960s, as empirical political science was starting to generate a vast amount of information about parties, it was becoming clear that political parties might be far less central to the democratic objective than the conventional wisdom of the first half of the century had suggested. Whatever their role in preserving stability in at least some capitalist countries – and Weimar Germany and the French Fourth Republic were among the notable exceptions – parties were themselves not exemplars of democracy in action. Furthermore, stimulated by the work of Anthony Downs (1957), increasing doubts were expressed about the ability of the electoral mechanism to allow citizens to choose how they were governed: party competition was, in brief, not an adequate device for effecting social choice. Because of their significance, it is worthwhile exploring these two points further.

The argument that parties themselves were unsatisfactory vehicles for mass democratic participation was not a new one. In his pathbreaking study of British and American parties, first published in 1902, Ostrogorski (1964) had pointed to the incompatibility between democracy and party organization. He was critical of the extra-parliamentary caucuses that had developed in Britain in the previous thirty years: 'The Associations have proved radically unfitted for serving as an instrument of political education; they have succeeded only in turning out electioneering machines' (Ostrogorski, 1964, p. 293). In 1911 Michels used his study of the Social Democratic Party in Germany to demonstrate 'the iron law of oligarchy': 'It is organization which gives birth to the domination of the elected over the electors, of the mandataries over the mandators, of the delegates over the delegators. Who says organization says oligarchy' (Michels, 1962, p. 365). For Michels, as for his fellow 'elite theorists', Mosca and Pareto, elites inevitably dominated institutions, so that the idea of control by the masses was simply an illusion. However, the great importance of these books as contributions to our understanding of political parties was not reflected in changing attitudes to parties at either elite or mass levels. There were several reasons for this. Many intellectuals remained unconvinced of the general applicability of the 'iron law of oligarchy'; Michels had, after all, chosen a German example, and since Germany was one of the most bureaucratized of the European societies he could be accused of choosing a highly favourable case to prove his 'law'. Again, while parties were obviously not controlled from beneath, many parties, especially socialist ones, did appear to be at least partially responsive to pressure from lower levels in their organizations. Finally, many, though not all, non-socialist parties in the twentieth century abandoned their wholly elite structures in favour of organizational forms which more closely resembled the mass-membership model pioneered by the socialists. In the terminology introduced by Duverger (1959) the caucus-cadre party of the nineteenth century had given way to the branch-membership party.[3]

By the 1960s, though, considerable doubts about the role of parties as democratic institutions were being expressed; in turn, this was to lead to much greater interest by the end of the decade in the practice of democracy in the workplace, in local communities, and in other arenas. A number of interrelated factors had helped to bring about this disenchantment with parties. The huge growth in the discipline of political science in the 1950s had generated a vast number of empirical studies, and parties were among the most studied institutions; research tended to confirm the belief that members of the lower echelons of many parties had very limited influence over the policy goals and strategies pursued by party elites. Evidence was

also emerging that in a number of parties, most notably in Britain, membership was starting to decline after the high levels of participation evident
in the years immediately after the Second World War. There were now
many more rivals, mostly outside the political arena, competing for the
time of the individual political activist. On the left, there was growing
impatience with the performance of parties in government. In many
Western European countries socialist governments had had periods in office
during the century, but with the partial exception of Sweden, socialist
policy objectives remained unfulfilled. Inequalities of wealth and income
remained high, state ownership of economic enterprises had not led to
worker involvement in the running of those industries, and with respect
to foreign policy most Western European countries were now even more
closely tied to the policies of the capitalist United States. Moreover, in
the hope of attaining power, a number of European socialist parties had
attempted to modify their socialist aims, so as to be attractive to newer
middle-class groups of voters. In West Germany the Social Democratic
leaders made an historic compromise in 1959, while in Britain there was
a divisive debate in the early 1960s about 'Clause Four' in the Labour
Party's constitution which committed the party to the nationalization of
the means of production.

At the same time, there was a widening discussion about the relevance
of party competition to the democratic aim of making government policy
a reflection of the interests of each citizen. Of course, some democratic
theorists, and in particular Schumpeter, had denied that the purpose
of elections was to provide a collective-choice mechanism. Yet most
democrats remained dissatisfied with this attempt to redefine democracy,
and persisted with the assumption that elections were of little value
if they did not contribute to the discovery of some kind of 'popular
will'. In the 1950s, though, academic interest in two related problems
burgeoned.

The first was the question of whether social choice was possible at all:
the publication of Arrow's 'Impossibility Theorem' (Arrow, 1951) had
thrown considerable doubt on this, and had stimulated an interest by
political scientists and theorists in rational choice analysis which is still
growing. Arrow had proved that 'no collective choice rule can satisfy certain
minimal conditions of workableness and ethical acceptability' (Colman,
1982, p. 209). Since then, other proofs have been generated to show that
any one of Arrow's original conditions can be omitted and a collective
choice rule is still impossible. Consequently, whether preferences can be
aggregated fairly in any situation depends entirely on the distribution of
preferences among people – there is no decision-making rule we can
introduce to provide for fair aggregation for certain distributions of
preferences.

The second problem which was part of this more general concern with rational choice was the relevance of models of economic competition to party competition. In 1957 the economist Anthony Downs produced a model of party competition which was derived from one applied to economic actors. Downs's model, and the conclusions that have been drawn from it, remain controversial, but it attracted widespread attention partly because it seemed to identify phenomena apparent in the real world of political parties. The model demonstrated that, with particular distributions of voters along an ideological spectrum (a distribution clustered around the centre of the spectrum), there was an incentive in a two-party system for parties to move to the centre of that spectrum. When voter opinion was more polarized, the parties had an incentive to remain away from the 'middle ground'. Again, with the very different distribution of voters supposedly found in multi-party systems (a more uniform distribution along the ideological spectrum), the parties would remain spread out along the spectrum. However, in this case, while the voter could be sure of some connection between her own views and the avowed intentions of her party, she still could not influence government policy because that would be worked out in secret negotiations between parties when forming a coalition government after an election. (Indeed, as later studies of 'consociational' democracy were to show, in countries like the Netherlands, party competition could be about the politics of division while government policy was directed towards accommodation by elites (see Lijphart, 1968).)

One conclusion which could be derived from Downs's model was that in both two-party and multi-party systems, electoral competition between parties was ill-suited as a device for effecting social choice. In two-party systems the parties were too alike to provide real choice, and in multi-party systems voter choice was linked only indirectly to the policy-making process. In turn, the debate following the appearance of Downs's book was to lead to considerable critical re-evaluation of two issues: do the Western polities' mechanisms for linking voters to policy outcomes actually make it possible for people to make choices between alternatives they find desirable, and could voting and electoral procedures be improved to make voter influence greater than it is in Western democracies? This debate was to be fuelled in the 1970s by growing evidence of popular dissatisfaction with the conditions under which choices were made, and with the range of choices effectively available. Dissatisfaction with party democracy took several forms. Survey evidence in the USA showed that the parties were the least respected political institutions (Dennis, 1975). In a number of European countries there was a rise of 'protest' voting – voting for hitherto minor parties, such as the Liberals in Britain; in Denmark a 'flash' party organized around protests against taxes made dramatic advances in the 1973 election.

It is against this background of the perceived failings of political parties and of party competition in helping to realize democracy that the remainder of this chapter is set. It focuses on three issues: attempts to democratize older parties, initiatives to provide democratic control of new parties, and the changing relationship between parties and pressure groups. All three issues have been the subject of considerable debate. For reasons of space, and because much less attention has been devoted to it in recent years, we must ignore the subject of how electoral procedures might be changed to provide for greater voter control over the policies pursued by parties. (We should note in passing, though, that, even here, the debate has not been entirely moribund: in the 1980s there has been considerable discussion among political scientists about a proposal for so-called 'approval voting'.) Section 5.2, then, will focus on the democratization of older parties, with particular attention being given to the Democratic Party in the USA. Section 5.3 examines the efforts by new parties to create more democratic structures than those found in older parties, and the principal example used is that of the 'Greens' in West Germany. Section 5.4 examines the relation of parties and pressure groups, particularly single-issue groups, and attention is given to the case of CND and the British Labour Party.

## 5.2 The democratization of old parties

Activist frustration at elite control of political parties, particularly in liberal and left-of-centre parties, has raised periodic debates about the democratization of party structures. An outstanding instance of this was the controversy which began in the Labour Party in the late 1970s.

There are three important features about demands for democratization in parties that are worth emphasizing. First, such demands are usually intertwined with the struggle by particular groups for control of a party. In the Labour Party case, for example, each faction's view of what 'true' democracy in a party involved was closely linked to the sort of arrangements which would best ensure their own control of the party. For example, those on the left of the party generally favoured maximizing the control of individual party members, among whom the left constituted a majority. Their schemes for democratizing the party gave no role to party voters, a group whose views were often rather different from those of the majority of active party members. Secondly, however, there is a danger that, if a party is made too 'open', then as an intermediary in the political process the party may partially collapse. This was not a likely outcome in the conflict within the British Labour Party, but it did occur in the Democratic Party in the United States in the early 1970s. We consider this example shortly. Thirdly, the potential for parties 'reforming themselves out of' a significant role in politics has been increased by the availability of new campaigning techniques. These have served both to strengthen elected representatives at the expense of party activists and to diminish the focus on policy issues in campaigns. Once again, the United States provides a good case study of the effects of these new techniques, and we consider this example after we have examined the attempts to reform the Democratic Party at the national level of politics.

To understand what happened in America between 1968 and 1976, it is important to emphasize at the outset two features of the context in which conflict developed. The first is that American parties have always been highly decentralized structures, with the state parties as autonomous entities; traditionally the national parties were never more than 'gatherings' of state parties. A second feature is that, for a variety of reasons, the local parties, which constituted the core of party strength, were already in the process of collapsing as the debate about democratizing the national Democratic Party began (see Ware, 1985).

Moves to democratize it commenced at the party's National Convention in Chicago in 1968 (see Ceaser, 1979; Crotty, 1978; and Shafer, 1983). That Convention was highly divisive because local and state party leaders were seen as foisting on the party a presidential candidate, Hubert Humphrey, who was unacceptable to many political activitists who had been mobilized on the issue of the Vietnam war. As a sop to this minority, it was agreed that a commission would be established to examine the procedures by which the party nominated presidential candidates. This commission (the McGovern-Fraser Commission) was not controlled by the state and local party leaders who had helped to nominate Humphrey, and the report it issued in 1971 outlined a number of major reforms intended to make the selection of delegates to the National Convention more democratic. Instead of county and state party chairmen being able to choose their own supporters – by not advertising caucus meetings, stacking them with their own loyalists, and so on – the Commission outlined a number of criteria which would have to be met in delegate selection. A central feature of this was the idea that delegations should be, as far as possible, microcosms of the Democratic electorate. At the 1972 Convention this was interpreted to mean that a quota system had to be operated, so that each delegation contained a certain proportion of women, ethnic minorities, and the young. (The disastrous defeat in the presidential election that year meant that the quota system was abandoned subsequently, and replaced by more informal means of generating 'balanced' delegations.) The crucial point, though, is that most of the Commission members wanted to retain one central feature of the older system of nominating presidential candidates; they wanted most of the delegates to be selected through caucuses, and county and state conventions. They did not want to increase the number of delegates selected directly by Democratic voters in primary elections.

The significance of this point is that the Commission wished to retain the party organizations as the channel through which participation would be directed. The problem with primary elections is that, unless they are used in conjunction with some form of pre-primary nominating convention, the power of nomination is largely removed from the party. In its place, the individual candidates become the central actors in the nomination process; they can use their own resources to mobilize an electorate directly. Clearly, in one respect, this is a democratic device because it is likely to increase the number of people involved in the selection procedures. However, if virtually any would-be candidate can enter a primary election and attempt to mobilize voters, then democracy can also be undermined. The *extent* of democracy is related both to the numbers of affected persons involved in making a decision and also to the distribution of power between them. The disadvantage of primary elections which virtually anyone can enter is that they provide a huge advantage to the candidates at the expense of other actors in the nomination process. Generally, most members of the McGovern-Fraser Commission were opposed to this imbalance being created.

In fact, the outcome was very different from the one they intended. Instead of democratized local and state parties nominating candidates, there was a huge increase in the number of states holding primary elections, so that by 1976 primaries were the most important element in presidential selection. The cause of this unforeseen development was the response of many state parties to the new regulations requiring 'balanced' delegations. Party organization leaders saw these regulations as too complex, and many of them believed that it would be difficult to ensure the creation of 'balanced' delegations even if all the participants were committed to this goal. Consequently, they proposed that their state legislators enact presidential primary laws; these would provide an easier way of complying with the new regulations. Primaries would also have the advantage of producing greater national publicity for the state party, because primaries, like sporting contests, are ideal 'media events'. Once Democratic politicians had opted for a presidential primary, the state Republican Party usually did so as well – often from fear of loss of publicity if it retained a caucus-convention system of nomination. By 1980 71 per cent of all Democratic Party delegates were selected in primaries, which bound them to vote for a particular candidate in the first ballot at the National Convention (Pomper, 1985, p. 9). In the early 1980s there were some modifications to the Democrats' nominating system which partially reversed these developments. For example, the number of delegates chosen in 'binding' primaries fell, so that in 1984 they constituted only 54 per cent of the total, and 14 per cent of the delegation places were reserved for elected and party officials (Pomper, 1985, pp. 9–10).

Unlike the case of the British Labour Party in the late 1970s, in which the debate about democratization was conducted against a background of declining party membership, a great many people who had previously been excluded from influence in the Democratic Party were 'brought into' the party by its reforms. Yet if this process has one of the features of democratization, it also has the undemocratic consequence of concentrating power in one group of actors in the nomination process – the candidates. Yet their position had already been strengthened by changes in campaign technology, and it is to this that we now turn.

The extension of the franchise to most Western European men from the late nineteenth century onwards led inevitably to the growth of parties. Only organizations of their size could provide the resources necessary to conduct campaigning among mass electorates, and one of their most vital resources was people – to canvass would-be voters and to get them to vote.[4] Of course, in many rural areas deference to social elites and the fear of losing a livelihood meant that electoral politics could continue to be conducted with minimal organization. But, in time, even here threats to local political monopolies brought greater organization and the absorption of local elites into national party structures. To be an effective political actor, the twentieth-century politician had to be a party politician. However, from mid-century onwards, a number of new techniques became available which, *in some circumstances*, could make the labour-intensive resources at the disposal of parties less essential for candidates for public office. These techniques included television, public opinion polling, and computer-controlled direct-mail solicitations. These devices would seem to have some potential for the advancement of democracy, in that they facilitate contact between leaders and led, making it more possible for the former to know the opinions and interests of the latter, and for the latter to ascertain the policies of the former. Yet this direct, 'neo-plebiscitary' form of democracy was also likely to change the relationship between voters and elected representatives in a way which disadvantaged the former. Whatever their limitations, parties had usually been required by their activists and by the demands of the electoral market to discuss public policy issues. A switch to candidate-centred campaigning would weaken these forces and give greater importance to the personality of political leaders and to the 'style' with which issues were presented to the electorate.

However, if these technologies could provide opportunities for individual politicians to separate themselves from the ties of party, this could happen only if three conditions were met.

First, there must be no restrictions, or only very weak ones, on the expenditure candidates are permitted to make on behalf of themselves. These technologies are expensive and are of little use to candidates facing low spending ceilings in a campaign. In Britain, for example, restrictions on expenditure are very tight indeed, and for individual candidates the new technologies do not constitute an alternative to the use of campaign workers in mobilizing an electorate.

Secondly, the party must have relatively low fund-raising potential compared with that available to candidates. If the party has considerable financial resources, it is likely to start purchasing the new technologies for party campaigning, thereby making individual campaigning less attractive. While declining party memberships in a number of countries have reduced party incomes, in some cases state funding of parties has more than made up for this. State funding was first introduced into Norway in 1970, and for all but one party it now constitutes by far the largest source of income (see Urwin, forthcoming).

Thirdly, there must be few limitations on the use of the technologies. For example, if candidates cannot buy advertising time on television, or if there are laws regulating the sending of unsolicited mail, then techno-logical advances do not work to the benefit of candidates.

Of the liberal democratic countries, in only one have these conditions been met fully. Over the past thirty years in the United States we find a significant shift from party-centred campaigning to campaigning by individual candidates. But this development must be placed in context. In the looser, non-branch party structures found there, some individual campaigning for offices had long been practised: for offices like the US Senate, the campaigns have contained a strong individualistic element from the time they first became directly elected offices (1913). Never-theless, there can be little doubt that the effect of new forms of campaigning has been to weaken parties as arenas of democratic participation. Individual candidates now build up their own campaign organization, they try to recruit activists who are loyal to them personally and are unlikely to work in other campaigns, and they try to divorce themselves from their parties. In many cases political advertisements on television do not even state which party the candidate is nominally representing. The parties themselves can offer little to attract would-be participants. For the most part, they now have only limited influence in the nomination of candidates – nomination is largely decided in primary elections fought by the organiza-tions of rival candidates. Parties contribute relatively little to campaigning; candidates spend far more than parties. Moreover, parties are relatively weak influences on the policy-making processes. Whatever the policy preferences of party activists, these activists have no leverage through the party structures on party representatives who will decide on these issues.

However, if the replacement of party campaigning by individual cam-paigning has not occurred outside the United States, this does not mean that the new technologies have not had an impact on parties elsewhere. Awareness of the potential of television, for example, has led to parties being more concerned with the way in which policies are presented to the public, and with the 'image' of the party and its leaders, and to some extent this has been at the expense of the discussion of issues. Moreover, it is clear that presentation does make a difference. In discussing the defection of party identifiers in the 1979 British General Election, Sabato argues:

Of the defectors from Labour, 26 per cent cited the Tory political advertisements as a reason for switching sides: none of the fewer defectors from the Conservative party named Labour broadcasts as influencing their decisions. The explanation for the disparity was not difficult to find. While the Tory party had been modernizing itself and its election machinery, the Labourites had been latter-day know-nothings, using little polling data, no thorough advance planning, no pretesting of what primitive media advertising there was. The Labour party leader and incumbent prime minister, James Callaghan, piously derided the Tory program, declaring: 'I don't intend to end this campaign packaged like cornflakes. I shall continue to be myself'. (Sabato, 1981, p. 61)

It goes without saying that such developments pose difficulties for parties as arenas of democracy. While party activists might be expected to have some contribution to make to the defining of policy objectives, and even, possibly, to the formulation of certain kinds of policies, it would seem that judgements about their presentation more obviously require professional expertise. Consequently, the new technologies pose two threats to parties as instruments of democracy even when they do not, as in America, contribute to the collapse of parties: they may focus attention away from the discussion of public policy objectives and they provide a lesser role for party activists, and a greater one for 'experts', in party decision-making.

### 5.3 Forms of democracy in new parties

For all the dissatisfaction with the centralized, branch-membership style of organization, and with the imitations of this style found among some conservative parties, there has been very little experimentation with new forms of party organization. The reason for this is quite obvious. Dissatisfaction has been most common among the lower party echelons, but usually these have been quite powerless to introduce new patterns of communication and control. For most party elites, institutional arrangements which limit the participation and power of the mass membership are to be welcomed. This point can be illustrated by a number of examples. In the 1970s, when both Spain and Portugal established liberal democratic regimes, the party organizations that emerged from the political groupings that existed under the dictatorships were very similar to those found elsewhere in Western Europe. The socialist parties had a formal branch structure, but elites were able to control the organization despite the democratic procedures built into the parties' constitutions; this has been especially true in Portugal. The right-wing parties in these countries have retained the more traditional form of caucus arrangement centred on party leaders. Again, to take a very different example, when the British Conservative Party changed its system for nominating a leader in 1975, no formal role was given to party activists. Instead, an informal system of consultation among party notables – from which a leader was supposed to 'emerge' – was replaced by direct election by MPs.

Just as old parties have generally been successful in resisting protests about the non-democratic character of intra-party relations, so too have most 'breakaway' parties resisted demands for mass control of the party structures. (In some cases, as with the British SDP, the party constitution was designed to prevent membership control over policies – one of the central controversies which had prompted the party leadership's exit from the Labour Party). Compromises with activists have usually worked to the advantage of the elites, so that participatory structures have been far less effective in practice than their proponents would initially have believed. This point is clearly demonstrated in the case of the Parti Québécois (PQ), which was founded in 1968. The party was a fusion of technocratic elites, who had split away from the province's Liberal Party, and a more radical group whose organizational blueprint for the party was derived partly from that of the Communist League of Yugoslavia. Fearful of being outvoted, the group surrounding the party leader, René Lévesque, agreed to the demands of the participationists. However, within a few years, the leadership had been able to circumvent the party structures that had been imposed on it:

> The PQ has made important innovations in two areas of Quebec politics. Control of the national council and the party convention has remained essentially in the hands of the members. The party's attempts at democratic financing by its members, without recourse to large company or union donations, have not only been successful, but have changed the whole character of political party financing in Quebec. But aside from the periods preceding conventions and financing campaigns, the participationists' hopes for mobilization of party members have been disappointed. Their goal of making the 'political' committee structure pre-eminent has not been achieved. On the contrary, the electoral goals and structures of the party have become increasingly predominant. (Murray and Murray, 1979, pp. 248–9)

Once in power in Quebec, the PQ became even less of a membership-oriented party.

A yet more radical attempt to provide for democratic control of a party than that of the PQ has been made by the 'Greens' in West Germany.[5] The Greens first put forward an 'alternative list' of candidates in 1977; they became a party in 1980, and since then have won parliamentary representation. A number of its founding members had been frustrated in their efforts to change the policies of the Social Democratic Party (SPD), and from the outset the party was designed to be very different from the bureaucratized SPD. However, as with the PQ, the search for an effective form of *democratic* party has so far proved elusive.

There were three related respects in which the Greens aimed at becoming a different kind of organization from the conventional parties competing in post-war Germany. First, they wanted greater participation in their party, with the party being open to anyone who wished to exert influence in politics: all party meetings were to be open to all interested persons or groups. Moreover, lower-level meetings were not merely advisory bodies, rather their resolutions were supposed to bring the parliamentary leadership to act in accordance with the wishes of these meetings. Parliamentarians would thus become mandated agents – the kind of representation which Edmund Burke, for example, had denounced in England in the eighteenth century. In opposition to representative democracy, in which 'trustees' try to protect the interests (as they see them) of their constituents, the Greens advocated *Basisdemokratie* or democracy from below. Secondly, the party's founders wished to avoid the experience of the SPD in creating a class of professional politicians within it – a development which, as we have noted already, was apparent to Michels by the early years of this century. A number of devices were introduced to prevent 'professionaliza-tion' of the Greens. Members of the Bundestag and of the *Land* legislatures would not remain as parliamentarians for the duration of a parliament, but instead they would be 'rotated' every two years. In part this would be made possible by the party list system of voting, which would permit the replacement of legislators without the risk of losing seats in by-elections. Another device was to forbid Green legislators from retaining more of their salary than a skilled worker in Germany would earn. The remaining portion of the salary was to be paid to the party. Again, multiple-office holding, a common feature in West German politics, was forbidden, so that no individual party leader could consolidate their position through control of a number of institutions. Finally, the party's founders did not want to create a party that would promote a particular vision of the *nation's* interests: it was to be part of a broader, transnational movement, promoting environmental and peace issues.

If the democratic objectives of the Greens were different from those of other parties in the Federal Republic, neither their objectives nor most of their proposed practices were highly innovative. In the nineteenth century many socialist parties had begun by espousing a 'mandate view' of democracy, only for this to be modified once they gained seats in national legislatures. Socialists had also been internationalist in their perspective before the First World War had demonstrated the problems of retaining mass support for internationalist goals. The idea that parties should be open to interested persons and groups, and not just to those who were prepared to commit their loyalty to a party, has been a well-established strand of anti-partyism in America. In the progressive era it resulted in the nomination process of parties in some states being open to all voters through the introduction of open primary elections. Moreover, in the USA the practice of elected public officials paying a proportion of their salary into party coffers had long been practised in a number of cities. (It is known there as 'macing'.) However, this differed in three important respects from the procedure advocated by the Greens. It was extended in the USA to appointed personnel, as well as elective ones; it covered all employees and not just party loyalists; and its purpose was to raise money for the party rather than to constrain the career ambitions of politicians. Nevertheless, the point remains that, while in the context of West Germany in the 1970s the Greens can be regarded as innovatory, they scarcely represent a complete break with the traditions of parties in liberal democracies.

As an electoral force, the Greens made considerable progress during their first few years. At the federal level they turned a 'two-and-a-half' party system into a 'two-and-two-halves' system, and they entered into a coalition government in Hesse. In other respects, though, they have been rather less successful. Although it may be possible that the policy of opening the party structures to all would-be participants may have mobilized some people who were not previously active in politics – and there are no data on this – a number of problems have been caused by this policy. Because membership was not a *sine qua non* for participating, there was little incentive for anyone actually to join the party. Consequently, and rather paradoxically for a party committed to democracy from below, the Greens have the lowest membership of all the major parties in West Germany; with only 25–30 000 members, they have fewer members per voter than any other party. Moreover, attendances at local meetings seem to have involved many 'irregulars' rather than being dominated by large groups of regular attenders. This has caused two problems for the party. On the one hand, it has made the principle of the mandate from below difficult to implement, because subsequent meetings have sometimes overturned the decisions of earlier ones. Even a legislator who was the most committed democrat would find it difficult to operate effectively if he was unsure whether current directives might be overridden later. This problem led to the abandonment of directives from the 'basis', and instead representatives in the Bundestag now follow the decisions of more central bodies, the Party Conference and the Federal Grand Committee. In fact, the latter seem to have been rather ineffective organizations in the making of policy, and power has accrued to the legislators. A second problem is that control of the party seems to have fallen into the hands of a relatively small group of functionaries. Just as American party reformers have been frustrated in the twentieth century, the German experience displays the difficulties of widening power in an organization when relatively few people are prepared, or are able, to commit the time for regular participation in it.

This weakness in the 'basis' has made still more complex the Greens' efforts at preventing the emergence of an elite of professional politicians, but it is certainly not the only reason for limited success in this area. Another factor has been the electoral system: while party list voting has both given the Greens legislative representation and permitted 'rotation' to be practised, it has meant that there is no *real* 'basis' for any Green members of the Bundestag to be accountable to, because none of them represent geographically defined constituencies. Rotation itself has been controversial. Although rotation has proceeded in some *Land* parliaments, a more flexible approach had to be adopted at the federal level, where the threat of resignation from the party could have cost the Greens their representation in the Bundestag. Some legislators resisted rotation, and indeed the costs to the party of losing from public view their most dynamic leaders had also become apparent and led to the modification of this policy. Now a Green member of the Bundestag may avoid rotation if 70 per cent of the relevant basis supports the proposal. Two prominent Greens, including the internationally known Petra Kelly, have not been rotated. Furthermore, there is an emerging problem in the paying of part of a legislator's salary to the party. Already the party's one minister (in Hesse) has indicated dissatisfaction with the agreement, and potentially there is a serious flaw in the practice. West German politics has been plagued by the policy of interest groups making payments to politicians. Even the public financing of parties did not prevent another major scandal emerging in the early 1980s, in which politicians of all parties (except the Greens) were implicated. If the Greens do increase their support and enter more coalition governments, their problems in controlling venality will be that much greater because of the relatively low salaries their members receive; the temptation to receive gifts will be even more than in the established parties. The Greens cannot expect that screening of their legislators, before they enter office, will be an adequate safeguard.

Finally, the prospects for making the Greens part of a wider international movement do not seem strong. Gatherings of more traditional parties may provide some publicity for the constituent parties, but bodies like the Socialist International do not have much influence in international affairs, and they do little to change the policy directions of national parties. (Of course, the publicity value of such gatherings should not be underestimated; this was one of the main reasons for the more recent establishment of the International Democratic Union, which serves as a conservative counterpart to the Socialist International). Equally, the formal arenas of party co-operation, such as the European Parliament, have been marked by the splintering of group cohesion on nationalist lines.[6] Moreover, both the particular combination of political issues supported by the Greens and the 'style' of politics they practise are firmly rooted in the experience of post-war Germany. While comparisons with CND and ecology movements elsewhere expose some important similarities with these other organizations, it may be doubted whether this is sufficient to make it likely that parties which are precise counterparts to the Greens will form in other countries. Political parties are essentially intra-state, rather than inter-national, political actors, because of the problems they face in organizing at the electoral and legislative levels in their own regimes.

## 5.4   Parties and interest groups

Until about twenty years ago a clear distinction was drawn in democratic
theory between political parties and pressure groups. Pressure groups were
seen as promoting narrowly defined interests or causes, did not offer
candidates in elections, and were separate from the state. Parties, on the
other hand, were bodies which aggregated interests, put forward slates
of candidates at elections and, in some respects, because they formed
governments, were part of the state. This rather neat model of the political
process was not wholly inaccurate, although its plausibility stemmed
partly from the fact that Anglo-American democratic theory drew mostly
on British and American examples of parties and pressure groups rather
than on those in other regimes in Western Europe. Nevertheless, in the
late 1980s it is apparent both that the distinction between parties and
pressure groups is more complex than was believed earlier and also that,
increasingly, the role that parties play in liberal democracies has been
threatened by two developments relating to interest groups.

The first is the emergence in a number of Western European countries of
what is often referred to as 'liberal', or 'neo', corporatism. Its key feature
is co-operation between government agencies and interest groups in the
formation and administration of policies, with the groups 'policing' their
own members to ensure that agreements with government are honoured.
In some European countries these arrangements are so well developed that
one traditional 'function' of parties which they shared with interest groups,
the articulation of interests, has been reduced. Moreover, parties are also
*seen* to have lost their importance in this respect. In his discussion of
Norwegian parties, for example, Urwin argues:

> What was most worrying, perhaps, was a facet revealed in a 1969 survey,
> where 46 per cent said that professional organizations were the best guardians
> of their interests: while 27 per cent regarded politicians as the most effective
> defenders of their interests, only 11 per cent saw the parties in this light.
> (Urwin, forthcoming)

Such developments have tended to undermine traditional 'party government'
models of liberal democracies, in which parties were at the centre of the
polity and interest groups were 'outsiders' competing for influence over
the central institutions: corporatist tendencies can lead to the peripheral-
ization of parties. It must be emphasized, however, that this is not
inevitable. In West Germany, for example, we find strong organizational
networks, but parties there have retained their role as important intermediaries in the policy process. Moreover, the political institutions of some
liberal democracies have been much less suited to neo-corporatism than
others. The United States is usually cited as the best instance of the failure
of corporatism, although even here the growing symbiotic relationships
between interest groups, federal government agencies and the congressional

committees which oversee their areas of policy-making have been observed by a number of political scientists since the 1960s (see, for example, Cater, 1964).

A second development which is threatening parties is the rise of 'cause' groups centred on a single issue or narrow cluster of issues. Such groups are not new, and indeed important instances of this kind of political organization can be found long before the rise of mass political parties. In Britain, for example, the Anti-Corn Law League was a major political actor in the mid-1840s, and in the debates about the second Reform Bill in 1867 it was on this kind of extra-parliamentary participation, rather than on parties, that attention was focused. Nevertheless, in the last twenty or thirty years a number of factors have contributed to their growing importance as articulators of opinion, at the expense of parties. Public frustration with parties is one factor which has benefited them. But as important as this have been changes in the media. Staging 'an event', whether it be a demonstration, a hunger strike, or even digging up a Test Match cricket pitch, can generate considerable publicity for a group through television coverage; they can gain far more attention than would be possible through print alone. While parties sometimes associate themselves with such events, the uncertain response of public opinion often makes them followers rather than leaders. Moreover, many of the issues that have attracted single-issue group activity are ones which cut across traditional lines of cleavage between the parties. Environmental issues and (in non-Catholic countries) abortion are two examples of this. (Sometimes, as with the Greens, a party may develop around the issue, but generally these parties have been minor ones.) The failure of major parties to articulate clear positions on such issues leads to activity through specially formed groups.

Yet another factor which has contributed to the rise of these groups is a change in the social environment facing party organizations. From their inception, mass party organizations were not just groupings of like-minded people; they offered facilities for their members to socialize with each other, by providing clubs with relatively cheap drinks, sporting contests, and so on. At the beginning of this century there were relatively limited alternatives to such social facilities, so that social activity and political idealism could merge quite easily. By mid-century greater affluence and a shorter working week, together with changing social values, helped to increase the alternatives people faced in deciding how to spend their time. Political parties became less attractive as arenas of social activity, and correspondingly a group promoting a single issue could more easily hope to mobilize those who did not especially want the 'social life' that a party could offer.

Although there are some respects in which it differs from the 'ideal model' of a single-issue group, the Campaign for Nuclear Disarmament

(CND) is a good example to consider in illustrating both the challenge such groups pose to parties and the limitations of this form of organization. CND was formed in 1958, when none of the major political parties was committed to unilateral nuclear disarmament. The issue was a relatively new one on the British political agenda, as the British government had tested its own atom bomb only in 1953 and testing of the British hydrogen bomb had commenced only in 1957. The issue partly, but not wholly, cut across lines of political division in the country. It was a cause which divided Labour Party voters and activists; it had virtually no support among Conservatives, and only much later was it to be a source of division in the Liberal Party. That the issue did not entirely cross-cut the political spectrum has posed problems both for CND and for the Labour Party. This was revealed in the early years of the organization, when an important faction in CND set its main objective as change in Labour Party policy on nuclear weapons. The pursuit of this strategy both restricted the ways in which appeals to the public were made (the campaign was linked very closely to the more general objective of disarmament, for example) and meant that CND was dependent on winning over the Labour Party. In fact, while the party did pass a unilateralist motion at its annual conference in 1960, this was reversed the following year. Two developments in the party then led to the dispute being defused, with CND having advanced its cause very little. The sudden death of Hugh Gaitskell led to the election of Harold Wilson as party leader; Wilson had left-of-centre support in that election, although he was not a unilateralist himself, so that CND now faced a leader who was less obviously a right-winger. Consequently, the split between left and right in the party became much less clear-cut and it became more difficult thereby for CND to maintain pressure on the party. A second development was that, following Wilson's accession, the party was engaged in a long 'run up' to the next general election and then took office. In its pursuit of a parliamentary majority the party avoided contentious issues, and, once in power, the administration was dominated by the so-called 'multilateralists' who opposed the CND position.

For the Labour Party the problem of facing a single-issue group which divided its own supporters, but not initially those of other parties, was twofold. First, there was the possibility that CND might try to appeal directly to the electorate – something which would obviously affect the Labour Party more than any other party. Although it did not try to offer its own candidates, one alternative which was discussed seriously in 1958 was the idea of a 'voter's veto' – that is, abstention at general elections. Labour Party members of CND, such as Michael Foot, argued against this strategy, which would certainly have harmed the party's chances at the next election. Secondly, to the extent that CND was a group putting pressure primarily on the Labour party, and to the extent that it was successful, it would reduce the party's flexibility in presenting issues to the electorate. Of course, this was not a factor in the 1964 election, but it did become a difficulty when CND re-emerged as a political force in the 1980s. Alone of the major parties, Labour went into the 1983 election with a nuclear policy which was highly contentious in the party and which opinion polls suggested was not widely popular with the electorate.

As an example of the potential for single-issue campaigns to attract attention for themselves, CND presents a classic case study. The Aldermaston marches at Easter in the late 1950s and early 1960s benefited enormously from the advent of television as a mass medium in the second half of the 1950s. The publicity that CND obtained from television was far greater than would have been possible with such a march before this period, and it provided a stimulus for other cause groups. Similarly, in the 1980s CND used the siting of new weapons at specific bases as a means of drawing attention to their cause by demonstrations, meetings, and so on. This contributed significantly to their ability to 'win' the public debate on defence policy.

The impact of CND on activism in the Labour Party is a more contentious problem, however. Our argument is that, in general, participation through single-issue groups helps to depress participation in parties by taking the time and resources of those who might otherwise contribute to parties. Certainly, in the case of the Labour Party, there was a continuing decline in party membership from the early 1950s through the early 1980s, and it cannot be denied that potential Labour Party activists were involved with CND. Nevertheless, groups like CND can scarcely be blamed for all of the difficulties the Labour Party faced in recruiting members. Indeed, it may even be that some Labour Party members joined because of the contacts they made through their involvement with bodies like CND. Yet there is no evidence that groups like CND have helped much to reverse the trend in declining participation in the party, and, of course, their presence has meant that the local parties have had less incentive to develop activities much beyond that of organizing for elections and acting as forums for socializing. Although individual issues seem to have become more prominent at the mass level of politics in the last thirty years than in the inter-war period, British parties have been remarkably passive in the channelling of support on these issues. While they are not the cause of this passivity, single-issue groups have enabled the parties to become minor actors in the process of mass mobilization around issues.

If single-issue groups have come to 'occupy territory' which parties might have occupied, there are still disadvantages in organizing political issues in this way. On the one hand, single-issue groups do not, in fact, avoid controversy about interest aggregation. There has been, and still is, a debate within CND as to whether it should be a single-issue group. Advocates of this approach stress the need to maximize the size of coalition support in promoting nuclear disarmament. Yet on two occasions the organization has formally adopted policy on other issues. In the 1960s it opposed the Vietnam War, while in the 1980s it has linked opposition to nuclear weapons to an anti-nuclear energy platform. The linking of issues in this way may satisfy a large majority of CND supporters, but, in making the single-issue group act more like a party, it reduces the flexibility of the organization in promoting a particular policy. On the other hand, while they can take on some of the functions of parties, organizations like CND do not have functions, which party organizations do, that enable them to survive the loss of salience or popularity of an issue. Very few single-issue groups can sustain intense interest in their particular cause for more than a few years. CND declined significantly both in terms of activists and public visibility after about 1962 or 1963. (One of the factors which contributed to the demise of CND was the successful conclusion to the Cuban missile crisis in 1962, an event which defused public concern about the possibility of nuclear war.) Before 1980, CND had spent more than three times as long in obscurity than it had as a focus for public attention. The coming to power of conservative administrations in Britain and the USA in 1979 and 1980 provided a great boost to its fortunes, but it is quite possible that the passing of these administrations might once again lead to the marginalization of CND. (This is not to say that CND would have failed to make an impact on British politics, and that it would become as marginal a body as it was from 1964 to 1980. In the 1980s it undoubtedly has helped to change public opinion far more than it did in the late 1950s.) However unpopular its leaders or policies, a party organization still has other functions to perform – in terms of organizing for elections – which keep it together during the 'lean' years. An electorally unsuccessful party is still in full public view, and can discuss political issues before a wide audience, while a small pressure group (like CND in the early 1970s) struggles to find an audience.

## 5.5   Conclusions

A cursory glance at the functions which political scientists have attributed to political parties might suggest that they are complex organizations with many facets. Supposedly parties do the following: structure the vote, integrate and mobilize mass publics, recruit political leaders, organize government, formulate public policy and aggregate interests.[7] Yet, in practice, most parties in liberal democracies have played a far more limited role in their regimes than this list of functions might suggest. In part, this is because, as Ostrogorski noted eighty years ago, party organizations have served primarily as instruments for mobilizing voters. Even socialist parties, with their public policy orientations, have been able to break out of this mould established by bourgeois parties in only modest ways. The blame for this cannot be laid entirely on the parties themselves, nor for placing the logic of the electoral market before other objectives. Nor can party leaders be held solely responsible for the limited role party structures play in the formation of public policy. One of the serious restrictions facing parties is that they have lacked the financial and other resources to act as 'governments in exile', in formulating new policies and strategies to implement when they return to office. Equally, the absence of political education from the activities of parties – a deficiency which, we have already seen, worried Ostrogorski – can be largely attributed to the skeletal nature of parties compared with economic organizations. Even in West Germany, where parties have better research and administrative facilities than in most other countries, they can play only a relatively limited role in the political process. Moreover, parties have lacked the potential to expand at their bases because of the absence of opportunities for direct popular democracy in the form of, say, industrial participation or neighbourhood level governments. Had liberal democratic regimes established such devices at the time mass parties developed, then undoubtedly parties may well have involved themselves extensively in activity at this level. But, of course, they did not, and parties adapted to the regimes they actually faced – regimes in which *representative* government was practised. Consequently, even those parties (such as socialist ones) which were supposedly committed to some form of control from the base found that the institutional structures they faced were ill-suited to this, and provided little opportunity for the expansion of party activity at the mass level of politics.

If we accept these arguments, then it is not surprising that democratizing a political party has proved so elusive. As we have seen in the cases of both the Greens and the Democratic Party in America, 'opening up' a party at its base poses severe difficulties. This is not to say, though, that the creation of parties which are more democratic is impossible. There are means of making parties more responsive to activists, as the present author indicated in an earlier study of the Democratic Party in Colorado (Ware, 1979). But what that study also demonstrated was that the balance between the provision of greater participation, the generation of more accountability of leaders, and the preservation of parties as significant electoral intermediaries, was a very delicate one. There are no simple proposals for reforming parties, or constituting new parties, which avoid the unfortunate 'side-effects' which can negate the democratization process or render the parties impotent as political actors. Constructing new and more democratic procedures in parties involves 'balancing' different objectives, yet very often the pressures which give rise to reform efforts and to the founding of new parties make these 'balancing' operations difficult to effect. For example, groups wanting to democratize a party also want power, and most often these are two incompatible objectives.

However, an alternative approach for those concerned about the undemocratic character of parties – the replacement of parties by some other mechanisms – is an unattractive solution. The absence of parties, or the presence of only very weak ones, as in the United States, gives more power to elective elites at the expense of activists than is the case in regimes with strong parties. Moreover, single-issue groups have disadvantages as devices for promoting issues compared with parties. While they can complement parties, they are scarcely a replacement for them because of the problems they face in maintaining pressure in support of an issue when it becomes unfashionable. One of the advantages of parties is that they are less subject to the pressures of short-term public popularity in promoting issues – an issue can remain on the political agenda, at least in some form.

This chapter has focused on parties in liberal democracies, and we must now consider briefly another possibility – that parties might be a channel for democracy in other kinds of regimes. For example, it has been argued with respect to both communist parties in Eastern Europe and one-party states in Africa that the single party can still be a democratic device. Most conservative writers have denied this and have asserted that parties can only promote democracy where competition between parties is permitted. In fact, this issue is rather difficult to resolve because other features of these one-party regimes hinder democratization. Most African states are perhaps too underdeveloped economically, and too diverse ethnically, to be able to survive the kinds of conflicts which open competition between political views can generate. On the other hand, most states in Eastern Europe have been burdened with a history of state domination that prevents the growth of extensive participation and representation of views through the party. There is, however, one example which might be used to test the argument that parties in one-party states can be vehicles of democracy, namely Yugoslavia. Curiously, its Communist Party has been little studied, but it does provide some evidence of a representational function. Since 1952 the party has attempted to reduce the proportion of party members who are also party officials, and today they constitute only about 0.2 per cent of all members. This policy, together with the fact that virtually any Yugoslav can join the party (there is no qualifying period of 'candidate' membership and about 13 per cent of adults are members) suggests that the party does provide *some* mechanism for participation. Moreover, while the party formally espouses 'democratic centralism', the orthodoxy of Soviet Union-influenced communist parties, it does not practise it in the Leninist way. In the context of this chapter, all we can do is to suggest that the case *against* the possibility of party democracy within a one-party state remains unproved.

For democrats, then, parties remain a source of frustration because they seem so central to the creation of more democratic societies, and yet devising suitable structures for realizing this objective seems elusive. Because there are so few experiments from which we can learn, even the apparent failures (such as the PQ and, perhaps, the Greens) are valuable because of the indirect evidence they supply about how the democratizing of parties might be carried out. As we have argued, though, we should not have overly high expectations about what is likely to be achieved in the short term.

## Notes

1. Although France had introduced manhood suffrage in 1848, cohesive political parties did not develop there until well into the twentieth century.
2. The term 'party democracy' has two quite distinct meanings. In this chapter we use it to refer to the practice of representative democracy involving competitive political parties. It is also used to refer to democracy *within* political parties; this was the meaning the present author used in an earlier work (Ware, 1979).
3. Duverger (1959) distinguishes between parties on two dimensions – organization and membership. In relation to organization, he identifies, among others, two important types – the caucus and the branch. The former is a closed, local group who do not seek to expand their number, while the latter branch-type parties are local affiliates of a central party structure. Cadre parties are 'groupings of notabilities' who conduct election campaigns, while mass membership parties seek to recruit as many dues-paying members as possible. Having constructed two dimensions on which we can analyse parties, Duverger (1959, p. 67) then argues: 'cadre parties correspond to the caucus parties, decentralized and weakly knit; mass parties to parties based on branches, more centralized and more firmly knit'.
4. Door-to-door canvassing, of the kind practised in Britain, is not practised universally. For obvious reasons it has not been a major feature of electoral campaigning in Norway, and it is actually illegal in Japan, for example.
5. I am very grateful for the advice of my colleague Willie Paterson in helping me to analyse the significance of the Green party. For a more comprehensive account of the Greens see Paterson (forthcoming).
6. In 1984 a 'Rainbow' group was formed from the Greens and other ecology parties in the European Parliament, but it remains to be seen how effective this will be.
7. These are the functions listed by King (1969, p. 120). King argues that parties do not perform many of the functions which political scientists had supposed they did. However, it can be argued that King overstates his case through the selective use of evidence.

## References

ARROW, Kenneth J. (1951) *Social Choice and Individual Values*, New York, Wiley.

CATER, Douglas (1964) *Power in Washington*, New York, Vintage Books.

CEASER, James (1979) *Presidential Selection*, Princeton, Princeton University Press.

COLMAN, Andrew (1982) *Game Theory and Experimental Games*, Oxford, Pergamon.

COMMITTEE ON POLITICAL PARTIES OF THE AMERICAN POLITICAL SCIENCE ASSOCIATION (1950) 'Towards a more responsible two-party system', *American Political Science Review*, 44, supplement.

CROOK, David Paul (1965) *American Democracy in English Politics 1815–1850*, Oxford, Clarendon Press.

CROTTY, William J. (1978) *Decision for the Democrats*, Baltimore and London, John Hopkins University Press.

DENNIS, Jack (1975) 'Trends in public support for the American party system', *British Journal of Political Science*, 5, pp. 187–230.

DOWNS, Anthony (1957) *An Economic Theory of Democracy*, New York, Harper.

DUVERGER, Maurice (1959) *Political Parties*, 2nd English edition, London, Methuen.

KING, Anthony (1969) 'Political parties in western democracies', *Polity*, 2, pp. 111–41.

LIJPHART, A. (1968) *The Politics of Accommodation: Pluralism and Democracy in the Netherlands*, Berkeley, University of California Press.

MICHELS, Robert (1962, first published 1911) *Political Parties*, New York, The Free Press.

MURRAY, Don and MURRAY, Vera (1979) 'The Parti Québécois: from opposition to power', in HUGH G. THORBURN (ed.) *Party Politics in Canada*, 4th edition, Scarborough, Ont., Prentice Hall.

OSTROGORSKI, M. (1964, first published 1902) *Democracy and the Organization of Political Parties*, Chicago, Quadrangle Books.

PARK, J. J. (1832) *The Dogmas of the Constitution*, London, Fellowes.

PATEMAN, Carole (1970) *Participation and Democratic Theory*, Cambridge, Cambridge University Press.

PATERSON, William, E. (forthcoming) 'West Germany: between party apparatus and basis democracy', in ALAN WARE (ed.) *Political Parties*, Oxford, Basil Blackwell.

POMPER, Gerald, M. *et al.* (1985) *The Election of 1984*, Chatham, NJ, Chatham House.

ROSSITER, C. (ed.) (1961) *The Federalist Papers*, New York, Mentor Books.

SABATO, Larry, J. (1981) *The Rise of Political Consultants*, New York, Basic Books.

SCHATTSCHNEIDER, E. E. (1942) *Party Government*, New York, Holt, Rinehart and Winston.

SCHATTSCHNEIDER, E. E. (1948) *The Struggle for Party Government*, College Park, Md, University of Maryland Press.

SCHATTSCHNEIDER, E. E. (1960) *The Semisovereign People*, New York, Holt, Rinehart and Winston.

SCHUMPETER, Joseph, A. (1943) *Capitalism, Socialism and Democracy*, London, Allen and Unwin.

SHAFER, Byron, E. (1983) *Quiet Revolution*, New York, Russell Sage Foundation.

URWIN, Derek, W. (forthcoming) 'Norway: parties between mass membership and consumer-oriented professionalism?', in ALAN WARE (ed.) *Political Parties*, Oxford, Basil Blackwell.

WARE, Alan (1979) *The Logic of Party Democracy*, London, Macmillan.

WARE, Alan (1985) *The Breakdown of Democratic Party Organization 1940–1980*, Oxford, Clarendon Press.

# 6  Mechanisms for Democracy
*Iain McLean*

## 6.1  What you can do with new technology

In November 1985 Ronald Reagan and Mikhail Gorbachev met at Geneva. The summit was unexpectedly friendly. Immediately after it was over, most of the media concluded that it marked a significant thaw in East-West relations. Furthermore, they asserted that the British public agreed with them. But did they?

Normally when journalists want to know what the public thinks they step out into their local shopping centre and ask the first ten people they see, whose opinions appear under a smiling picture in the next day's paper. When politicians want to know they ask their local party or the taxi-driver who takes them from the station (Stanley Baldwin believed in station-masters).[1] But these methods are ludicrously unscientific. The people you meet in the street may be quite unrepresentative; the members of your local party almost certainly are.

Until recently the only way to take a scientific poll of public opinion was to send interviewers out with strict instructions to call on a number of voters whose names had been randomly selected from the electoral roll and find out what they – and only they, not their husbands, wives, nephews, nieces, friends or anybody else – thought. This was slow, cumbersome and uncomfortable; and interviewers who could not face going out on December nights to sample public opinion were always tempted to fill in the forms in a pub.

The Reagan-Gorbachev summit enabled the BBC to try out a newish technique of opinion polling. A panel of television viewers each had a monitor with a key-pad like that on a push-button telephone. When asked on air what they thought of the summit they could key in their answers straight away. Within minutes the BBC could announce that the proportion of voters who thought a nuclear war was 'almost certain' within twenty years had dropped from 6 per cent to 2 per cent as a result of the summit, and those thinking it 'quite likely' had dropped from 31 per cent to 23 per cent (*Sunday Times*, 24 November 1985).

That BBC programme was just one example of interactive television, which is certain to grow enormously in the everyday life of citizens of advanced countries in the next twenty years. In the UK, interactive television began in 1982 in the Granada region, where the first sample of homes acquired the monitors that enabled viewers to talk back to the programme. They have been in regular, trouble-free use since then. At the moment the information passes down telephone lines. Telephones and computers are converging rapidly. Although the vast majority of messages going down the lines are still conversations which are coded into digital messages, a telephone line is just as capable of transmitting any other data between one computer and another. A telephone is one sort of specialized computer and the TV monitor is another. Some homes are linked by another network: cable. Although cable has progressed far more slowly than some overexcited pundits predicted in the early 1980s, it is still thought that some 10 to 20 per cent of UK homes will be interactively cable-linked within the next twenty years. Cable has many times greater capacity than telephone lines and would enable people to give far more elaborate messages back to the television programme they were watching.

Is interactive television a blessing or a curse? You may already be comparing it with the unforgettable telescreen in *Nineteen Eighty-Four* – the inescapable witness that 'Big Brother is watching you'. Some of the uses to which it has been put are almost as gruesome. For instance, a nationwide panel of viewers was put on line to Granada's 'Fame Game' (a talent-spotting programme) in January 1985. They were invited to vote seven times. In one of the votes a number of comedians were contesting for the dubious honour of reappearing the following week: 'After a fixed percentage of the voters had voted against a comedian a hook came through the electronic door and whisked off the clown. The comedian who survived the hook longest was the winner for next week' (Clemens, 1985, p. 17).[2]

However, the subject must be discussed rationally as well as emotionally. (By the way, telescreens on which They can watch You all your life are not on the feasible agenda, so you need have no nightmares on that score.) Interactive communication is an instrument of very great power. Like nuclear fission, it can be used for good or evil, but it is morally neutral in itself, and (as with nuclear fission) refusing to think about it will not make it go away.

Interactive information technology (henceforth IT) makes it much easier to take votes and test opinions. Anybody who is on line can take part. Anybody who has a telephone or interactive cable television is on line. Eighty per cent of households in the UK have telephones. Thus it would almost be possible to conduct the next General Election entirely by telephone. So far, interactive television has been used not for elections but for opinion polling. In this role it is very valuable if used properly and very dangerous if used irresponsibly. Unless the organizers use reputable sampling techniques, it is irresponsible to present the opinions of a few people and claim that they are representative. The purest sampling technique would be to start with the whole population, assign one unique number to each person, get a computer to pick about 2000 random numbers from the range and interview those 2000 people. The laws of statistics would then enable us to say that there was a very good chance

(95–99 per cent) that the distribution of opinion in the sample was close (within 2 or 3 per cent) to the distribution of opinion in the population at large.

Of course, there is no guarantee that any particular sample is not wildly unrepresentative, but the better one's sampling technique, the lower the chance of that happening.[3] A pure sampling technique is unobtainable in the real world. But interactive television sampling is potentially much purer than all previous methods providing it can overcome three problems. First, are all members of the population truly eligible to be sampled? This will not be true unless and until everybody has access to a television. Well over 95 per cent of the British population do, but any practical surveying technique would have to modify its results to allow for the views of the tiny minority who do not. Second, are those willing to go on-line to the polling computer an inherently unrepresentative group? People who like playing video games might be overrepresented, and people who always turn away double-glazing salesmen from the door before they have finished their first sentence might be underrepresented. Third, might a sample which was representative to begin with become unrepresentative just by virtue of being sampled, for instance by being exposed to far more political information than most people? First tests on the Granada panel suggest that this has not happened, but they are not conclusive.

Obviously, any proposal to use IT in large-scale elections or referenda would have to ensure that those who did not have a telephone, or whose telephone was out of order on the day, were able to vote, and that nobody was able to vote more than once. These are not insuperable problems. For instance, you can guard against fraud by issuing each voter with a password or codenumber like those used by banks to let you use their money machines. For the rest of this chapter I shall assume they have been solved. (Even if you think the assumption is unrealistic, bear with me; this chapter is not really about technology but about logic.) For many elections in bodies smaller than a nation there is already no problem. They could be run on terminals to a mainframe computer, or a series of net-worked micros. Suppose we had workplace democracy, for instance. There would be no difficulty at all in letting each employee of a firm, or each member of a co-operative, have access to a terminal on which to record his or her vote. Furthermore, it would be possible to have a truly interactive general meeting, in which people did not merely cast a single vote but watched proposals for debate come up on their screens, proposed amendments to them if they wished, and voted on as many of the different proposed courses of action as they wished. There are limits to feasible democracy of this sort, but they are not to do with the inadequacies of IT. We shall see later in this chapter that they are not technological at all, but logical.

A computer counts votes as well as recording them. The votes we have mentioned so far have been 'first-past-the-post' votes. Viewers were asked only to choose one out of the more than two options available. First-past-the-post is, of course, the electoral system in use in the UK at the moment. It produces results that are difficult to justify: for instance, in the General Election of 1983 the SDP/Liberal Alliance gained 26 per cent of the votes but only 3.5 per cent of the seats. Defenders of the system complain that proportional representation (PR) systems are hard to explain to the voters and hard to count. IT demolishes this argument (although there are other arguments against PR which IT does not affect). The programme could ask first: 'Which candidate(s)/course(s) of action do you favour most?' After the voter had keyed in one or more of the options the programme would ask: 'Which candidate(s) [etc] do you favour next most?', and so on until the voter had said something about every option on offer. Notice that the 'something' could perfectly well be 'I don't care' or 'A plague on all your houses'. To give this answer, the voter need only list all the options in answer to the very first question. Alternatively, the programme could ask the question: 'Is there any candidate or candidates you are not prepared to have at any price?' before asking anything else.

With this information, the computer would have a record of each voter's preference schedule. A preference schedule is a complete, ordered list of all the alternatives. Table 6.1 is an example of the notation that will be used in this chapter to show preference schedules. At the head of each column is a number: this is the number of voters who have the schedule listed underneath it. Options, or candidates, are listed in descending order from best to worst. The procedure could treat 'none of the above' as if it were an option. This would enable the views of the 'plague on all your houses' voter to be taken fully into account. (This modification was first suggested by the earliest English voting theorist, Lewis Carroll. See Black, 1958, pp. 214–34.) If voters are indifferent between two or more alternatives, those alternatives are listed at the same level.

TABLE 6.1   *Preference schedules: an illustrative example*

| No. of voters: | 3 | 2 | 2 | 2 |
|---|---|---|---|---|
| | $a$ | $b$ | $c$ | $a$ |
| | $b$ | $c$ | $a$ | $b,c$ |
| | $c$ | $a$ | $b$ | |

In Table 6.1, for instance, the three voters in the leftmost column each prefer $a$ to $b$ and $b$ to $c$. The two voters in the rightmost column each prefer $a$ to $b$ and $c$ but are indifferent between $b$ and $c$.

Preference schedules are a basic building block of voting theory, but you have probably never come across them. So why are they needed? The answer comes in two parts. The first part shows that democracy requires more than information about first preferences; the second part shows that it must settle for less information than, for instance, somebody comparing car prices has available.

When there are only two alternatives on offer, it is quite straightforward to say that the one for which a majority voted was the people's choice. But whenever there are more than two, a count of first preferences can lead to a result that is very hard to call 'democratic'. The Conservatives won the 1983 General Election with 42.4 per cent of the vote. Suppose (only for the sake of argument) that every single Labour voter put the Alliance second, and that every single Alliance voter put Labour second. The combined Labour and Alliance vote was 53 per cent. Democracy, literally, means 'the people rule'. Could we really say that this result was 'democratic'? Over half of those who voted would have thought that the party that won was the worst alternative. It is not necessary to believe that what I have just described actually did happen in 1983, only that it could, in order to agree that a democratic theorist must know more than just every voter's first preference.

When we compare objects, we can sometimes say not just that one is bigger than another, but by how much: 'this car is twice as expensive as that', or 'Janet is six inches taller than John'. So why not allow 'how much?' information into voting theory? Suppose I think *a* is twice as good as *b*, but *b* is a million times better than *c*. You think *c* is only just better than *b*, which is only just better than *a*. A preference schedule like that shown in Table 6.1 cannot show that information. Your preferences exactly cancel mine out if they are added up using a method based on preference schedules. This does not seem fair at first sight. But the trouble is that there is no objective standard for measuring 'how much' information on preferences. Janet really is six inches taller than John, and a tape-measure can prove it. But if I say I think *b* is a million times better than *c*, you might say that you think *c* is a quintillion times better than *b*. There is no tape-measure of intensity of preference. Preference, in other words, cannot be measured cardinally, but only ordinally.

A preference schedule, then, is an ordinal list of the voters' preferences. How do we add them up ('aggregate them')? There is no one universally agreed way. But there are two families of procedures, named after the two Frenchmen who invented the mathematical theory of voting just before the French Revolution: the Marquis de Condorcet and Jean-Charles de Borda. A *Condorcet* procedure compares each alternative against every other in turn. If there is one option which beats every other in a pairwise vote, it is called a *Condorcet winner*. From a preference schedule a computer can instantaneously calculate the *Condorcet score* of every option – that is, the number of the other options it beats in pairwise votes. A *Borda* procedure gives each option a score based on how high it appears in each voter's ranking. The simplest is that which, when there are $n$ options, gives $n - 1$ to a voter's first preference, $n - 2$ to the second, and so on down to 0 for the lowest. Adding these scores up gives each option a *Borda score*. When a voter ranks options equally, their Borda scores are the average of what they would have obtained if they had not been ranked equally. In Table 6.1 the Condorcet scores of the options are $a$, 2; $b$, 1; and $c$, 0. The Borda scores are $a$, 12; $b$, 8; and $c$, 7. (Do not take my arithmetic on trust. Go back to Table 6.1 and work it out for yourself. The exercise may help you to understand what is going on.) Thus $a$ comes top on both criteria, so it has a strong claim to be 'the preferred option'. A computer could, of course, get there very much quicker than you or I. But it needs a human being to tell it whether to use a Condorcet rule, a Borda rule, or some other rule. Before we tackle this question, we must examine the ancient argument between direct and representative democracy, to see where it ought to go in the light of new technology. This will gradually reveal the logical problems I have warned of. Only after they have been revealed, in the final sections of this chapter, can we come back to the question of choosing a voting procedure.

## 6.2 Direct versus representative democracy

Democracy began in ancient Greece. Greek democracy was direct democracy. In ancient Athens for instance, the assembly (*ecclesia*) of the people was sovereign. Every citizen was a member of the assembly. By no means everybody living in Athens was a citizen. Women, resident aliens, and slaves had no votes, and a citizen could be disfranchised for neglecting his parents, military cowardice, squandering property, or having been a prostitute as a boy.[4] The assembly had maybe 10 000 members. The assembly agenda was prepared by the council (*boule*). The council had 500 members, not elected but chosen by lot from among the citizens. In turn, they chose a rotating presiding committee, which chose its presiding officer, again by lot. So every citizen of Athens might be President for a day. Such a system flies in the face of two pieces of modern conventional wisdom: that an enormous public meeting cannot take real decisions, and that executives must either be trained experts or elected politicians. It was controversial in its own day, but it did work. Several Athenian writers in Rodewald's (1975) collection give vivid pictures of democracy at work.

Democracy disappeared with Greek and Roman civilization; when it reappeared it was in representative form. Every important writer (except Rousseau) assumed that representative democracy was the only possible form in any large society, and that direct democracy was simply impracticable. Some, notably Edmund Burke, added that politicians should in any case not 'represent' their electorate too closely. As Burke said to the electors of Bristol in 1774, 'your representative owes you, not his industry only, but his judgement; and he betrays, instead of serving you, if he sacrifices it to your opinion'. (This may have been good political philosophy, but it was not a tactful thing to say in an election campaign; Burke lost the seat.) Only Rousseau put the opposite view. In a famous passage in *The Social Contract*, he wrote: 'The people of England think they are free. They are quite wrong. They are free only while they are electing members of parliament; as soon as they are elected, the people are slaves, they are nothing'. Rousseau was Swiss, and Switzerland was the only European country in which direct democracy existed in his day. Some Swiss cantons were small enough to allow every adult male citizen who so wished to meet to pass laws.

Only in the last twenty or thirty years has anybody else started to take direct democracy seriously. Many radical writers of the 1960s rediscovered Rousseau's ideas, not always knowing that Rousseau had had them first. So there has been a revival of interest in (actual or supposed) direct democracies like kibbutzim and communes. Rousseauvian radicals reluctantly accept that modern states, firms and student bodies are too big to be ruled by general meetings. So they demand that representatives be as subservient as possible to general meetings, for instance by making them subject to recall at any time.

There is more direct democracy around in modern Western societies than is often realized. For instance, a parish in England and Wales may choose whether to have a parish meeting (direct democracy) or elect a parish council (representative democracy). Some towns in New England are still governed by town meetings, to which any citizen may go. Student unions often give general meetings an important place in their constitutions, and may give the general meeting the power to recall or give binding instructions ('mandates') to the executive. Oxford colleges are formally direct democracies: all fellows are expected to attend sovereign governing body meetings three times a term. Cambridge colleges tend to be representative democracies, in which fellows choose the governing body, but are not automatically members of it. (However, Oxford students are in the same position as Athenian slaves.)

Opponents of direct democracy often dismiss it with a wave of the hand: 'It can't be done. Decision-making would take far too long. Anyhow, you can't discuss options at mass meetings'. Now that IT opens possibilities that were unsuspected only a few years ago, this will no longer do. Therefore, the next section looks at the traditional argument between direct and representative democracy. However, the traditional arguments on both sides are not very clearly put, and, beginning with Section 6.4, I shall reorient the discussion around a number of 'key problems for democrats'.

## 6.3    For and against direct democracy: traditional arguments

The commonest argument for direct democracy is very simple. It is that no other version is truly democratic at all. Representatives can misrepresent. We have elected the present government, but we have no control over what it does. The only constraint on it is that, if it wants to get re-elected, it must do just enough of what sufficient voters want to get a bare plurality in the next election. If, as in the UK at present, there are three parties of roughly equal strength, 40 per cent of the votes cast should be enough to get the incumbent party re-elected. That falls a long way short of the literal meaning of democracy: 'the people rule'. For a direct democrat, as Rousseau said, the people of England are free only on General Election day. If there must be representatives, the direct democrat wants them to be bound hand and foot by their mandate: they are free only to discuss what their electors authorize them to discuss, and if any new proposals are made, they must report them back to their electors for instructions on how to vote. Such individuals are, in fact, normally called 'delegates' rather than 'representatives'.

A second argument for direct democracy stresses the educational value of participation. Opponents of direct democracy view participation as a burden; supporters view it as good in its own right. Both Rousseau and J. S. Mill (who disagreed with Rousseau on everything else) saw participation as good in itself, and many modern democratic theorists (e.g. Pateman, 1970) agree with them. Participation, it is said, broadens the mind. It makes you see the other person's point of view. It makes you understand the value of compromise and tolerance. If you have helped to make a decision yourself, rather than just helped to elect representatives who took the decision, you may feel better even if it was a worse decision. (I feel prouder of shelves I put up incompetently myself than of shelves I paid a carpenter to put up competently.)

The main argument against direct democracy is time and unwieldiness. If a large meeting takes decisions, it will usually spend a long time taking them. If you have ever attended, say, a busy student union meeting, you will be familiar with the procedural mess that usually occurs when more than two propositions have been put forward: votes on whether to vote, votes on what to vote on, votes on whether to accept the chairman's ruling on whether to vote or what to vote on. . . Most normal people vote with their feet, sometimes before the meeting even gets to the actual vote on a substantive proposition. The Rousseau–Mill–Pateman claim that participation is intrinsically valuable looks fragile to anybody who has witnessed such scenes.

Another objection is that direct democracy can lead to inconsistent decisions. If you ask the people assembled whether they would like to pay less tax, they will vote in favour. If you ask them the following week whether they would like more money spent on the NHS, they will vote in favour again. Or if you ask them one week whether every group in society, including gypsies, should have decent housing and ask them next week to agree to have a gypsy site on the village green, you again risk getting inconsistent answers. To caricature Rousseau, there is a General Will in favour of gypsy sites, but a sum of particular wills against locating them anywhere. Elected politicians, it is said, not only can but must sort out inconsistencies like these.

A third criticism of direct democracy goes right back to the Ancient Greeks: 'democratic assemblies are liable to being manipulated by unscrupulous orators'. Plato hated the democratic Athenian Assembly because it put Socrates to death. Again and again in his dialogues, Plato recurs to the argument that democracy is corrupt because those who win votes are professional orators, not professional statesmen. This 2500 year-old argument suddenly seemed relevant again in the era of Hitler's Nuremburg rallies.

A fourth objection is broader than either of the last two, but it includes elements of both. It is that direct democracy is bad for liberty and toleration. This idea influenced both Burke and the framers of the US Constitution. Its most influential twentieth-century advocate was the Austrian economist and politician, Joseph Schumpeter. As a young man, Schumpeter had experienced both fascism and Bolshevism; the experience left him bitter about dictators who claimed to personify the will of the people. Therefore Schumpeter claimed that direct, participatory democracy was not only unattainable, but undesirable. He deplored not only mass meetings but even lobbying and letter-writing campaigns aimed at persuading politicians to change their minds by threats to mobilize votes against them. Most modern opponents of direct democracy do not go as far as Schumpeter, but scratch one and you will usually find a Schumpeterian just below the surface.

Much of this is a dialogue of the deaf. The two sides ignore each other's points, or argue in a way that can only be inconclusive. For instance, Pateman and her allies say that participation broadens the mind, and cite some examples which they claim bear them out. Schumpeter and his allies say that participation at best wastes time and at worst encourages mass hysteria, and cite some examples which they claim bear them out. Something might come of this argument if somebody designed a very large and very ingenious experiment to compare the incidence of the two opposite effects. But, so far, nobody has even tried, nor does either side seem interested in trying. Again, when Plato's successors cry 'Mass meetings encourage demagogues!', direct democrats retort 'So do elections!' Each side alleges that the other's favourite method is more likely to be exploited by the mendacious or the corrupt, but no tests are proposed. Therefore, before we can measure democratic theory and new technology against each other, we need a fresh start. In the next section I suggest four key problems for democrats, and examine how far new technology gets round them. In Section 6.5 I return to discuss direct versus representative democracy in the light of these findings.

## 6.4  Four key problems

*Problem A: the existence of cycles*
Suppose there are three voters and three options *a*, *b*, and *c*, say candidates for a job. The voters rank the options as shown in Table 6.2.

TABLE 6.2   *A cycle: the 'paradox of voting'*

| No. of voters: | 1 | 1 | 1 |
|---|---|---|---|
| | *a* | *b* | *c* |
| | *b* | *c* | *a* |
| | *c* | *a* | *b* |

Suppose now that each option is compared with each other. This is the Condorcet procedure introduced in Section 6.1. You will see from Table 6.2 that *a* will beat *b* by two votes to one, and that *b* will beat *c* by two votes to one. You would therefore expect *a* to beat *c*, but in fact *c* beats *a* by two votes to one. Which one is the people's choice?

This phenomenon is known as a 'cycle'. If there is a cycle among the top three (or more) options, there is no Condorcet winner and there is a problem for democratic theorists. Often, when people first meet Table 6.2, they dismiss it as a trivial irritation – or entertainment, according to their cast of mind. Do cycles matter? Do they ever happen in real life? There are two sorts of answer, theoretical and empirical. It is not hard to work out how frequently cycles would occur for any given number of options and/or voters if we assume that any preference ordering is as likely to occur as any other. There must be at least three voters and three options before cycles can occur at all. If there are three of each, there is a 5.6 per cent chance that there will be a cycle. If there are three alternatives, the chance rises towards 8 per cent as the number of voters goes towards infinity. The chances of cycles occuring rise more sharply with the number of alternatives than with the number of voters. For instance, if there are seven alternatives and three voters, the chances of a cycle are 23.9 per cent; for seven alternatives and an infinite number of voters, the limit is 36.9 per cent.

There are many examples of cycles in real life. In both houses of the US Congress, the Democrats are often deeply divided, with white-supremacist southern Democrats voting very differently to their northern counterparts. When Congress votes on a proposal to spend public money in the South, somebody often proposes an amendment to make the spending conditional on the fair treatment of blacks. This can lead to a cycle. Northern Democrats prefer the amended proposal to the unamended to the *status quo*; southern Democrats prefer the unamended proposal to the *status quo* to the amended; and Republicans prefer the *status quo* to the amended; and Republicans prefer the *status quo* to the amended proposal to the unamended. (For examples see Farquharson, 1969, pp. 52–3; Riker, 1982, pp. 152–6.) There is no predicting what will happen in such cases. It depends on which faction is most astute: whichever option is picked out in the first vote will lose.

One way to break the deadlock when there is a cycle (i.e. no Condorcet winner) is to count the Borda scores of each option. But Borda scores have problems too. Consider Table 6.3.

TABLE 6.3  *Borda scores and inconsistent results* (1)

| No. of voters: | 3 | 2 | 2 |
|---|---|---|---|
| | a | b | c |
| | b | c | d |
| | c | d | a |
| | d | a | b |

A fourth candidate, *d*, has entered the lists, and there are now seven voters. There is still no Condorcet winner: in fact all four candidates are in a cycle in which *a* beats *b*, *b* beats *c*, *c* beats *d*, and *d* beats *a*. So we see if a Borda score breaks the deadlock. It does: *a* gets 11, *b* gets 12, *c* gets 13 and *d* gets 6. So *c* wins. But now suppose that candidate *d* had conducted a private poll just before the election, and found out that every single voter preferred *c* to him. He might decide that there was no point in standing. His withdrawal produces Table 6.4.

TABLE 6.4  *Borda scores and inconsistent results* (2)

| No. of voters: | 3 | 2 | 2 |
|---|---|---|---|
| | a | b | c |
| | b | c | a |
| | c | a | b |

Again, there is no Condorcet winner. But this time, the Borda score of *a* is 8, *b* gets 7, and *c* gets 6. A candidate who had no hope has withdrawn; nothing else has changed; and yet the ordering of the remaining three has been turned upside down!

This puzzle suggests two things. First, the paradox of voting is deeper than meets the eye. If you try to get round it by using Borda scores, you merely hit another paradox instead. We have not (yet) seen whether there is a way round it which does not hit another paradox, but perhaps there is not. Second, the Borda procedure is open to manipulation. Candidate *c* has a strong incentive to bribe no-hoper *d* to stand, and candidate *a* has an equal incentive to bribe him to withdraw. Lucky *d* has found an easy way to make money, but everybody else is left to ponder on another problem for democrats: strategic manipulation.

## Problem B: strategic voting and misrepresentation of preferences

There is a more obvious way to manipulate Borda counts, which is worth bearing in mind if you take part in a Borda-count election, and if you think you are the only voter who has read this book: put the candidate you expect to be the strongest challenger to your favourite at the bottom. A recent poll among heads of political science departments in US universities asked them to name the best departments in the country, excluding their own. Unfortunately, many of the respondents knew all about Borda counts. One openly admitted to having played the strategy just described. Others may have played it without admitting that they had. If everybody does it, the effect is nullified, and the resulting choice is nonsensical. When somebody pointed out to Jean-Charles de Borda that his scheme could be manipulated like this, he replied plaintively that it 'is only for honest men'.

This may seem remote from ordinary elections, but it is not. The first-past-the-post system forces large numbers of voters to consider a 'strategic' vote. A strategic vote is any vote which does not truly represent the voter's preference schedule, but which is cast in the hope of improving the chances of a candidate high on the schedule against one low down on it. Millions of people in the General Election of 1983 knew that their favourite party (often, but not always, the SDP/Liberal Alliance) had 'no chance' in their constituency. So they voted for their second-best to keep out their worst. All three parties egged voters on to vote tactically in their favour, and condemned tactical voting against them as immoral.

Electoral reformers have always condemned this feature of first-past-the-post. They claim that a form of PR called Single Transferable Vote (STV) is proof against manipulation. It was (re)introduced in Northern Ireland in 1973, in order to ensure that the minority community got their fair share of seats (not a consideration that seems to apply in the rest of the UK). All parties promptly announced that they could get round it, and urged their voters to vote tactically in various ingenious ways. None succeeded. But although nobody could manipulate STV in those particular elections, it can be manipulated. The so-called Gibbard–Satterthwaite theorem has proved that there is no such thing as a non-manipulable voting system.[5] Some are easier to manipulate than others, but there is no point in looking for one that cannot be manipulated: none exists, and none will ever be invented.

*Problem C: who decides what questions to ask?*
Consider again the problem of inconsistency. Obviously, the questions 'would you like to pay less tax?' and 'would you like the NHS to be improved?' are inadequate. The proper question is something like 'would you be willing to give an extra 5p in the pound from your income to pay for improvements in the NHS?' Any such question would be complicated, but not impossibly so. Opinion polls now regularly ask people whether they would rather pay less tax (and get fewer benefits), or maintain (or increase) tax and benefit levels, and people give intelligent answers. But the power to set the questions is both great and open to abuse. Many democracies have provision for referenda. But it is not clear whether a regime with provision for referenda is 'more democratic' than one without. It depends who has the power to ask the questions. In the UK citizens have no right to demand a referendum (on anything important), but politicians may decide to have one. The record shows that they decide according to calculations of party advantage. In 1910, the Conservatives proposed a referendum on reforming the House of Lords, not to find out what the people thought, but to try to delay the Liberals' proposals in the hope that the Liberals would lose the next election. The referendum on Britain's entry to the EEC in 1975 was held in order to stop the deeply divided Labour government of the day from falling apart. The referendum on Scottish and Welsh devolution in 1979 was imposed as a wrecking measure by opponents of devolution. These were all exercises in manipulation, not democracy. What about states where a certain proportion of the electorate has a constitutional right to demand a referendum on a question of their choice? The best known examples are Switzerland and a number of US states, especially California. Switzerland has had a tradition of direct democracy since before Rousseau's day, and parts of the USA have always been proud of the direct democracy of the town meeting. The fear is sometimes expressed that this form of referendum, too, is undemocratic: that it may be demanded by special interests (particularly those of the rich) and that the people are hoodwinked into voting for it, perhaps because of an over-simple question. The famous Proposition 13 in California in 1978 asked voters to approve a low ceiling on state property taxes. It did not point out that a ceiling on taxes implied a ceiling on expenditure, and

some of its proponents actually denied any connection, presenting it entirely as a measure to cut 'waste'. It was carried, and gave rise to a chorus of liberal disapproval for being misleading and/or unfair to the poor. But as it turned out, Proposition 13 did not lead to a general tax revolt; nor is there any evidence that popular referenda consistently favour the rich (see Butler and Ranney, 1980).

### Problem D: the cost of voting and under-representation of the poor

Nevertheless, all elections, including referenda, tend to show a common pattern: that the poor are less likely to vote than anybody else. In the UK, the lowest General Election turnouts are always in poverty-stricken inner-city constituencies whose voters, one might think, had more to gain than anybody else from a change of government. Nevertheless, it may be entirely rational for a poor voter to abstain. It is incredibly unlikely that one vote will make the difference between one party forming the government and another. A rational voter would have to ask: 'is the value to me of the government I want, multiplied by the probability that it is my vote that brings it in, greater than the value of doing anything else with my time?' For everybody, rich or poor, the answer is almost certainly 'no'. But the poorer you are, the more resounding a 'no' it is. This is especially true if it costs money (bus fares, petrol, shoe leather) as well as time to vote. If new technology makes voting cheaper, it may reduce the bias against the poor; but if it depends on gadgetry that not everybody has, it may increase it.

### 6.5  New technology and the key problems

Let us now go back to imagining new technology at work, first on a large scale and then on a small scale. The General Election of 1995 is being conducted interactively on television. Before the campaign starts, all the parties have commissioned telephone poll or viewdata companies to establish what the public thinks of the main issues of the day, and what are the strong and weak points of each party. Through their own computer networks, they have also polled their own members. Somehow, they have reconciled the very different views of the public at large and their own members into a manifesto. Every day during the campaign an opinion poll is conducted on-line, so that every family knows the nation's voting intentions. Each evening the leaders of the main parties sit in a studio, defending their manifesto policies and attacking those of their opponents. They also answer questions sent in by viewers all over the country, a computer in the studio selecting randomly from the hundreds of thousands of questions in the stack the dozen that can be dealt with in one programme. At 00.01 hours on polling day, the voting lines open. Voters dial first the number assigned to their constituency, then the individual identifying numbers known only to them. Once the equipment indicates that it is ready to receive their votes, they press '1' on their phones to vote Labour, '2' for Alliance, '3' for Conservative or '4' for Monster Raving Looney Party. If, by 1995, Parliament has enacted a measure of electoral reform, they will actually be asked to record their preference schedules. The lines close at midnight: at 1 a.m. the result is announced and the new Prime Minister arrives at Buckingham Palace at 9 a.m. to kiss the Queen's hand and form a government. (However, if there has been an electoral reform, it is almost certain that no party will have won half of the seats, so forming a government may take a little longer.)

Everything described in the last paragraph will probably be technically possible in 1995. If it happened that way, it would change the lives of many people, but would it be more democratic than our present way of running a General Election? It would be a clear improvement in terms of Problem D (the cost of voting). Everybody, not just those who read the heavy papers, would have the chance to become well-informed about the issues from unbiased sources – or from sources whose biases cancelled each other out. The parties would find out much more accurately and more cheaply both what the electorate wanted and what their own members wanted. Voting would take much less time, and would be easier for the elderly, the sick and the disabled, whose interests are particularly likely to be overlooked at present because they are less likely to turn out and vote than others. It could make a small contribution to solving Problem C (who asks the questions?), because the questions asked in the campaign would come direct from the electorate and would not be filtered through the 'news values' of television presenters or press barons. It would have an ambiguous impact on Problem B (strategic voting). Everybody would have access to much more accurate and unbiased information about everybody else's intentions than at present. Would that increase or decrease the incentive to vote strategically? It is impossible to tell without more information. If there was electoral reform, strategic voting would probably decline (because although all systems are manipulable, none forces as many voters to consider voting strategically as first-past-the-post does). But more people would be tempted to make their vote conditional on what everybody else was doing, and if everybody did that, the result would be utterly unpredictable. Without electoral reform, there would be no progress on Problem A (cycles). With it, the computer would be able to announce if there was no Condorcet winner among the parties. What happened next would be up to Parliament to decide. Unfortunately, Parliament has never in its history discussed electoral reform in an informed way (it has discussed it in an ill-informed way in 1917, 1930–1, and sporadically since 1974), so nobody knows what Parliament thinks.

Now for a change of scenario. The fifty members of a snark-making co-operative are meeting for their 1995 AGM. Ten of them are at the snark-ore mine in Argyllshire, thirty at the snark factory at Skelmersdale, and ten at the snark sales office and showroom in Bond Street. At each site are enough terminals to the co-operative's computer system to give every co-operator access to a keyboard within a few seconds. The co-operators first elect a Chair for the meeting. There are three candidates. The voters' preference scales show that none of them is a Condorcet winner, so the computer's vote-counting package breaks the tie by running a Borda count. The winner of that takes the meeting through the legal requirements for an AGM: approval of the directors' reports, the appointment of auditors, election of the co-op board for 1995–6. Then the meeting has to decide on the allocation of the year's surplus between reinvestment in the business and bonuses to co-operators. Members key in a number of suggestions for the share to go to reinvestment. They run from 20 to 80 per cent. The computer picks the median figure of those proposed (that is, the figure with as many others below it as above), which it knows from Black's theorem (Black, 1958, pp. 14–25) must be the Condorcet winner. The median proposal is 55 per cent, so the other 45 per cent goes in bonuses. There is a proposal that bonuses should be distributed in proportion to educational qualifications rather than length of employment. This would be a constitutional amendment, which would require a two-thirds majority to be approved. It is passed, but without the necessary majority, so it falls. When the Chair declares the meeting over, the computer wishes every member of the co-op a Merry Christmas before signing off.

All this is perfectly feasible already. The hardware exists, and it would not take long to write the vote-counting software (indeed, it is time somebody did). Does it make industrial democracy easier than it used to be? It clearly helps with Problem D. Not all those entitled to attend the meeting need be in the same place. They do not have to compete for the chairman's eye from the floor of a large meeting. Both of these factors help to reduce the bias towards the rich and the extrovert that exists at present. It may help, for the same reason, with Problem C. To some extent, the selection of questions can be done by the programme rather than by exercise of the chairman's discretion. It probably exacerbates Problem B. Each member of the meeting knows much more about the others' views than at present; but that is not all gain. The more they know, the more they can manipulate. For instance, somebody who wanted most of the surplus to go in bonuses would have an incentive to encourage others to put in bogus 'bids' for a reinvestment of 1 per cent, 2 per cent, 3 per cent, etc. This would obviously turn a lower bid into the median than if everybody voted sincerely. As to Problem A, it is neither solved nor exacerbated, but it is likely to be revealed. The more proposals are under discussion at once, the more likely there is to be a cycle of preferences among them. All manuals for chairmen (e.g. Citrine, 1952) insist on binary procedures. Only one proposal can be before a meeting at any time. If there are two, one must be considered as an amendment to the other and disposed of before turning to the other. Even skilled chairmen sometimes sink into procedural bogs where nobody knows whether the vote is on a resolution or an amendment, or a motion that the motion be now put, and so on. When a meeting descends into chaos, people often think it is the chairman's fault. Sometimes, however, the root of the trouble is that there is a cycle which the traditional binary procedure has failed to pick up. So everybody feels dissatisfied with the outcome, but nobody can say why. The reason is that there was at least one other proposal which would have beaten the one actually adopted; but they were never pitted against one another.

A programme which tested all the proposals at once to see if there was a Condorcet winner would show up cycles at once. It would thus reveal the true problem rather than what people mistakenly think to be the problem. If that is a gain, then we should thank new technology for it. But it might be a Pyrrhic victory. It forces us to confront a deeper problem than we have yet done.

## 6.6 The inescapability of cycles

How serious a problem is cycling? Most people have never heard of it. It was discovered by the Marquis de Condorcet and forgotten again; rediscovered by Lewis Carroll in the 1870s and forgotten again (Carroll circulated his pamphlets for comment but nobody understood what he was talking about); and then re-rediscovered by Duncan Black in the 1940s and not taken seriously for at least ten years after his first attempts to publish it. Now the tiresome little mathematical curiosity is threatening to turn into a monster which devours the whole of traditional democratic theory. First of all, Kenneth Arrow (1951) used it to prove that no voting procedure can satisfy four very undemanding requirements at once. Every procedure, familiar, unfamiliar or not yet invented, must violate at least one of Arrow's conditions. Then came the Gibbard–Satterthwaite theorem mentioned above, which proves that no voting procedure is proof against manipulation. Then, in a series of increasingly depressing theorems, Richard McKelvey and Norman Schofield have shown that cycles are almost inescapable in any complex voting decision. The latest conclusion is that not just cycles, but global cycles, are prevalent: that is, cycles embracing every single option, so that no matter which is chosen, it could have lost on a simple majority vote to another. All these theorems are quite difficult, but they are explained for non-mathematicians by Riker (1982) and Dummett (1984).

This is the hidden explanation of a common frustration. Theorists have often underestimated how long and complicated a process decision-making is. Lenin, for instance, envisaged that under communism 'All citizens [will] become employees and workers of a single country-wide state "syndicate"... The accounting and control necessary for this have been... reduced to... extraordinarily simple operations – which any literate person can perform... the need for government of any kind begins to disappear altogether'. He wrote that before the Bolshevik Revolution, which did not quite work out like that. Of course, Lenin defined democracy in a very peculiar way. But many who do not have made the same mistake. The most famous producers' co-operative of the 1970s, Kirby Manufacturing and Engineering, collapsed 'partly because it had lousy constitutional arrangements' (Eccles, 1981, p. 380). In eighty years' discussion of industrial democracy, nobody has produced a coherent scheme for democratic self-management. As Eccles, whose book is compulsory reading for industrial democrats, concluded in exasperation, 'Management isn't mysterious; it's just difficult' (p. 392). In direct democracy, the problems caused by cycling are frustratingly obvious, even if their origin is not. Meetings last a long time; the procedure for dealing with resolutions and amendments cannot cope; at the end of it people are left feeling that they would have preferred something other than what was decided. They are almost always right. It is hard to take in the conclusion that this applies to every possible course of action, but that is exactly what the McKelvey–Schofield theorems mean.

In representative democracy, the universality of cycling is more deeply hidden. At a General Election, we are not offered a choice between the possible different ways of running the country. There are uncountable trillions of those, and they are probably all in a cycle. We are offered a choice – like it or lump it – among at most three or four of them. But if those are in a cycle with others, politicians always have an incentive to bring new policies into their manifestos in order to beat the current alternatives. Riker (1982) offers a challenging re-interpretation of American political history on the basis of this insight. He concludes that cycling was the cause of the American Civil War. Interpretations need not be as bleak as his. But the universality of cycling forces us to ask what democracy can and cannot reasonably be asked to achieve.

## 6.7 How to avoid cycling: implications for democracy

There is a ray of hope. Consider again the vote on the co-operative's surplus. I said then, without explaining myself, that 'Black's theorem' states that there must be a Condorcet winner, and hence no cycle, on that vote. The reason is that all the possible options lay along one ideological dimension – in that case, the relative importance of reinvestment and distribution to co-operators. When there is an agreed ideological dimension, there are only two rational positions to take. One is to prefer one of the extreme options, and like each other option less and less as it gets further from one's favourite. The other is to prefer some non-extreme option, and to rank the others in two chains of diminishing preferences going towards the two extremes. If everybody ranks the options in one of those ways, the distribution of opinion is called 'single-peaked'. Figure 6.1 gives an example.

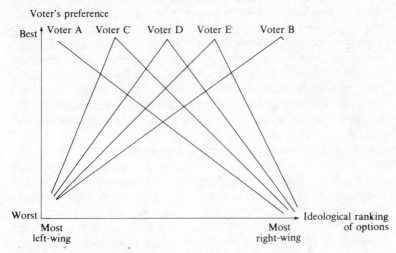

FIGURE 6.1   *A single-peaked distribution of opinion*

In Figure 6.1 there are five voters and numerous options. The options can be ranked from the most left-wing to the most right-wing. Voter A is an extreme left-winger and B is an extreme right-winger. C, D and E hold intermediate views. In this example, the policy preferred by Voter D is the Condorcet winner.

How common is the situation pictured in Figure 6.1? Notice that for there to be a guaranteed Condorcet winner, it is not necessary for everybody to agree. Voters A and B disagree as completely as it is possible to do. It is necessary for there to be an underlying dimension such that all the options can be ordered along it to produce a single-peaked distribution of opinion. Left-right is one such dimension. At one time it was thought that it dominated the politics of both political activists and ordinary citizens. That idea has been exploded, even though many politicians and journalists continue to believe in it. The people of Britain cannot be listed in order from the most left-wing to the most right-wing. But there are some small communities whose members can be ranked from leftmost to rightmost, just as drinkers can perhaps be ranked from real ale lovers to lager lovers; trade unionists from most pro-differential to most egalitarian; painters from most traditionalist to most modernist; and so on. Direct democracy within such groups is in principle feasible, and new technology makes it easier. Furthermore, if most members of a group are in agreement about the group's ultimate aims, even if they disagree violently about the means to get there, it is likelier that they will treat each other with good faith and not seek to manipulate voting.

Even if we could break society up entirely into groups which each operated along an agreed ideological dimension, there would still have to be a national government or some body to co-ordinate the activities of the groups. So there must be a place in any large society for representative democracy. In a large group, cycling can only be avoided if there is only one ideological dimension, which most voters recognize and use. Failing this, as in modern Britain, cycling is unavoidable. There are some incurable diseases, and cycling in multi-dimensional politics is one of them. Electoral reform is obviously needed, but it is not a panacea. But some 'reformed' electoral systems are better than others. What sort of electoral reform is appropriate for Britain in the age of information technology?

## 6.8  Information technology and electoral reform

The first step is to decide whether you want constituencies or not. The case for them is that each MP represents some locality, and will normally be prepared to work for anyone in that locality; and voters know for sure who is 'their' MP. The case against is that they distort representation. Even a result which was 'fair' in every constituency, as the present system obviously is not, would not necessarily be fair nationwide. Suppose the 1983 General Election had been fought on single-member constituencies, but instead of electing the first candidate past the post, the procedure had sought a Condorcet winner if there was one, and, failing that, elected the candidate with the highest Borda score. Any guess as to the result is unreliable, but mine is that the SDP/Liberal Alliance would have won perhaps three-quarters of the seats under such a rule. Each constituency result would appear fair, but the aggregate of them would be unfair to the other parties.

With IT, a direct, non-constituency election would be very easy, as was shown in Section 6.5. However, the UK is not a presidential democracy, and I shall assume that any electoral reform leaves intact the idea that the voters elect MPs with party labels, the parties elect their leaders, and the leader of the party which can command a majority in the House of Commons forms a government. I shall also assume that some element of local representation at least is bound to stay, so that the whole country is not treated as one constituency (as in Israel).

In multi-constituency elections, there are three electoral systems, or families of systems, worth taking seriously: Approval Voting, the Single Transferable Vote (STV) family, and the Additional Member family. With Approval Voting, you have not just one vote, but as many votes as there are candidates in the constituency. You vote for as many of them as you approve of (although there is no point in voting for them all, since this has the same effect as not voting at all). Approval Voting sounds bizarre, but it has a number of technical advantages. It is less liable to be manipulated than other systems which do not use preference information.

But its fatal defect is just that it does not use preference information. It forces you to treat somebody you really want like somebody you can only just stand. Although it has influential academic support in the USA, I think Approval Voting will remain an oddity.

STV, used in Ireland and Malta, operates in constituencies with between three and seven members each. This has produced a rough proportionality of seats to voters' preferences in Ireland since 1920, although proportionality is not absolutely guaranteed. In the last General Election in Malta, for instance, the STV system awarded more seats to the party which got fewer first preference votes. But that could happen under any constituency system. A more serious defect is that STV is non-monotonic. 'Non-monotonic' means, roughly, that a candidate can become more popular but have reduced chances of winning; for a more precise definition see Brams and Fishburn (1982, pp. 143–6). In my *Introduction to Public Choice* (McLean, 1987, Chapter 8) I give an example of how this can occur under STV. However, STV does have one big advantage: it is good at protecting minority blocs if they are sufficiently concentrated. Non-white UK citizens are an example. There are about four million of them, but not a single black MP. Many black Britons do not want to be represented by separate parties. But any who do are in a hopeless position at the moment. In a five-member seat under STV, any group of at least one-sixth of the electorate would be guaranteed an MP if all members of the group listed their candidate first. Thus, if you think that large social or geographical minorities (blacks, gays, Ulster loyalists, Irish nationalists . . .) ought to be guaranteed representation, you should go for STV.

There is no right and wrong on such questions, only different opinions. If you do not think minorities have a right to be protected in this way, you should not go for STV, as its failure to be monotonic is a serious defect. That leaves the Additional Member (AMS) family of procedures. AMS is a variant of the electoral system in West Germany which was proposed for Great Britain by the Hansard Society in 1976. Under AMS, three-quarters of MPs would be elected in single-member constituencies as at present. The remaining, 'additional', seats should be allocated to the parties in such a way as to ensure that their total representation, from constituency and additional MPs combined, was proportionate to their shares of the vote. The additional MPs would be the 'best losers' of their parties. Thus, if there were to be forty additional Labour MPs, they would be the forty unsuccessful Labour candidates with the highest share of the vote in their respective constituencies.

The main defect of AMS is that it relies on summing the first-past-the-post votes in each constituency to calculate the parties' 'fair shares' of seats. But those are hopelessly incomplete and inaccurate as expressions of preference. If AMS is adopted, therefore, it should be modified to incorporate information from voters' preference schedules. One way to do this would be to run a Borda count on all the parties standing in the election, and allocate seats to the parties in the same proportion as their Borda scores above some threshold (the West German threshold is 5 per cent). For example, in the 1995 election the total Borda score for all candidates might be 180 million. Suppose this comprised (dividing throughout by one million) 65 for the Conservatives, 60 for Labour, 50 for the Alliance and 5 for other parties. The other parties would be below the threshold, and the additional seats would be distributed to give the three main parties seats in the proportion 65:60:50. In a 640-member House of Commons, this would work out as 237 Conservative, 219 Labour and 183 Alliance MPs. The national voting computer would be able to work these figures out within minutes of the close of poll.

Teachers of computing like to begin with the statement: 'A computer is a high speed moron'. It is a useful warning. A computer can only do what human beings tell it to do, although it can do it very quickly. It cannot do things that are logically impossible, such as design a manipulation-proof voting procedure. Nor can it make value judgements. Questions like 'Do we want to entrench minority rights, or is majority rule to be sovereign?' are, and must remain, for human beings. New technology can bring into the open issues for democrats which all too few political theorists have ever thought about. It can do things which used to be physically impossible. But it cannot achieve the logically impossible, and it does not relieve us of the need to think about the age-old disputes of political theory. We have technology which Plato, Rousseau and Mill never dreamed of; but we have not settled the arguments among them.

## Notes

1. During the crisis over the abdication of King Edward VIII in 1936, Winston Churchill opposed the efforts of Stanley Baldwin, the Prime Minister, to get the King to abdicate. Many Tory MPs were initially sympathetic to Churchill and the King; but over the weekend of 5–6 December 1936 their support for the King suddenly melted away as they found out (what Baldwin already knew) that opinion in their constituencies was overwhelmingly against him. 'I have always believed in the weekend', Baldwin said later. 'But how they do it I don't know. I suppose they talk to the stationmaster' (Ramsden, 1978, p. 208).
2. I am most grateful to Mr John Clemens of London AGB Cable and Viewdata Ltd for showing me unpublished material about his firm's operations.
3. Pollsters commonly 'stratify' their samples to improve their representativeness. To stratify means to split up the population into social groups and ensure that there is the same proportion of each social group in the sample as there is known to be in the population. A television sample can be stratified as easily as one obtained by house-to-house interviewing.
4. Aischines, *Against Timarchos*, 27–32, translated by Rodewald (1975), p. 12.
5. The theorem is too hard to prove in a book like this, but it is introduced and discussed in, for example, Barry and Hardin (1982), pp. 11–14, 213–28, 355–66.

# References

ARROW, K. J. (1951) *Social Choice and Individual Values*, New York, Wiley.

BARRY, B. and HARDIN, R. (eds) (1982) *Rational Man and Irrational Society?*, London, Sage.

BLACK, D. (1958) *The Theory of Committees and Elections*, Cambridge, Cambridge University Press.

BRAMS, S. J. and FISHBURN, P. C. (1982) *Approval Voting*, Boston, Mass., Birkhauser.

BUTLER, D. and RANNEY, A. (eds) (1980) *Referendums*, Washington DC, American Enterprise Institute.

CITRINE, W. (Lord) (1952) *ABC of Chairmanship*, London, NCLC Publishing Co.

CLEMENS, J. (1985) 'Interactive television: tomorrow's instant referenda', mimeograph, London, AGB Cable and Viewdata Ltd.

DUMMETT, M. (1984) *Voting Procedures*, Oxford, Clarendon Press.

ECCLES, T. (1981) *Under New Management*, London, Pan.

FARQUHARSON, R. (1969) *Theory of Voting*, Oxford, Blackwell.

HANSARD SOCIETY FOR PARLIAMENTARY GOVERNMENT (1976) *Report of the Commission on Electoral Reform*, London, Hansard Society.

MCLEAN, I. S. (1987) *An Introduction to Public Choice*, Oxford, Blackwell.

PATEMAN, C. (1970) *Participation and Democratic Theory*, Cambridge, Cambridge University Press.

RAMSDEN, J. (1978) *The Age of Balfour and Baldwin*, London, Longman.

RIKER, W. H. (1982) *Liberalism Against Populism*, San Francisco, Freeman.

RODEWALD, C. (ed.) (1975), *Democracy: Ideas and Realities*, London, Dent.

# 7 Democracy and Bureaucracy
*Christopher Pollitt*

## 7.1 Introduction

What guidance do contemporary scholars offer concerning the relationship(s) between 'bureaucracy' and 'democracy'? Bureaucracy, says Eva Etzioni-Halevy, is 'by no means a sufficient condition for democracy, but it is certainly a necessary one' (Etzioni-Halevy, 1983, p. 227). Denis Thompson (1983, p. 236) concurs: 'No-one has yet shown that the quality of life that citizens in modern democracies demand can be sustained without bureaucracy, or a form of organization very much like it'. The influential 'new right' economist, William Niskanen, also seems to agree that bureaucracy is a 'standard fixture'. His acceptance is, however, heavily qualified: 'All bureaus are too large', he says, 'efficiency incentives are lacking, and sweeping restructuring and reform are required (Niskanen, 1973, p. 33).

Harsher verdicts are not hard to find. Both the 'new right' and the 'new left' offer visions of new worlds in which the social space currently occupied by conventional bureaucracies will be radically reduced. By privatizing many public industries and services and reconstituting the remaining state bureaucracies on a fragmented, mutually competitive basis, new right theorists claim that it will be practicable greatly to relieve bureaucratic stagnation and increase both citizen control and citizen choice. 'Decentralization' is also popular – in different forms – with the new left. For them, too, the large, centralized state bureacracies (agents of democratic progress for an earlier, Fabian generation) are now seen as hostile to true democracy. Under monopoly capitalism, according to Poulantzas (1978, p. 226), we have seen 'the emergence of the administrative and governmental apparatus as the dominant state structure', an apparatus which 'perfectly embodies...the hermetic insulation of power from democratic control'.

Clearly, then, contemporary scholars thoroughly disagree among themselves. Their analyses of how democracy and bureaucracy are currently related to one another vary considerably. Their prescriptions for the future are equally diverse. Furthermore there are other theories not yet mentioned here. To make some sense of this variety, by offering a partial 'map', is my first objective. Mapping will inevitably entail a preliminary discussion of definitions (unsurprisingly, different scholars do not use 'bureaucracy' and 'democracy' in any uniform fashion). In the second half of the chapter, once the 'map' is sketched, my objective will be to begin an evaluation of the main theories of the bureaucracy/democracy connection. As part of this evaluation reference will be made to empirical evidence, mainly from the USA and the UK. Such evidence cannot clinch the arguments in favour of one particular theory or theorist, but it can perform at least two very useful functions. First, historically, it can reveal where bureaucracy is now, and the route it took to get here. It can show, for example, whether the pattern of bureaucratic growth over time has varied much from country to country. It can show, for one or more countries, which parts of the bureaucracy have grown recently, and which diminished. Second, by the careful empirical study of existing, but rare or experimental, types of organization we can sometimes form more discriminating judgements about the consequences and desirability of the 'alternatives' to bureaucracy which many contemporary writers propose. My third (and final) objective is to develop my own account of the prospects for bureaucracy. This is done in Section 7.6. It will not be radically different from the other models but will draw on many of them. Together, these three objectives already constitute an ambitious task for a single chapter. Regrettably, although the study of bureaucracy boasts a rich history, it perforce must go almost entirely unmentioned here (but see Albrow, 1970; Brown *et al*, 1979; Dunsire, 1973).

## 7.2 Definition and scope

For the purposes of this chapter my working definition of bureaucracy will be fairly conventional. Unless otherwise specified, I shall take a 'bureaucracy' to be an organization which exhibits:

1.  A hierarchy of authority, i.e. the authority wielded by officials is graded by horizontal strata, with maximum power and discretion being located 'at the top'.
2.  Functional specialization, i.e. a complex subdivision of labour by task.
3.  Rule-orientation. Explicit (usually written) rules describe (potentially all) the rights and duties of each official.
4.  'Impersonal' relationships, in the sense that no personal likings or dislikings (favouritism/victimization) are supposed to influence the service provided to clients, the hiring of new officials, or the career advancement of those already employed.
5.  A tendency to develop standardized operating procedures (SOPs) using uniform criteria for classifying and processing a wide variety of situations.
6.  A tendency to secrecy (because this is a way of preserving one of the bureaucracy's major power resources – its command of specialized information, including information about its own, often very complex, rules).

It should immediately be noted that actual organizations may exhibit any one of these elements to greater or lesser degree. Empirically, it makes more sense to write of *degrees of bureaucratization*, rather than attempting to impose a black-or-white 'is a bureaucracy/isn't a bureaucracy' dichotomy. My working definition is very much in the Weberian tradition, though it should be noted that Weber himself never quite offered a single, generic definition of the term (Albrow, 1970, pp. 40–9).

Evidently, then, 'bureaucracy' and 'bureaucratization' are complex, multi-concepts, with multiple empirical referents. Any attempt to fix an 'immortal', final and authoritative definition is at best 'Quixotic' (Albrow, 1970, pp. 120–5). Rather, 'bureaucracy' and 'bureaucratization' may be regarded as labels denoting a family of interrelated issues, concerns which, historically, have grown up together and which have appeared to many researchers and thinkers to be logically and empirically interconnected.

Weber himself saw bureaucratization as a process taking place in *both* the state ('public') and non-state ('private') sectors. Indeed, only that part of the private sphere constituted by household and personal relationships seems to escape this ubiquitous process (see, for example, Jacoby, 1973). Many organizational sociologists have continued to work in the Weberian tradition, studying bureaucratization in private sector corporations as well as state agencies (e.g. Gouldner, 1954; Ferguson, 1984). However, some of the thinkers we shall be examining take a sharply different line. On the right, Niskanen and other 'public choice' theorists start from an entirely non-Weberian definition of bureaucracy and – not surprisingly – therefore arrive at a different set of 'problems' and recommended 'solutions'. Niskanen's is an *economic* definition of bureacracy as an organization in which:

(a) Their owners and employees do not appropriate any part of the difference between revenues and costs as personal income...

(b) Some part of the recurring revenues derive from other than the sale of output at a per unit rate.

So 'bureaus are non-profit organizations that are financed, at least in part, from a periodic appropriation or grant' (Niskanen, 1973, p. 8). This approach sharply distinguishes bureaucracies from profit-oriented private sector corporations, and even self-financing nationalized industries. The norm for the new right is the market-oriented, competitive, profit-seeking organization. Bureaucracy is seen as a problem principally because it diverges from this norm.

In many important respects (not least in the presumption of explicitly political direction), state bureaucracies no doubt *are* different from private sector corporate bureaucracies such as ICI, Unilever or IBM (Allison, 1983). Nevertheless, as Weber well knew, state bureaucracies cannot be satisfactorily studied in isolation from other sectors of society. At the level of case studies, the frequent 'capture' of state agencies by business and other interests is now well documented (see, to take just one of many examples, the discussion of the US President's suspicion of the federal bureaucracy in Maidment and McGrew, 1986). And at a more general level the 'special relationship' between the liberal democratic state and corporate business interests has now been fully acknowledged even by the neo-pluralists (Held, 1986, Chapter 6). In this chapter, therefore, 'bureaucracy' will not be as narrowly construed as it is in Niskanen's work.

It should also be borne in mind that bureaucratization is not exclusively associated with the nation state and corporate business. Since the Second World War one of the fastest arenas for bureaucratization has been the international and transnational one (Negro, 1987; Weiss, 1982). The European Community, for example, has achieved the doubtful distinction of serving as a new focus for a whole suite of anti-bureaucratic jokes. Some of the theorists interrogated in this chapter pay little or no attention to international bureaucracies. More generally, it seems that the distinctive qualities of these organizations have hitherto been noticeably under-theorized (Jonsson, 1986). While I cannot hope to remedy such a large deficiency here, I shall at least endeavour to point to its implications wherever they seem most significant.

Finally, one major exclusion from the present account is that of bureau-cracies in the communist states. There is a fascinating literature on bureaucracy in the Soviet Union, Eastern Europe and China (e.g. Nove, 1978; Urban, 1982) but regrettably I have no room to pursue it. My focus remains on bureaucracy in the liberal democracies of the West.

## 7.3 Bureaucracy: advantages and problems for democracy

I have selected six contemporary theorists. The selection is inevitably personal, but (I hope) reasonably representative. Each theorist 'represents' a major school of thought ('new left', 'new right', etc.). For each I offer a summary, concluding with an account of the main issues which the theorist in question identifies in the bureaucracy/democracy relationship.

The first theorist is *Nicos Poulantzas*, a neo-Marxist and noted representative of the 'new left'. In his last major work, *State, Power, Socialism* (1978) Poulantzas had a good deal to say about 'state administration'. His basic stance was hostile towards bureaucracy. Although he certainly did *not* see it in vulgar Marxist terms (as just an automatic arm of the bourgeoisie) he nevertheless held it to be ineluctably secretive, authoritarian and anti-participatory. No formal definition of 'bureaucracy' is offered, but the discussion is clearly focused on the governmental or state apparatus, not on bureaucracy in the private sector. As far as 'democracy' is concerned, he shares the fundamentally critical stance which all Marxists take towards the liberal democracies of the West. Opportunities for popular, mass participation are severely limited. The main political parties are becoming less and less 'representative' of working-class and petit bourgeois people.

Instead these parties 'now constitute veritable transmission belts for executive decisions, rather than being centres engaged in political elaboration and in working out compromises and alliances around a more or less precise programme' (p. 229). The real centre of political decision-making has moved:

> under the authority of the Executive, the state bureaucracy is becoming not merely the principal site, but also the principal *actor* in the elaboration of state policy . . . The various economic interests are now directly present as such within the administration. (p. 224)

This centralization of power is principally the consequence of the economic concentration of monopoly capitalism. This compels the state to intervene more and more (and in a more detailed and partial manner) in the economy (see Held, 1986, Chapter 7). However, while the tendency to centralization 'derives from socio-economic and political changes, it also flows from the specifically bureaucratic logic according to which statism begets statism, and authoritarianism begets authoritarianism' (p. 227). Poulantzas's concept of *democracy* embodies the usual Marxist preference for direct democracy, but he also values some representative institutions. Bureaucracy, it seems, is antagonistic to democracy, and should be minimized, 'transformed'.

Kathy Ferguson is also of the new left. In her book, *The Feminist Case against Bureaucracy* (1984), she is centrally concerned with the *psychological* impact of bureaucracy. This impact is felt by both bureaucratic clients and bureaucrats themselves. Ferguson employs a familiar Marxist framework – for example, she asserts that the biggest bureaucratic benefits flow to corporate and business interests (pp. 128–9). On the whole, however, she does not spend much time exploring the economic dimension. Rather, she emphasizes the *personally* disabling features of bureaucratic modes of discourse and action:

> Any orginality of thought or action requires that we be rooted in shared existence; but the more firmly rooted one is in bureaucracy, the less likely one is to think differently, to act differently, or in any way to make a new beginning. In bureaucratic settings the requirements of creativity – that is to be linked to others – stifle creativity; the very process of self-creation is threatened. Put another way, in conditions of administered life, individuals, both bureaucrats and clients, come to see each other and themselves as the objects of administration. The source of the norms and rules governing their behaviour . . . is precisely the rules of the organization itself. (Ferguson, 1984, p. 14)

Of course, Ferguson is far from being the first to express anxiety about the psychological impact of bureaucratization. Nor have such concerns been confined to feminists: for example, in his book *The Bureaucratization of the World*, Henry Jacoby partly attributed the growth of alienation and indifference to the decline of participation, as more and more of the contexts in which individuals found themselves turned out to have been 'organized' for them by bureaucrats (Jacoby, 1973, especially pp. 201–8). And there are many texts bewailing the defensive over-caution which the bureaucratic environment is widely perceived as encouraging. 'Play safe and ignore the long-term consequences for others' might be the bureaucrat's rule of thumb (Beneviste, 1982). Ferguson does, however, offer a specifically feminist slant on the 'bureaucratic pathology'. She suggests that, psychologically, the process of bureaucratization is like the process of feminization. Just as male (patriarchal) dominance encourages women to see themselves as relatively passive, as needing to please, as customarily subordinate and of secondary importance, so does bureaucratization inculcate similar attitudes in officials (towards their hierarchical superiors) and clients (towards officials). In each case, a sense of personal creativity, efficacy and autonomy is submerged. (Ferguson, 1984, Chapter 3). These qualities (isolation, defensiveness, image-manipulation, etc.) Ferguson perceives as running counter to those required for effective participation in democratic political activity. Since her definition of democracy appears to be heavily participative and 'developmental', she therefore sees bureaucratization as a major constraint on democratization. The achievements of 'human service' bureaucracies (e.g. social security and public health and housing agencies) are dismissed as forms of social control in disguise. The reformist strategy of capturing power within bureaucracies is criticized because 'women need power in order to change society, but power within bureaucracies is not change-making power. The organizational forms and discourse of bureaucratic capitalism institutionalize modes of domination that recreate the very patterns of oppression that feminism arose to combat' (p. 203).

On the new right, *William Niskanen* is not so unremittingly hostile to state bureaucracy. Its sin is not so much its authoritarian, anti-participatory character as its tendency to supply more of its services than the average member of the electorate wants (Niskanen, 1971, 1973). According to Niskanen, the special protections enjoyed by bureaucracies in supplying their goods and services enable them to oversupply at anything up to twice the rate the citizenry, given the choice, would prefer. Each bureau is headed or supervised by a political 'sponsor'. But in the sponsor–bureaucrat relationship the bureaucrats have more specialized information, more time, and are usually in the position of monopoly suppliers of their services. 'It is not the preferences of the constituents that are important to the bureau, rather their influence on the revealed preference of its sponsor' (Niskanen, 1973, p. 15). What is more, in so far as bureaucratic performance is reviewed by congressional or parliamentary committees, these tend to contain a disproportionately large percentage of Congressmen/ MPs enthusiastic for the services in question (in Niskanen's terms, representative of the 'high demanders' among the population as a whole).

Although Niskanen's analysis is rooted in observation of US practice, he clearly believed much of it to be more widely applicable. This belief was quickly taken up by 'new right' politicians and academics in Britain. For example, the (British) Institute of Economic Affairs publication of his ideas contained a commentary by Nicholas Ridley, later to become a prominent member of Mrs Thatcher's Cabinet, in which Ridley claimed that 'Professor Niskanen has produced a paper of devastating importance' (Ridley, in Niskanen, 1973, p. 87).

What disciples of Niskanen noticed less often about his ideas was that their prime thrust was not actually to do with efficiency at all, but with 'the *quantity* of output of a public service' (my emphasis) and 'the preferred combination of public services' (1973, p. 51). As far as efficiency was concerned, Niskanen was not by any means an implacable opponent of public bureaucracy. Indeed, he thought that *if* his proposed reforms (see later) were implemented, 'A large part of the bureaucracy would probably survive this challenge by improving its performance to equal or better than that of other forms of organization' (1973, p. 59).

Not only is Niskanen's definition of bureaucracy very different from those in the Weberian or Marxist traditions, but so is the scope of his concern. He is scarcely concerned with the role of bureaucracy in relation to social and political cleavages, with whether very large and complex organizations can in fact be held accountable to elected representatives, with whether there is 'enough' citizen 'participation' or 'self-government'. He discusses 'bureaucracy', but he does not really discuss 'democracy'. Representative democracy is, by implication, fairly satisfactory, and his work is silent on the possibility or desirability of forms of direct democracy. It is not just that he is an economist; rather that he is a very particular kind of economist, a 'neo-classicist', taking the competitive market as *the* normal and desirable way of satisfying preferences and enquiring very little into how those preferences arise and change (see also Perlman, 1982).

*Eva Etzioni-Halevy's* concerns are much more in the Weberian tradition of broad socio-political analysis. In her text *Bureaucracy and Democracy: a Political Dilemma* (1983) she defines bureaucracy as 'a hierarchical organization of officials appointed to carry out certain public objectives' (p. 85). She acknowledges that 'I have adopted Weber's insights and a modified elitist perspective' (p. 3). This perspective is outlined as follows: 'I consider political power as crucial in its own right rather than as an offshoot of ownership or economic power and I view political and economic elites who wield power as basically serving their own interests rather than those of property-holding classes' (pp. 3–4). It is, of course, pertinent to ask what kind of 'democracy' it is to which she is referring. The book is admirably clear on this point. The author offers a distinctly Schumpeterian and instrumentalist definition (see Held, 1986, Chapter 5):

*Democracy*... is defined as the institutional arrangement whereby two or more organized groups of people (or parties) participate in the contest for power (or for elite positions) on the strengths of their advocated policies and/or their projected images and whereby they acquire such posts on the basis of free elections by the whole of the adult population (Etzioni-Halevy, 1983, p. 86)

Etzioni-Halevy argues that bureaucracy performs vital functions for democracy. It reduces political corruption and provides a non-partisan watchdog to safeguard democratic procedures. In allocating the vast resources commanded by the modern state, bureaucracy operates by 'general categories of need or entitlement', thus preserving the citizenry from the ever-present danger of allocation based on the party political criteria of 'potential or actual political support of the recipient for the donor and his [sic] party' (p. 91). Yet there are also major tensions between bureaucracy and democracy. Bureaucracy may be used by political elites to increase their domination, or even to construct a repressive state. Alternatively, bureaucracy may slip beyond the control of the elected political elite, using its technical expertise and exploiting the inevitable ambiguity of the rules demarcating the 'political' from the 'administrative' in order to pursue its own interests. Again, examples are not hard to think of, and unlike either Poulantzas or Niskanen, Etzioni-Halevy includes extensive case study material from several countries. This material shows that bureaucrats may be more or less 'progressive' than their political leaders, more or less authoritarian, more or less conservative. To be effective, bureaucracy has to enjoy a certain degree of autonomy, of discretion, yet for the polity to qualify as 'democratic' (even from this elitist perspective) officialdom must also be subject to political control. This is the paradox, the constant tension that Etzioni-Halevy sees at the heart of the bureaucracy–democracy relationship.

This account offers a salutary reminder of the risks of patronage and corruption once the ideal of an impartial bureaucracy (however imperfectly realized in practice) is abandoned. Second, it draws attention to the considerable powers of initiative often possessed by the bureaucracy. Like a number of other elite theorists (notably Nordlinger, 1981) Etzioni-Halevy argues that the bureaucracy cannot accurately be characterized simply as a tool of some particular class or class fraction. elsewhere, however, her analysis seems sketchier. She does not delve as deeply as Poulantzas into the economic links between big business and the state apparatus. She says little of the impacts of technological change and less still of the 'psychological costs' of bureaucracy – the personal consequences of following such rule-bound existences as do many middle-rank and junior officials.

My fifth theorist, the neo-pluralist *Charles Lindblom*, is much less sure that we can do without bureaucracy. It is one of the curiosities of the cast-list of academic political science that the arch-pluralists – Robert Dahl and Charles Lindblom – should turn up again two decades later as the arch *neo*-pluralists (see Held, 1986, Chapters 6 and 7). Here I shall be considering Lindblom in his 'neo' persona, principally through examination of his book, *Politics and Markets* (1977). This elegant text is of extremely broad scope, as the sub-title, *The World's Political-Economic Systems*, indicates. Lindblom dissects both Western liberal democracies and communist regimes in terms of three 'elemental mechanisms of social control': exchange, authority and persuasion (pp. 11–12). Exchange is 'the fundamental relationship on which market systems are built' (p. 12), while 'the authority relationship is the bedrock on which government is erected' (p. 13). In America (and elsewhere) Lindblom believes there has been an unplanned but revolutionary growth in hierarchical authority structures:

> In the early nineteenth century, four out of five Americans were self-employed; the number is now less than one in ten. Assuming all but the smallest corporations are bureaucratically organized, over half the gainfully employed work in bureaucracies...Millions of people are also members of bureaucratically organized labor unions, employer groups, fraternal orders, veterans associations, and farm organizations; and their children are encouraged to sample bureaucracy in the Scouts and Little Leagues. (Lindblom, 1977, p. 28)

For Lindblom bureaucracy is not just *any* organizational structure using authority as its principal means of social control. Only hierarchical (or 'pyramidal') organizations qualify. He says these tend to share certain characteristics, and then goes on to produce a very Weber-like list, including task specialization; the assignment of authority to posts rather than individuals; the standardization of problems, procedures and solutions; the assignment of co-ordinating functions to the higher echelons; tendencies towards 'goal displacement' (means becoming ends in themselves); and growing rigidity over time. Despite these latter tendencies 'bureaucracy [in both the governmental and the private sector] is a powerful multipurpose tool. It routinizes problem solving to an extreme degree and frees it from dependence on any unusual skills or initiatives' (p. 27). Bureaucracy can be clumsy ('strong thumbs, no fingers', as Lindblom puts it) and overall co-ordination is a special difficulty. Market/exchange systems, by contrast, transform complex co-ordinating problems such as 'what should we produce?' into very simple ones: 'should I buy or sell?' Nevertheless, bureaucratic co-ordination is potentially a *strong* tool, strong enough to produce high growth rates in some communist countries, and impressive feats of wartime planning in the liberal democracies.

Thus Lindblom sees bureaucracy as useful and increasingly pervasive, though characterized by unfortunate tendencies to develop its own goals and to become increasingly inflexible with age. But how does he see 'democracy'? He specifically avoids labelling the family of Western nations 'liberal democracies' and instead calls them 'polyarchies'. A polyarchy ('rule by the many') is a set of authoritative rules which 'limit the struggle for authority, specifying a particular orderly and peaceful process to replace armed conflict, threat of force or other crude contests' (p. 133). Distinctively, top authority is assigned by elections, in which each citizen has a vote of equal weight. Distinctively also, polyarchic citizens have the rights, protected by special rules, to:

> inform and misinform themselves, express themselves wisely or foolishly, and organize into political groups in order to decide how best to cast their votes and to influence others. They are also authorized to communicate their wishes to political leaders and in other ways influence them. In all polyarchies, these authorizations are to a significant degree effective...They are, however, not effective for all, nor equally effective, nor always effective. (p. 133)

One serious discrepancy in effectiveness is the privileged position of business. Lindblom concludes with this striking peroration:

> It has been a curious feature of democratic thought that it has not faced up to the private corporation as a peculiar organization in an ostensible democracy. Enormously large, rich in resources, the big corporations...command more resources than do most government units. They can also, over a broad range, insist that government meet their demands, even if these demands run counter to those of citizens expressed through their polyarchal controls. They are on all these counts disproportionately powerful...The large private corporation fits oddly into democratic theory and vision. Indeed, it does not fit. (p. 356)

Lindblom refers to a 'veto' because, he argues, polyarchies are increasingly threatened by the power of business to cast an effective veto (p. 347). The market system (social control through *exchange* rather than through *authority*) has evolved in a way that has afforded business too many protections, too much freedom from the electoral controls of polyarchy. More recently, another prominent pluralist-turned-neopluralist has echoed some of Lindblom's anxieties. Robert Dahl now argues that: 'a system of government Americans view as intolerable in governing the state has come to be accepted as desirable in governing large economic enterprises' (Dahl, 1985, pp. 161–2). The authoritarianism of corporate bureaucracies, in Dahl's view, constitutes a severe constraint on the core democratic value of self-determination.

For Lindblom, Dahl and the neo-pluralists, therefore, bureaucracy poses one huge problem and one lesser one. The huge problem is that of the *private sector* corporate bureaucracy, which is effectively organized to wield *both* control through exchange in the market-place *and* political control through its veto over the exercise of authority by the polyarchically constituted state. The secondary problem is that governmental bureaucracies have the distressing habit of becoming set in their ways. Though not as free to explore new functions as private (corporate) bureaucracies, they do tend to try to perpetuate themselves beyond their original *raison d'être*. They also age ungraciously, resisting changes in the ways of doing things in which they have invested their expertise and resources. Lindblom seems to suggest that political leaders can minimize these secondary problems by continuous administrative reform and restructuring, and that bureaucracies in any case set some limits to each other's exercise of authority. Thus, in the USA, several federal, state and local bureaucracies commonly find they have interests in the same problem (public transport, health, Central America). Effectively, concerted action can only be achieved by persuasion, the exchange of information, and the creation of an ongoing bureaucratic network through which 'favours' are swapped and mutual obligations created.

In sharp contrast *John Burnheim's* unusual work, *Is Democracy Possible?* (1985), is dedicated to showing how democracy might work without much at all in the way of a central government. Burnheim addresses problems at all levels – local, national, international (see the final chapter of this book) and even that of the psychology of individual participation. Unlike any of the five texts previously referred to, it is explicitly a blueprint for change. (Accordingly I shall have more to say about Burnheim in Section 6.8.) Burnheim advocates a highly decentralized scheme which he terms 'demarchy'. He defines bureaucracy as 'that form of permanent organization of social action that is directed by a central authority. It is characteristic not only of state instrumentalities but also of large non-state institutions' (Burnheim, 1985, p. 51). Bureaucracies operate through hierarchical chains of command and are generally staffed on a permanent and full-time (i.e. 'career') basis. They 'are no doubt always imperfect... But since organization is indispensible, so is bureaucracy, at least where there are permanent functions to be carried out and controlled' (p. 52). Having set out this general argument for bureaucracy, Burnheim turns to arguments against. These (which he appears to find more persuasive) include:

1. Bureaucracy's inflexibility.
2. Its inhibiting effect on novelty.
3. Its distortion of information/messages as they pass up or down hierarchies.
4. Its resistance to measures of performance based on the actual *impact* of its services.
5. Its tendencies to 'empire-building', 'goal displacement'.

In sum, 'Even most bureaucrats do not like it very much. They feel constrained by all those rules even when they are seen as having great power' (p. 54). What model of democracy informs this critique? This is where Burnheim is most startling, because he argues for the relinquishment of elections as a central feature:

> Let the conventions for deciding what is our common will be that we will accept the decision of a group of people who are well-informed about the question, well-motivated to find as good a solution as possible, and representative of our range of interests simply because they are statistically representative of

us as a group. If this group is then responsible for carrying out what it decides, the problem of control of the execution process largely vanishes. (Burnheim, 1985, p. 114)

The notion of *statistical representation* is crucial. For Burnheim's vision of 'demarchy' comprises a large number of modest-sized functional agencies, each one run by a random statistical sample taken from a larger group of those who (a) have volunteered *and* (b) have a legitimate material interest in the function in question. He is against elections because they lend themselves to exploitation by increasingly professional, irretrievably oligarchical party machines. Equally, he maintains that 'Nobody *should have any input into decision-making where they have no legitimate material interest*' (p. 5, original emphasis). By stressing 'material' interest Burnheim intends to exclude those who simply wish to tell others how to live their lives, or what is good for them. By *'legitimate'* he means that claims to material interests must be morally sound, e.g. not based on theft or forced expropriation.

Burnheim's conception is therefore one of a form of democracy embodying much broader citizen participation than is common in contemporary liberal democracies. But it is not participation by *all* in *everything*. Rather it is participation by a regularly changed representative sample of those with specific interests in each particular function (health, education, etc.). Burnheim sums up as follows:

> most of the decisions that are now taken by centrally-controlled multi-function agencies ranging from nation states down to municipalities could be taken by autonomous specialized agencies that are co-ordinated by negotiation among themselves or, if that fails, by quasi-judicial arbitration, rather than by direction from a controlling body. (p.7)

Demarchy, then, is founded on a profound mistrust of centralized, multi-purpose authority. Burnheim's main thrust 'is not only anti-state, but anti-communalist, directed against giving sovereignty or anything like it to *any* geographically or ethnically circumscribed group' (p. 8).

The first step in mapping the bureaucracy-democracy relationship is now concluded, Table 7.1 offers a summary of 'the story so far'.

## 7.4 Meanwhile, back at the office...

What relations do the theories sketched above bear to trends in real-world bureaucracies? None of the six chosen texts contains much empirical material. Poulantzas and Burnheim have least to offer in this regard. Niskanen produces some figures for the growth of the government sector relative to private business, but these are scarcely sufficient to support even his own theory of 'oversupply'. Ferguson refers to many empirical studies but makes no systematic statement of the current extent of bureaucratization or of any changes that may already be taking place. Etzioni-Halevy gives a

TABLE 7.1   *Bureaucracy and democracy: six contemporary theorists*

| Theorist | Definition of bureaucracy | Conception of democracy | Bureaucracy–democracy relationship |
|---|---|---|---|
| Poulantzas (neo-Marxist, 'new left') | No formal definition. State bureaucracy the principal 'actor' in policy-making. Bureaucracy inherently authoritarian and secretive. | Increasing gap between the masses and the state machine. Normative model is highly participatory, still with some representative institutions but also many (unspecified) forms of direct democracy. | In a fully participatory democracy there would be very little bureaucracy. Consistently supposes a fundamental antagonism between bureaucracy and democracy. |
| Ferguson (radical feminist; 'new left') | No formal definition, but bureaucracies are characterized as rule-bound, authoritarian, hierarchical, secretive and uncreative. | Normative model heavily participatory, with an emphasis on direct and developmental rather than representative and instrumental modalities | Similar to Poulantzas, but much greater emphasis on the *personally* disabling effects of bureaucratization. Likened to the processes of 'feminization', whereby patriarchal men attempt to maintain women as deferential, subordinate, needing-to-please (etc.). |
| Niskanen (neo-classical economist; 'new right') | Non-profit organizations financed principally by periodic appropriations or grants. | Not much discussed. By implication, representative democracy is reasonably satisfactory. But tends to overrepresent groups with higher-than-average demands for bureaucratically supplied services. | Bureaucracy necessary but has strong tendency to oversupply its services. Various institutional changes hold prospect of curbing this. |

TABLE 7.1 *continued*

| *Theorist* | *Definition of bureaucracy* | *Conception of democracy* | *Bureaucracy–democracy relationship* |
|---|---|---|---|
| Etzioni-Halevy (neo-elitist) | Broadly Weberian: 'a hierarchical organization of officials appointed to carry out certain public objectives'. | Schumpeterian: elite groups compete for power by advocating attractive policies and projecting attractive images at periodic elections. Popular participation largely limited to choosing the most promising team of leaders. | Bureaucracy vital for democracy. Allocates resources etc. impartially, thus reducing political patronage and corruption. But elite groups may use bureaucracy to repress opposition. Bureaucratic elites may grow beyond control and pursue their own interests. Eternal vigilance the price of democracy. |
| Lindblom (neo-pluralist) | Broadly Weberian. Sees bureaucracy as a particular type of social control mechanism, one based on *authority* distributed in a *hierarchical* manner | Normative model not much discussed. Descriptive model of liberal democracies as '*polyarchies*' with special rules governing the acquisition and exercise of authority. | Private, corporate bureaucracies much too powerful (also Dahl, 1985). Able to veto state authority in many important areas. Governmental bureaucracies manifest pathologies (inflexibility, self-perpetuation). On the positive side, bureaucracies can be used as powerful, multi-purpose tools in the sometimes necessary exercise of government authority. |
| Burnheim (demarchist) | Centralized, hierarchical authority systems, found in both public and private sectors. | Advocates '*demarchy*', a system of highly decentralized, fragmented functional authorities. Each to be run by a random sample of those citizens with a legitimate material interest who volunteer for nomination. | Centralized, multifunctional authorities inherently oligarchic. Their internal structures systematically distort flows of information. Big, centralized bureaucracy inhibits democratic creativity and participation. |

good deal of space to some interesting case studies, but does not attempt any empirical overview. Lindblom is more concerned with studies of political participation and of business influence in government to focus specially on the condition of governmental bureaucracy. One must look elsewhere to see what has been happening, and when one does a number of interesting features appear. In brief, it seems that bureaucratic growth has been much faster in some *countries* and some policy *sectors* than others. Furthermore, the *character* of bureaucracy may be quite diverse – and may be changing, at least as far as its internal structures are concerned. Neither of these features seems to have been adequately acknowledged at the level of the 'grand theories' mapped above.

Almost everyone is agreed that bureaucratization has been increasing in the Western liberal democracies, in both state and private sectors. In the USA, for example, total government employment increased from 5.8 million in 1947 to 16.1 million in 1983. In the UK, enormous growth has taken place since the 1870s – more in some periods than others (Pollitt, 1979).

The post-war growth of public employment in the USA and the UK has in fact been noticeably *slower* than in most other liberal democracies, as Table 7.2 makes clear.

TABLE 7.2   *Public employment as a percentage of national employment (adapted from Rose, 1984, p. 132)*

| Country | 1951 | 1980 | Change |
|---------|------|------|--------|
| Sweden | 15.2 | 38.2 | +23.0 |
| Britain | 26.6 | 31.7 | + 5.1 |
| Germany | 14.4 | 25.8 | +11.4 |
| Italy | 11.4 | 24.3 | +12.9 |
| USA | 17.0 | 18.8 | + 1.8 |

Nor should we believe that the seemingly relentless cuts of conservative administrations such as Mr Reagan's or Mrs Thatcher's have substantially changed this general picture. As yet the overall effect of their onslaughts have been marginal, which is not to deny that the margins are real, and painful. There are strong reasons to believe that they will not easily be able substantially to reverse the governmental growth of the past thirty years (Rose, 1984).

It is also noteworthy that the number of elected representatives per elector has declined. This has been true for all Western democracies

(Rose, 1984, p. 177): in the UK, for example, there were 8519 voters per MP in 1885 and 64 716 in 1979. Similarly, in most countries, the jurisdictional size of local government units has increased over the post-war period (Rose, p. 159). Taken together, one can understand from these trends – more bureaucrats per elected representative, larger administrative units – why neo-Marxists like Poulantzas (and other radicals) see 'a loosening of the ties of representation' and an 'irrepressible shift in the centre of gravity towards the state bureaucracy' (Poulantzas, 1978, pp. 221, 227).

Of course, there are large definitional and data problems with most figures of this kind. Not all public employees work in organizations which manifest all the characteristics listed in my working definition. Some are highly independent, politically active community workers. Others are lone forest rangers, or fisheries inspectors operating with extensive personal discretion, far from the nearest 'hierarchical superior'. Others still may be coal miners or steel workers in nationalized enterprises – hardly stereotypical 'bureaucrats'. Unfortunately, however, we often have to accept 'public employment' as the best proxy for 'bureaucracy' that the available data permits us to use. There are no records which show – even for one country, let alone comparatively – how many jobs altogether exist within organizations with the six characteristics given in Section 7.2.

In the private sector the situation is no better. Two kinds of figures are commonly used to indicate corporate bureaucratization. First there are figures for 'concentration', that is for the percentage of the workforce employed in large organizations (the presumption being that larger firms are much more likely to be bureaucratic). Since the Second World War private sector 'concentration' has been on the increase in most Western countries, though it has gone further and faster in some countries (e.g. the UK) than others (e.g. France or Italy). The share of UK net manufacturing output accounted for by the hundred largest firms rose from 22 per cent in 1949 to 37 per cent in 1963 to over 40 per cent by the 1970s (Prais, 1976, p. 4). The other kind of index of bureaucratization is the 'A/P ratio'. An A/P ratio is the ratio of 'administrative' to 'production' employees (this is roughly the distinction between salaried 'staff' and waged 'workers'). The higher the percentage of 'A' employees, the more bureaucratized the firm is supposed to be. Studies of A/P ratios commonly yield a picture of rapid bureaucratization. For example, in 1947, for each 'administrator' in US manufacturing industry there were five 'production workers', while by 1983 there was only one (Meyer *et al.*, 1985, pp. 37–9). The lion's share of this 'bureaucratization' took place in larger ('multiunit') establishments. A/P ratios have consistently been higher in manufacturing than non-manufacturing industry.

Where, though, has the growth come in the *governmental* sector? The evidence here indicates considerable *commonalty between the liberal democracies*, despite differential *starting points* and *rates* of growth

(Table 7.3). The major growth – in money and staff – has come in the now well-established programmes: income maintenance (social security and pensions), and education and health (Rose, 1984, pp. 208–13). 'In the past quarter-century, "armies" of social welfare workers have replaced armies of soldiers as the characteristic employees of government' (Rose, p. 136).

TABLE 7.3   *Percentage changes in numbers in employment in major functional programmes 1951–80 (adapted from Rose, 1984, p. 136)*

| Programmes | UK | Germany | Italy | Sweden | USA |
|---|---|---|---|---|---|
| Education | 161 | 225 | 298 | 123 | 270 |
| Health | 167 | 217 | 289 | 628 | 209 |
| All social programmes[1] | 163 | 182 | 283 | 455 | 244 |
| Defence | −54 | n.a. | −19 | −10 | −39 |
| All nationalized industries | −13 | 65 | 120 | 76 | 134 |
| Total change, all programmes | 22 | 111 | 123 | 217 | 72 |

[1] Including programmes other than education and health, e.g. personal social services.

This pattern has a relevance for several of the theories we have been examining, for the typical representative of recent bureaucratization has not been, as some theorists would seem to apply, a faceless official pushing paper in a remote office. It has been a nurse, a teacher or a social security clerk. What is more, two of the largest growth programmes, health and education, are dominated by professionals who, though certainly subject to many rules and regulations, usually possess wide powers of discretion and initiative. The rule-bound zombie may be an untypical stereotype. There is also the question of public attitudes to bureaucracy. It is sometimes implied (or assumed) that 'bureaucracy' is very unpopular. Certainly many of us (*mea culpa*) occasionally *speak* disparagingly of bureaucracy. Yet the services provided by the biggest and fastest growing state bureaucracies turn out to be among the most popular features of the liberal democratic polity. 'The public strongly supports the heartland services of the welfare state' is the recent conclusion of one expert on UK public attitudes to welfare services (Taylor-Gooby, 1985, p. 91). Not that all aspects of the welfare state are equally popular. In Britain, while pensions, education and (above all) the NHS call forth high levels of public approval, popular support for local authority housing and for benefits directed at the unemployed, the low paid or single parents is much less pronounced (Taylor-Gooby, 1985). Nevertheless, the overall theme is hardly one of universal hostility to bureaucracy or even bureaucratic growth. Impatience with delay, resentment of obscurantism or high-handedness: these reactions are no doubt commonplace. But if survey and electoral evidence is to be believed, the public in Western countries can and do discriminate between particular incidents of this kind and the *general* desirability of many of the services bureaucracies make available.

Yet this is still less than the full picture. True, growth in the 1960s and 1970s was concentrated in the relatively 'benign' welfare bureaucracies. Defence establishments usually declined in terms of absolute numbers employed. They remain, however, very large, especially in the USA, which devotes an unusually high percentage of its governmental spending to defence. What is more, the Thatcher administration in Britain and the Reagan administration in the USA have each sought to reverse the previous relative contraction in defence spending. Between the 1981 and 1986 financial years, US defence appropriations rose by 40 per cent in real terms, and both military and civilian defence personnel increased their numbers. In any case, expenditures had never shrunk at the same rate as staff numbers – the growing technological complexity of weaponry saw to that. Defence forces became more 'money intensive'. Yet at the time of writing it remains true that the overall scale of these recent increases is dwarfed by the huge expansion of welfare spending in the previous two decades. There is, however, another factor. Both defence and domestic public order forces (police) have steadily enhanced their intelligence-gathering and -processing capacities. Such an intensification of (usually secret) surveillance – of domestic populations as well as the activities of military rivals – must be a cause for concern to those interested in the maintenance of freedoms from state interference (Giddens, 1985, p. 310).

So it is not only the *dimensions* of bureaucracy that have changed. Internal structures and procedures are constantly evolving, and some recent changes appear both widespread and relevant to the continued usefulness (or otherwise) of conventional definitions of bureaucracy. I will restrict my discussion to just three developments which seem particularly significant.

## 7.5 Professionalization

It has already been remarked that some of the fastest growing sectors of state bureaucracies are also highly professionalized. Professionals do not fit all the features of a conventional Weberian definition terribly well. They tend to develop relatively 'flat' hierarchies, and to stress 'collegiality' rather than lines of command. To the conventional assumptions of a vertical, 'command' structure of authority they oppose claims of authority founded on expertise. Further, public service professionals often lay considerable emphasis (partly but not *only* rhetorically) on maintaining the *trust* of their 'clients'. They therefore aspire to develop individual relationships with those with whom they deal. Certainly they develop highly specialized skills, but the tendency to adopt 'standard operating procedures is limited by claims (at least in medicine and teaching) that each client is unique, and that the professional's task is to identify and act upon the best interests of that individual. It is certainly true that the image of most professions has suffered somewhat since the late 1960s and that they can be tenacious defenders of their own interests (Pollitt, 1984). Yet it also remains the case that professionals are frequently accorded considerable trust and status. This, together with the popularity of bureaucratically provided health, education and pensions, poses some problems for both 'new left' and 'new right' interpretations. Neo-Marxists are sometimes driven to assert that this popularity is some kind of ideologically programmed 'false consciousness'. However, this requires the unflattering assumption that the great majority of people are duped – that they lack the 'penetration' to see that state welfare is, as Ferguson among others insists, principally a form of social control operated by the state on behalf of monopoly capitalism. The new right also has difficulties. Mrs Thatcher's government may have encouraged private health care, but it has not dared to try a frontal attack on the resiliently popular NHS.

### 7.6  Technological change

While 'professionalization' may still be waxing, other elements in our bureaucracies have quite recently begun to wain. Weberian definitions of bureaucracy commonly stress the way in which work is 'routinized', that is, organized into a comprehensive set of categories, each one of which has its own pre-set procedures for decision or action. Work routinized in this way is often suitable for partial or total computerization, usually with corresponding 'staff savings'. In fact large volumes of standardized work are exactly what suit computers (Brown, *et al.* 1979). This may have a number of consequences. It is already clear that, under current political and economic pressures, many large state bureaucracies are shedding jobs in the lower, clerical grades. At the same time 'middle management' (including new technical experts such as computer programmers and systems analysts) often *increases* its size. So bureaucratic 'pyramids' are becoming mis-shapen, with thinner bases and bulging middles. Quite soon (it may have happened already) this may produce a levelling-off of the relentless growth of public sector employment illustrated in Table 7.2 (because more jobs are computerized at the bottom than added in the middle). It can also dilute the power of those at the top of an organization to *command* the lower grades:

Once they commit their operations to computerization their chains of authority must run through the programmers, the technically qualified operators, and the research directors. But what more can this authority amount to than the right to ask the computer staff whether the desired results are technically feasible?. . . both the desirability of, and the opportunities for, maintaining a pyramidal hierarchy of command authority are much diminished. (Brown *et al*. 1979, p. 149)

Indeed, specialist teams may form and re-form within bureaucracies (the 'multi-disciplinary project teams' beloved of much management literature) partly relacing the fixed pyramid of command authority with temporary agglomerations of 'horizontal', expertise-derived authority. Such teams may also (in some cases definitely do) develop group loyalties and collective satisfactions which lessen the alienation made so much of by writers such as Ferguson and Jacoby.

Computerization may have other consequences, too. It has greatly assisted state agencies wishing to expand their surveillance activities. In 1985 the British Police National Computer contained details of all the country's thirty-three million vehicles and owners, including special listings of vehicles in such vague categories as 'seen or checked in noteworthy circumstances'. More generally, it permits massive concentrations of information which *may* be disseminated or *may* be used to seek sectional advantage.

### 7.7 Decentralization and participation
Specialist project teams represent just one way in which decentralization may be achieved within bureaucratic organizations. Decentralization is virtuous, fashionable. Some schemes, like project teams, are purely administrative. Others involve – in a host of different ways – some degree of public participation, either in policy formulation, policy implementation, or both. Even the purely administrative schemes may have important implications for democracy. For example, Mrs Thatcher's administration introduced a whole series of Whitehall reforms, notable among which was the Financial Management Initiative (FMI). FMI innovations included the delegation of more personnel management functions to civil servants in line management, and the creation of 'cost centres' and similar devices whereby heads of divisions and sections were given greater independence in handling resources – they were able to move money and staff around more freely. Despite occasional official denials, it seems obvious that all this has implications for ministerial and parliamentary control (Plowden, 1985). Discretion over decisions concerning money and staff (and therefore patterns of activity) is being more widely dispersed. The constitutional fiction that ministers are personally responsible for everything their departments do thus becomes even more threadbare.

Many tasks have escaped the departmental model altogether. Britain is not the only country to have experienced a rapid post-war growth in the number of quasi-governmental organizations (QUANGOs) (Pollitt, 1979, pp. 103–4). These bureaucracies vary enormously in size and significance (the NHS is one of the largest) but they share the characteristic that they perform public functions without the benefit of any directly elected element. Decentralization *may*, therefore, lead to a diminution of democratic accountability.

Decentralization has been even more popular at the level of local and municipal government. 'Such decentralization has formed part of the administrative reforms initiated by a very large number of modern states' (Smith, 1985, p. 166). Many of these reforms have aimed at creating 'neighbourhood', 'community-based' or 'street-level' units, which are supposed to shed the remote, introverted and inflexible qualities associated with conventional centralized bureaucracies. Some have specifically included citizen 'participation' among their aims. One might almost suppose that, what with council tenant self-management groups, community health projects, community development projects, neighbourhood councils and a host of other innovations, a wave of participation was rapidly washing away all the old evils of remote centralized control.

Such a conclusion is not warranted. Despite the success of some schemes, Smith concludes that, overall,

> Participation in neighbourhood government has largely meant providing the authorities with information on the attitudes of deprived groups... It has often meant absorbing dissent by involving activists in time-consuming bureaucratic delays. It has been a means for politicians and planners to educate the public in an appreciation of the resource constraints on local authorities. Ultimate control has remained with the existing authorities. (Smith, 1985, p. 182).

In the United States, where President Johnson's 1964 'War on Poverty' programmes specified 'maximum feasible participation' by the poor themselves, enormous conflict was created. In some cities, like Chicago, the new initiatives were quickly brought to heel by existing party machines (Greenstone and Peterson, 1973). In others, such as San Francisco, delays ensued as open political rows broke out over *which* 'poor' were to be represented, *how* and *by whom* (Etzioni-Halevy, 1983). Soon, both Congress and the presidency began to reduce their support for these programmes, and particularly for the 'participation' clause. At the centre, the sponsoring Office of Economic Opportunity was finally killed off by the Nixon administration in 1973. Effective public participation in the formulation and delivery of decentralized services is evidently not impossible, but it is extremely difficult and rarely achieved (Davis and Schoen, 1978, Chapter 6, offer a vivid account of both failures and at least one success).

## 7.8 Remedies

Given that all see at least *some* problems in the bureaucracy–democracy relationship, what remedies do our six theorists propose? Some, (Lindblom and Etzioni-Halevy) are much more concerned with analysis of the *status quo* than with recommending specific changes. Others (Niskanen and Burnheim) are determined to advance specific proposals. Poulantzas and Ferguson stand somewhere in between, indicating general directions for change but avoiding detail.

Broadly speaking, one may divide the proposals for 'what is to be done about bureaucracy?' into three categories:

1. sweep it away;
2. strengthen the 'countervailing powers' within the political system, so that bureaucracy is better supervised or controlled;
3. change the character of bureaucracies by internal reforms.

Poulantzas and Ferguson both find bureaucracy so antipathetic to democracy that they believe it must be largely (not altogether) swept away. Ferguson is perhaps the most optimistic. She believes that alternative forms of organization are already plentiful: 'Countless examples of genuine member-controlled collectives exist and have existed' (Ferguson, 1984, p. 206). Such problems as the lengthiness of truly collective debate and the frustration of the verbally less skilled and confident can be overcome: 'Feminist groups have developed strategies for dealing with these problems: rotating the chair; integrating social and organizational activities; electing one delegate to canvass less active members' (p. 207). Co-ordination between these small, face-to-face groups can be achieved by voluntary co-operation and by election of delegates within a federal structure. There are as yet no blueprints for *large* non-hierarchical organizations, but there are 'numerous indications' (unspecified) that such are possible. Other writers, not all of them socialists, also place most of their faith in small, face-to-face participatory groups. Thayer (1981) says that hierarchy is the root of alienation, and must be dismantled. The world of organizations will then become a structured set of 'innumerable small face-to-face groups characterized by openness, trust and intensive interpersonal relations' (p. 5).

Poulantzas's vision is more cautious, and more complicated. He insists on a large element of uncertainty: we do not yet possess clear models of what can be, especially of what combination of direct and representative institutions is best calculated to safeguard democracy. 'History has not yet given us a successful experience of the democratic road to socialism: what it has provided – and that is not insignificant – is some negative examples to avoid and some mistakes upon which to reflect' (Poulantzas, 1978, p. 265). Referring to co-operatives etc. as 'the self-management movement', he warns that, though possibly a useful strand in a broader strategy, *exclusive* pursuit of self-management is likely to degenerate because technical experts, through wielding their indispensability, will gain too much influence. Instead he advocates a dual strategy, with struggles to control representative and bureaucratic state institutions on behalf of the masses *and* 'the development of popular movements, the mushrooming of democratic organs at the base, and the rise of centres of self-management' (p. 260). All this, he concedes, 'presupposes the continuous support of a mass movement founded on broad popular alliances' (p. 263). Similarly Abrahamsson, also of the 'new left', concludes that the struggle against bureaucracy must take place *both* through wider economic developments *and* by participatory reforms within conventional bureaucracies. Economic growth 'is a prerequisite for extending the resources of underprivileged groups, and for creating economic equality which, in turn, contributes to the implementation of democratic rule' (Abrahamsson, 1977, p. 228). As for participatory mechanisms, he harks back to Marx's *The Civil War in France* and recommends 'a delegate system based on conditional mandates, immediate recall of delegates; information duty for delegates vis-à-vis their basic organizations, and rotation of mandates' (p. 229).

Central to all these new left accounts is the idea that society itself must be transformed before the problem of bureaucracy can be fully tackled. Even the optimistic Ferguson acknowledges 'that one could not move towards the alternatives that I am suggesting simply by replacing existing welfare bureaucracies with something else, and leaving the systemic context intact. Given existing class inequalities, these inequalities will make their way into welfare organizations no matter what their form' (Ferguson, personal communication, 1985). Such a broad transformation is only likely to come about with the kind of active popular support for radical change to which Poulantzas refers. Yet even with economic and legitimation crises as deep as those afflicting the liberal democracies since the mid-1970s, the looked-for mass movement towards socialist solutions remains elusive. Popular discontent, scepticism and disappointed expectations abound, but they do not seem to add up to the kind of mass determination that could trigger a 'transformation' (Held, 1986, Chapter 7).

Furthermore, the new left conspicuously underdiscuss questions of *scale* and *co-ordination/control*. Even if small face-to-face groups can be made to work as effectively as Ferguson suggests, how are vital services to be delivered in uniform and equitable fashion to large (and widely dispersed) populations? Feminist groups, even self-managed Yugoslav enterprises, may perform their own functions exquisitely, but they are a long, long way from being capable of delivering, say, health care, education or pensions to millions of people. Yet fair allocations over whole populations are a crucial ingredient in the socialist vision of democracy. What is more, these services are, as we have seen, both major recent growth points for bureaucracy and among the most popular aspects of the liberal democratic state. Even where scale is not such a problem, co-ordination may be. Federal bodies of delegates from a host of small or medium organizations may not be enough to stop the interests of the local water authority colliding with those of the local agricultural collective, while both find it hard to keep pace with the district housing and education authorities. Voluntary co-operation is the recipe offered by Ferguson, Thayer and a number of other radicals, but experience with the present workings of public agencies entitles the reader to some scepticism about whether this alone will be enough. New left theorists, both Marxist and feminist, seem to have rather little in the way of concrete proposals here. When, occasionally, they *do* offer prescriptions these not infrequently turn out to be more reformist than the rest of their analyses – advocacy of elected community health boards, better representation of parents in school government, and so on. Marxists in particular have fought shy of detailed analysis of specific bureaucratic procedures and mechanisms, and how these could be altered – in advance of a general transformation – so as to offer more purchase for democratic values.

There are also important sectoral problems facing radical 'de-bureau-cratizers', namely those of military security and public order. Unless the world is transformed out of all recognition, there will still be a need for military and police forces. Here the problems of co-ordination and control are at their most acute. How 'decentralized' and 'community-based' are we prepared to make decisions concerning, say, crowd control, anti-terrorist planning, or, at the extreme, nuclear war? One has only to pose the question to see how much of the new left prescription is implicitly confined to the bureaucracies of the welfare sector. Indeed, in political practice it tends to be the left that insists most vigorously on tight, central-ized political control of the means of surveillance and violence. Nor is this problem confined to the theorists of the new left. Within professional military circles the problem of maintaining communications in the violently unusual context of modern war has spawned an anxious debate. How, in an age of possibly very sudden military action and of highly dispersed forces armed with all manner of nuclear weaponry, is political (or even senior military) direction to be preserved?

Etzioni-Halevy is almost silent as far as 'improvements' are concerned. She concludes that the tension between bureaucracy and democracy has no ready-made solution. Bureaucracy must continue, it is necessary to democracy. Democracy must not become too 'unlimited', or corrup-tion and inefficiency will flourish. No doubt some modest reforms would help – greater freedom of information, more training of senior politicians in the running of large departments, more effective ombudsmen and other restraints on bureaucratic abuses – but the basic tension is built into the symbiotic relationship between competitive, elitist democracy and non-partisan, effective bureaucratic organizations. Like Niskanen, Etzioni-Halevy's focus excludes broader changes in relations between social classes. This wider framework remains off-stage.

Lindblom is more forthcoming. Polyarchy may simply continue; its 'crippled' form of democracy may be the best we can do (Lindblom, 1977, pp. 353–4). On the other hand (and this is clearly where Lindblom's own inclinations lie) there is always the *possibility* that we will learn new ways of conducting our arrangements. Groups and individuals could even learn more 'self-restraint', a kind of strategic understanding of their inter-dependence with others, and the sense, therefore, of not always pushing their own short-term material interests to an extreme. Lindblom sees some interesting possibilities (though also plenty of flaws) in the Yugoslav experiments in self-managed enterprises. (Dahl is even more enthusiastic about these.) Here the *market* is used to co-ordinate the decisions of hundreds or thousands of small or medium-sized self-managing units. To co-ordinate this bureaucratically would have needed a central authority which would have perpetuated 'just those elements of authority, hierarchy, and bureaucracy against which the participatory democratic movement is a protest' (Lindblom, p. 338). The appeal of this solution is that it separates out the valuable co-ordinatory qualities of the market from the specifics of private ownership (in which both he and Dahl see the threat to democracy of unaccountable business power). 'The most fertile soil for a more partici-patory democracy appears to be in industry, perhaps because the potential for democracy is large in an arena in which authoritarianism has been for so long universally practised and little questioned' (p. 334). Thus Lindblom inclines towards – though he forbears specifically to recommend – a polity in which governmental bureaucracy is reduced, though not swept away, by extensive use of markets. At the same time participatory democracy is extended, and the political veto of corporate business elites lessened, by the extensive practice of industrial democracy. For the lesser sins of bureaucracy – secrecy and self-perpetuation – he has no novel remedies, but these, in his view, are not the main problem anyway.

Both Niskanen and Burnheim can be classified as falling mainly into the 'countervailing powers' category, although their remedies also include elements of internal reform. Both deem it essential to break up the huge, centralized bureaucracies they see as characteristic of modern government. Both see centralized rule-making and planning as having grown far beyond the limits of their usefulness (see also van Gunsteren, 1976). Furthermore, both wish to strengthen political supervision over officials. Beyond that, however, their remedies diverge sharply. Burnheim is clearly of the left, in that he believes the 'central requirement' is 'that the working class should become conscious of the need to abolish the source of class division at every level of social life' (Burnheim, 1985, p. 12). Niskanen, by contrast, believes profoundly in the positive virtues of precisely those competitive markets which play such a large part in producing class divisions.

Niskanen wishes to see bureaucracies that will *compete* with one another (not *co-operate* as in the new left and demarchist scenarios). Like other 'public choice' theorists (see, for example, Ostrom, 1977) he favours the disaggregation of large bureaucracies with a monopoly in the supply of their services. These would be broken down into a larger number of autonomous units which would offer citizens more opportunities for comparison and choice. Competition could be encouraged by such devices as vouchers which citizens would use at the school or hospital or transport facility preferred. What is more, many public functions could be partly or wholly 'privatized' to give established state bureaucracies another competitive jolt:

> Private firms could bid to manage the postal services, the fire protection services, the terminal air traffic control system, or, possibly, even the police services in a local community. . . A management contract is probably preferable to one which includes the supply of the major assets, in order to retain government ownership of the major assets and to ensure the necessary standardization (Niskanen, 1973, pp. 57–8).

Against this background of increased intra-bureaucratic competition, Niskanen proposes a variety of other reforms. He gives details of a number of alternative procedures whereby senior bureaucrats could receive personal rewards proportionate to the amounts by which they managed to hold their agency's costs below its awarded budget. He is also concerned to strengthen the legislature's committees, which review bureaucratic activity; Bureaucracies should be subjected to sets of public, quantified indicators of performance (especially in respect of their success in keeping within their budgets). The legislative review committees (much more powerful in the US Congress than the British Parliament) should have their members *randomly* selected from the broader body of elected representatives. Unlike Burnheim's use of randomization, Niskanen's is aimed at *preventing* these committees from becoming packed with individuals who have strong personal interests in the functions they supervise. Such individuals, Niskanen believes, tend to want higher levels of bureaucratic service provision than the *average* voter would wish. Both members of review committees and the political heads of departments (ministers and secretaries of state) should be periodically and randomly re-assigned to other posts, so that they do not become too 'cosy' with 'their' bureaucrats.

Burnheim begins by noting that bureaucratic state socialism has been discredited, and that 'the lack of any clear and plausible view of how a democratic socialist society might work is. . .the main obstacle to significant radical activity' (p. 13). Such a view will not magically 'emerge' from political struggles; it will have to be thought out in detail, in advance. He then proceeds to elaborate his suggestions for a large number of modest-sized autonomous functional agencies (p. 169 above). The co-ordination problem is solved by voluntary co-operation *and* by giving higher bodies constitutionally entrenched powers of arbitration (but *not* policy-making).

The frequent weakness of current political supervision is overcome by (a) reducing the average size and complexity of bureaucracies (making them easier to supervise), and (b) the system of random selection of political directors from volunteers with a material interest in the function in question (so that they have a strong personal motive to gain a good grasp of the subject). The idea of 'policy' begins to dissolve; instead, local functional agencies will focus attention on the tangibilities of particular projects: 'it is very much easier to get agreement about which solution to a given problem is best in the circumstances than it is to get soundly-based agreement on a comprehensive policy that purports to supply a general criterion of what is best' (p. 59).

Of course, there is still the problem of scale. Some problems (channel tunnels, airborne and maritime pollution, access to rare mineral resources) demand resolution on a global or at least continental scale. Burnheim does not say much about this in *Is Democracy Possible?*, but he does develop his ideas further in the final chapter of this book.

A full evaluation of the detailed remedies advanced by Burnheim and Niskanen cannot be completed within the confines of this chapter. Burnheim's demarchy is particularly ingenious. My doubts about it are threefold. First, I wonder whether random selection from a pool of interested volunteers actually will provide effective political supervision of the experts. True, the agencies will be mono-functional and probably smaller than they are today. But will the 'interested', limited-term, random appointees be a match for the doctors, teachers, engineers, lawyers and computer specialists whom they are supposed to control? Second, just how small and local are functionally defined agencies likely to be? Many important functions may turn out to have rather large optimal jurisdictions. Water supply, transportation, defence, much health care, energy, higher education, and income support are just some. The British District Health Authority, with an average population of in excess of 200, 000 is now widely recognized as being too small to provide the full range of modern medical services. So a high percentage of Burnheim's functional authorities may actually grow rather large. This will also exacerbate the first problem. Third, and most serious, there is the problem of co-ordination. There is the fundamental empirical question of whether Burnheim's formula (voluntary co-operation plus arbitration) will be enough to cater for the high level of functional interdependency which we see all around us. My suspicion – and that is all it is – is that in Burnheim's scheme the higher level arbitration bodies will require wider authority than he allows. There are also the rather special co-ordination problems of defence and public order. Burnheim's few references to security issues seem optimistic to the point of naivety. Nevertheless, demarchy is a fascinating proposal. It has yet to be probed, interrogated and (I hope) experimented with.

Niskanen's remedies display considerable inventiveness, but the critical debate – and practice – of the last two decades have left parts of the new right's formula looking implausible. Analysis has raised doubts about Niskanen's basic thesis of a *general* oversupply of bureaucratic services (Goodin, 1982). Furthermore, competition may be much more difficult to ignite than he allows. According to economic theory, it would pay a small number of 'competing' agencies actually to collude in a secretive and oligopolistic share-out of the 'market'. In these and other respects Niskanen's model is 'flatly wrong' (Goodin, 1982, p. 38). Even if competition worked, what kind of 'choice' would the citizen be offered?

> To many groups for whom public services are especially important...the 'right' to move to a preferred 'bundle' of services and taxes is empty. To the aged, the unskilled worker, the one-parent family, the unemployed and the ethnic minority, the recommendation to move to Long Island or Gerrard's Cross is either cruel or stupid...Alternatively, who is going to 'prefer' Toxteth or Harlem, even though the costs might be lower? (Smith, 1985, pp. 34–5)

However, while big choices such as moving to another area might be impractical for many people, this does not deprive the new right's emphasis on citizen choice of all its force. It may be much easier to increase choice on smaller but still significant issues: where children are schooled; which GP to attend; which types of public housing should be provided, and so on. Increasing these kinds of choice not only appears a popular move, it may also be used to jolt bureaucratic providers out of their occasional complacency, and to give citizens some sense of personal efficacy. Under the stimulus of new right ideas, many politicians and administrators, by no means all themselves of the same political persuasion, have proposed or introduced more client-choice across a range of bureaucratically provided public services.

Finally, there is once more the co-ordination/interdependence issue. For example, spillover effects from transportation and land use decisions by small jurisdiction authorities soon seem to require a wider metropolitan, regional or even national authority to reduce duplication, inequalities and waste. The American health care system gives some idea of what can happen when such co-ordination is weak: surplus hospital beds and doctors in the wealthy parts of many cities while, a few miles away, the ethnic ghettos have only a few, crumbling facilities (Pollitt, 1982).

## 7.9  Concluding comments

It remains for me to offer a few observations of my own on the 'map' now unfolded, First, a word of caution about generalizations at the very high level represented by the theories discussed above. It is entirely possible that *all* the advantages and disadvantages attributed to bureaucracy by our six main thinkers are true in some cases and to some degree. Some bureaucratic jobs *are* alienatingly and demeaningly narrow. Some bureau-cracies *are* rigid and unlearning. Some do 'tame' their political chiefs rather than being tamed by them. Many are secretive. Others, however, provide widely needed and much appreciated services, sometimes in sensitive and efficient ways. Some officials find a 'calling' in public service and demonstrate an independent-minded creativity in interpreting their roles. Some bureaucracies undoubtedly help restrain partisan political corruption. What is lacking, in all the accounts surveyed, is evidence concerning the *relative extent* of these different attributes, and the particular conditions conducive to them. To put it bluntly, we seem to have only scattered and impressionistic evidence with which to meet the question 'are our bureau-cracies becoming more (or less) powerful, more or less humane?'

Related to this, I suggest that there is in our six accounts a certain neglect of the opportunities offered by *changes which are happening anyway*. This is in no way to deny the long-term strategic importance of some kind of 'transformation', whether to demarchy, socialism, a Lindblom-style redesign of the exchange/authority mix, or whatever. If a radically different polity is desired, then radical changes must be envisaged. But that does not mean that lesser alterations should be spurned. 'Participation' alone seems most unlikely to be 'enough' (Thompson, 1983). As Poulantzas says, the struggle for democracy must be carried on at many sites, within and across the state apparatus as well as 'from outside'. Unfortunately, neither he nor any of the others take this thought very far. Bureaucracies are currently becoming professionalized, computerized and middle-heavy. They are among the targets for equal opportunites and 'affirmative action' employment policies (see, for example, Sigelman *et al.*, 1984). They are being increasingly subjected to elaborate sets of quantified 'performance indicators' (Pollitt, 1986). The volume of judicial and other external scrutiny is on the increase. All these developments, and more, offer opportunities (only *opportunities*) for democratization, but are little discussed in the 'grand theory' about bureacracy and democracy.

Imagine, for a moment, a large social security agency where 'affirmative action' hiring has produced numbers of women and ethnic minorities *at each grade* roughly proportionate to their representation in the population as a whole. In social security offices in localities where the ethnic minorities are concentrated, most of the staff are drawn from those same groups. The bureaucrats are therefore statistically 'representative' of the community they serve (Krislov, 1967). They work flexible hours and share jobs. Additionally, creches and other facilities are provided to make paid employ-ment more easily compatible with domestic responsibilities (for women *and* men) than it has usually been in the past. Citizens wishing to make a benefit claim can choose which local office to go to and, when they arrive, can choose whether to give their information to an official or to key it into a computer with very 'user-friendly' software. (Experiments in GPs' surgeries in Glasgow have shown that ordinary, untrained people are perfectly able to enter quite complex medical symptoms to computers, and that many of them actually *prefer* this to seeing the doctor: 'The computer is capable of being developed for *consumer* convenience' – Dunsire, 1985, p. 71.) Claimants have a statutory right to a print-out of all the information held about them, the details of the calculation of their benefit, and the rules and administrative codes of practice relevant to their case. They can also use the computer (or the official at the desk) to register complaints. The workings of the agency are scrutinized by a standing parliamentary select committee, and there is an ombudsman (-woman?) with powers to go in, inspect the files and question individual officials. These and other scrutiny bodies are aided in their work by the existence of freedom of information legislation and by a sophisticated (again computerized) system of 'performance indicators'. The latter show, for each local office, not only information about running costs and staffing levels, but also how many complaints there are per thousand applicants, how many successful appeals, how long on average it takes to get money to claimants, and so on. This information is publicly displayed and, since claimants can choose which local office to go to, results in the boycotting of overpressurized, inefficient or slovenly offices.

This vision, which relies, note, solely on the further development of practices already in place or long under active discussion, is clearly not the rigid, overpowering organization conveyed by some of the new left's accounts. Nor is it Niskanen's inefficient oversupplier, with a semi-captive review committee. Nor yet is it Etzioni-Halevy's elite organization facing a powerless and largely apathetic citizenry. The approach of each of these theorists *can* result in attention being focused exclusively on big, sweeping changes, so that smaller opportunities are missed. To take one recent trivial-but-indicative example from the real world, when VDUs are installed on social security office counters, will they be fixed so that *only* counter staff can see the screens, or will they face both ways, so that claimants, too, may read the information displayed?

It is not difficult to push the vision a little further, beyond the territory of familiar administrative reforms, to incorporate more directly participationist aspirations. Such changes are generally seen as much more radical than the kind of administrative reforms described above, but are in no way incompatible with those more modest, yet still significant, developments. Claimants could be given rights to full voting representation on all the project teams responsible for designing and redesigning local offices and their procedures. More radically still, each region could be run by a Burnheim-style statistically representative executive of interested parties. If we were considering a heavily professionalized service like education or health (or even defence), attention would need to be given to democratizing the training, career development and accountability systems under which the professionals worked (Pollitt, 1984).

It should be stressed, however, that the problem of maintaining democratic control over those possessing specialist knowledge is a pervasive one. The power of the professions is merely one particularly obvious manifestation of it. Possession of specialized information about almost *anything* can be converted to the currency of obstructiveness or 'escape' from political, group, or customer control. Consider the garage mechanic, the photocopier maintenance technician or the procedurally versed counter clerk. It is not only doctors, computer experts and the commanders of nuclear submarines who can baffle those they nominally work 'for'. Specialized know-how of many varieties is secreted in every nook and cranny of most bureaucracies. Thus, for example, international bureaucracies tend to gain enhanced autonomy the more technically complex their subject matter (Jönsson, 1986). Specialization thus poses control problems for selected ministers, for senior bureaucrats and for 'middle managers' – and would still do so for Burnheim's statistically chosen representatives. Burnheim's many single-function agencies – or the new right's competing bureaucracies – might well generate *diversity*, thus solving the centralization/uniformity problem. But unless they were very small indeed (unlikely, for reasons already adduced) they would not avoid this problem of *control and co-ordination*. Neither do any of the other theorists interrogated here offer a terribly convincing solution. One can certainly manipulate the balance between specialist knowledge and popular control, but there are many functions where a radical shift in favour of the latter would appear to risk very serious penalties in efficiency and effectiveness. As Alan Ware indicated in Chapter 5 on political parties, even the West German 'Greens' have found it difficult to withstand tendencies to specialization and professionalization among their delegates and spokespersons. Beyond a certain point this may be a trade-off – a dilemma rather than a problem.

Can we, then, go so far as to eliminate large, bureaucratic organizations? I cannot yet share the optimistic beliefs of Ferguson, Thayer or even Burnheim that we already know how to do without them. Yet it is striking how widespread is the call for the control exercised by our present representative institutions to be supplemented (perhaps, eventually, to some degree replaced) by more direct, participatory mechanisms. Of the six, widely divergent, theorists 'mapped' here only two, Etzioni-Halevy and Niskanen, do not lend their support to this 'remedy'. The neo-Marxists, neo-pluralists, feminists and demarchists display infinite differences of detail but all present a broadly similar conclusion. All see developments in *both* the state *and* the 'private' sectors as essential. All insist that the participation must be real, not cosmetic. That means, of course, that new participatory organs *will* sometimes act unpredictably and *will* take decisions which are not those the central authorities would have wished for. This degree of scholarly agreement, albeit at a high level of generalization, is impressive. There may well be special difficulties in the areas of defence and public order, and in respect of international organizations. Yet, acknowledging these, there remains wide scope. In many existing bureaucracies we could go a long way, it seems, before co-ordination would be seriously impaired, or effectiveness catastrophically undermined. If we wish to enhance liberal democracy, and lighten the 'dark side' of bureaucratization, then greater direct participation should be our direction of travel.

## References

ABRAHAMSSON, Bengt (1977) *Bureaucracy or Participation: the Logic of Organization*, London, Sage.

ALBROW, Martin (1970) *Bureaucracy*, London, Pall Mall Press.

ALFORD, Robert R. (1969) *Bureaucracy and Participation: Political Cultures in Four Wisconsin Cities*, Chicago, Rand McNally.

ALLISON, G. T. (1983) 'Public and private management: are they fundamentally alike in all unimportant respects?', in J. L. PERRY and K. L. KRAEMER (eds) *Public Management: Public and Private Perspectives*, California, Mayfield Publishing Co.

ARCHER, Clive (1983) *International Organizations*, London, Allen and Unwin.

BENEVISTE, Guy (1982) 'Survival inside bureaucracy', pp. 154–66 in Anthony G. McGREW and M. J. WILSON (eds) *Decision Making: Approaches and Analysis*, Manchester, Manchester University Press.

BLAU, Peter M. (1973) *The Dynamics of Bureaucracy: a Study of Interpersonal Relationships in Two Government Agencies* (revised edition), London, University of Chicago Press.

BROWN, Robert, KAMENKA, Eugene, KRYGIER, Martin and ERH-SOON TAY, Alice (1979) *Bureaucracy: the Career of a Concept*, London, Edward Arnold.

BURNHEIM, John (1985) *Is Democracy Possible? The Alternative to Electoral Politics*, Cambridge, Polity Press.

DAHL, Robert A. (1985) *A Preface to Economic Democracy*, Cambridge, Polity Press.

DAVIS, Karen and SCHOEN, Kathy (1978) *Health and the War on Poverty: a Ten Year Appraisal*, Washington, Brookings Institution.

DUNSIRE, Andrew (1973) *Administration: the Word and the Science*, Oxford, Martin Robertson.

DUNSIRE, Andrew (1985) 'Why administer? The moral dimension of administrative reform', pp. 64–72 in Leo KLINKERS (ed.) *Life in Public Administration*, Amsterdam, Kobra.

ELGIN, D. S. and BUSHNELL, R. A. (1977) 'The limits to complexity: are bureaucracies becoming unmanageable?', *The Futurist*, December, pp. 337–48.

ETZIONI-HALEVY, Eva (1983) *Bureaucracy and Democracy: a Political Dilemma*, London, Routledge and Kegan Paul.

FERGUSON, Kathy E. (1984) *The Feminist Case Against Bureaucracy*, Philadelphia, Temple University Press.

GIDDENS, Anthony (1985) *The Nation State and Violence*, Cambridge, Polity Press.

GOODIN, Robert E. (1982) 'Rational politicians and rational bureaucrats in Washington and Whitehall', *Public Administration*, Vol. 60, No. 1, pp. 23–41.

GREENSTONE, David J. and PETERSON, Paul E. (1973) *Race and Authority in Urban Politics: Community Participation and the War on Poverty*, New York, Russell Sage Foundation.

GUNSTEREN, Herman R. van (1976) *The Quest for Control: a Critique of the Rational-Central-Rule Approach in Public Affairs*, London, Wiley.

HELD, David (1987) *Models of Democracy*, Cambridge, Polity Press.

JACOBY, Henry (1973) *The Bureaucratization of the World*, Los Angeles, University of California Press (translated from the German by Eveline L. Kanes).

JÖNSSON, Christer (1986) 'Interorganization theory and international organization', *International Studies Quarterly*, Vol. 30, No. 1, March pp. 39–57.

KRISLOV, Samuel (1967) *Representative Bureaucracy*, Englewood Cliffs, NJ, Prentice Hall.

LINDBLOM, Charles E. (1977) *Politics and Markets: the World's Political-Economic Systems*, New York, Basic Books.

McSWAIN, Cynthia J. (1985) 'Administrators and citizenship: the liberalist legacy of the constitution', *Administration and Society*, Vol. 17, No. 2, August, pp. 131–48.

MAIDMENT, Richard and McGREW, Anthony (1986) *The American Political Process*, London, Sage.

NEGRO, Josephine (1987) 'International institutions', Block IV, D308 *Democratic Government and Politics*, Milton Keynes, Open University Press.

NISKANEN, William A. (1971) *Bureaucracy and Representative Government*, Chicago, Aldine-Atherton.

NISKANEN, William A. (1973) *Bureaucracy: Servant or Master? Lessons from America* (with commentaries by Rt Hon. Douglas Houghton, MP, Maurice Kogan, Hon. Nicholas Ridley, MP, Ian Senior) London, The Institute of Economic Affairs.

NORDLINGER, E. A. (1981) *On the Autonomy of the Democratic State*, London, Harvard University Press.

NOVE, Alec (1978) *The Soviet Economic System*, London, Allen and Unwin.

OSTROM, Vincent (1977) 'Structure and performance', pp. 19–46 in V. OSTROM and F. P. BLISH (eds) *Comparing Urban Delivery Systems*, London, Sage.

PERLMAN, M. (1982) 'The economic theory of bureaucracy', pp. 167–76 in ANTHONY G. McGREW and M. J. WILSON (eds) *Decision Making: Approaches and Analysis*, Manchester, Manchester University Press.

PLOWDEN, William (1985) 'What prospects for the civil service?', *Public Administration*, Vol. 63, No. 4, Winter, pp. 393–414.

POLLITT, Christopher (1979) 'The development of government in Britain', Block 1, Paper 4, D336 *Policies, People and Administration*, Milton Keynes, Open University Press.

POLLITT, Christopher (1982) 'Corporate rationalization of American health care: a visitor's appraisal', *Journal of Health Politics, Policy and Law*, Vol. 7, No. 1, Spring, pp. 227–53.

POLLITT, Christopher (1984) 'Professionals and public policy', *Public Administration Bulletin*, Spring, pp. 29–46.

POLLITT, Christopher (1986) 'Beyond the managerial model', *Financial Accountability and Management*, Vol. 2, No. 3 Autumn, pp. 155–70.

POULANTZAS, Nicos (1978) *State, Power, Socialism*, London, New Left Books.

PRAIS, S. J. (1976) *The Evolution of Giant Firms in Britain*, Cambridge, Cambridge University Press.

ROSE, Richard (1984) *Understanding Big Government: the Programme Approach*, London, Sage.

SIGELMAN, Lee, MILWARD, H. Brinton, SHEPHERD, Jon M. and DUMLER, Michael (1984) 'Organizational responses to affirmative action: "elephant burial grounds" revisited', *Administration and Society*, Vol. 16, No. 1, May, pp. 27–60.

SMITH, Brian C. (1985) *Decentralization: the Territorial Dimension of the State*, London, Allen and Unwin.

TAYLOR-GOOBY, Peter (1985) 'The politics of welfare: public attitudes and behaviour, pp. 72–91 in RUDOLF KLEIN and MICHAEL O'HIGGINS (eds) *The Future of Welfare*, Oxford, Blackwell.

THAYER, Frederick C. (1981) *An End to Hierarchy and Competition: Administration in the Post-Affluent World* (2nd edition), London, New Viewpoints.

THOMPSON, Dennis F. (1983) 'Bureaucracy and democracy', pp. 235–50 in GRAEME DUNCAN (ed.) *Democratic Theory and Practice*, Cambridge, Cambridge University Press.

URBAN, Michael E. (1982) 'Bureaucratic ideology in the United States and the Soviet Union: some empirical dimensions', *Administration and Society*, Vol. 14, No. 2, August, pp. 139–62.

WEALE, Albert (1985) 'Why are we waiting' the problem of unresponsiveness in the public social services', pp. 150–65 in RUDOLF KLEIN and MICHAEL O'HIGGINS (eds) *The Future of Welfare*, Oxford, Blackwell.

WEISS, Thomas G. (1982) 'International bureaucracy: the myth and reality of the international civil service', *International Affairs*, Vol. 58, No. 2, Spring, pp. 287–306.

# 8 Reasons of State
*Steve Smith*

## 8.1 Introduction

One area of political activity that has consistently posed a problem for democratic theory is foreign and defence policy.[1] Traditional democratic theory argues that the form of political activity within a polity will be reflected in the ways in which decisions and policies are made. This has led to typologies of political systems, with a popular continuum being that of the totalitarian and liberal democratic dimension of political systems. The implication is clear: the extent to which a political system is either liberal democratic or totalitarian will affect the ways in which policies are made in that system.[2] The object of this chapter is to examine the extent to which the defence and foreign policy areas are ones in which this assumption is appropriate. This will provide the basis for looking at the degree to which new forms of democracy may allow these areas to be opened up to democratic control.

Before discussing the problems that foreign and defence policy issues pose for democratic theory, it is necessary to say a few words about the concept of democracy itself. Although there are many ways of defining democracy, the definition used in the literature on international relations equates it with public control and accountability. This is not unproblematic, and it is certainly a narrow interpretation of democracy which can be contrasted with radical calls for more participatory forms of political arrangements. Yet even this narrow definition allows us to make two introductory comments about the link between defence and foreign policy issues and democracy. The first is that traditional democratic theory (as found in the works of Locke, Rousseau and Mill, for example) tends to ignore these dimensions of state activity, and it will be argued that this is because of the way in which traditional democratic theory has defined the state. The second is that international relations theory has itself been concerned with the link between democratic practice and foreign and defence policy. Although we will concentrate mainly on those accounts of international relations that treat the external setting of the state as the major determinant of foreign and defence policy (the realist or systemic theorists), there is a powerful school of thought, known as idealism, that argues that the democratization of societies is a prerequisite to the attainment of international peace and harmony. We will return to these two introductory comments later in this chapter. For our purposes, though, it is useful to note that realists tend to adopt a more elitist or narrow view of democracy, while idealists define democracy in a wider participatory or radical sense. There is, therefore, a link between forms of democratic theory and views of international relations.

The problem for traditional democratic theory arises out of the fact that most theories of democracy treat the state as a kind of analytical ceiling to enquiry (Easton, 1953; Downs, 1957). Different forms of democratic practice are examined, and preferred, in terms of the ways in which they allow greater public control over the policy-making process. In all this, the state is the body that is the focal point of enquiry: theories of democracy pose differing definitions of the state, of how it is to be related to public control, and thus say something about the relationship between democratic structure and the processes of political behaviour. For example, in the 1950s and 1960s most discussions of democratic theory posited a dichotomy between liberal democracy and totalitarianism. This dichotomy implied that the liberal democratic or totalitarian nature of a society would be reflected in the ways in which policies were made in those societies and in the nature, and extent, of public control and accountability. Although there have been many attempts to examine the issue of the possible conver-gence of these types of political systems (towards, for example, an advanced industrial society), this dichotomy still dominates most Western democratic theory. Not only does such a distinction carry crucial normative implications, most evident in Dahl's conception of pluralism (Dahl, 1971), but it also involves a critical empirical implication: that were we to observe political practice in liberal democratic and totalitarian societies, we would see policies being made in very different ways. At the risk of over-simplifying, we would see a contrast between a bottom-up pattern of democratic practice and a top-down one. In liberal democracies policies would, in the final analysis, depend on public acceptance via the ballot box; in totalitarian societies policies would be decided on outside the political process deemed to be central to democracy in the West.

Of course, this view is both ethnocentric and value-laden, but it is introduced not as a straw person to knock down but as an example of the *form* of analysis common to democratic theory. Historically this has concentrated on the mechanisms that link political practice to the nature of representation and accountability. Such a focus seems inappropriate when we look at political practice in the foreign and defence areas. This is because there is ample evidence that the liberal democratic nature of a society is not crucial in determining how policies are made in these areas. Constitutional lawyers and politicians might well claim otherwise, but it is difficult to support the claim that democratic control extends to the foreign and defence areas in most Western liberal democracies. To be sure, the ballot box does exist, and there is the legal and constitutional possibility of democratic control being exercised in foreign and defence areas. But the evidence indicates that this is rarely the case in practice. To pose the question provocatively: is there any more democratic control over foreign and defence policy in the United States than there is in the Soviet Union? In terms of the focus of this book we might also ask whether there is any possibility of extending public control over these areas.

We will start by examining the orthodox literature on this topic before turning to look at the limitations of the conventional account. There is a very good reason why political practice in the foreign and defence policy area does not accord with the assumptions of democratic theory. This is because the state – the ceiling of democratic theory's enquiry – also exists in another environment, the society of states that together comprise the international political system. For democratic theory, the state and the persons who occupy its key roles are to be understood in terms of the linkages and constraints that democratic structure impose on them: that is, the leaders face inwards; what they do and their freedom of manoeuvre are crucially related to the form of democracy existing within that state. Yet these same leaders, and these same states, also have to face outwards: they must be concerned with the constraints and freedom of manoeuvre imposed on them by virtue of the state's location in the international political system. In this regard, the state is not only an analytical ceiling, but is also an analytical floor, the starting place for an explanation of foreign and defence policy.

## 8.2   International society

To understand the implication of this dual role of the state one must comprehend the substantial differences that exist between international society and domestic society (see Bull, 1977; Donelan, 1978; Mayall, 1982; and Butterfield and Wight, 1966). The key point is that the two societies have very different structures. International society is in a literal sense anarchical. It is a society in which the members possess an attribute – sovereignty – that is not possessed by the individuals who comprise domestic society. Indeed, the major recurrent issues in political theory concern the ways in which individuals gave up sovereignty in order to form political society and acquired the rights, duties and obligations that result as a consequence. Unlike domestic society, international society has no sovereign body above the constituent members that can carry out the functions of rule-making, implementation and adjudication. In such a society each state is judge in its own cause. This does not mean that international society is automatically condemned to a constant war of all against all, since there are mechanisms for ensuring order and stability, but the central consequence that results from the structure of international society is that states face a security dilemma (Beitz, 1979). Since there is no international body above the constituent members of international society to enforce international law, the leaders of states are required, in the final analysis, to act to ensure the security of their own state. If the state is attacked there is no guarantee that any other state will come to its aid, and if such aid is forthcoming it can only be as a result of the definition of self-interest held by the leaders of that other state. So, as a consequence of the structure of international society, the leaders of states have to undertake measures to provide for the security of the state they represent. The security dilemma results from the problems faced in achieving this goal without increasing the perceptions of insecurity of any adversaries or neighbours, and thus, for example, leading to an arms race.

Another consequence of the structure of international society is that the very division of the human race into units called states means that there is a sense in which it is possible for leaders to talk of the members of a state having interests in common. This can be contrasted with the greater difficulty in trying to claim such a commonality of interest with regard to domestic policy issues. Because the state is the unit of international society, it can be argued that any given state has 'national interests' in any particular conflict, in a way that has no such obvious parallel in domestic political activity. One effect of this seeming commonality of interests is that the ability to define the 'national interest' provides governments with a kind of trump card in political debate. Historically, foreign and defence policies have been largely bipartisan in the Western liberal democracies, with governments left to define what is in the interests of the state with little political debate. This tendency is exacerbated by the role played by secrecy in the foreign and defence areas: governments often claim that they have information that cannot be revealed but which shows the validity of their definition of what is in the interests of the state. It is a brave politician indeed who tries to argue that this definition is inaccurate. Because of their role as guardians of the security of the state, government leaders hold all the cards in such a discussion.

The final consequence of the structure of international society for democratic theory concerns the ways in which that structure impacts on the behaviour of states. There are two aspects of this. First, it is evident that the anarchical structure of international society creates a network of interactions in which foreign policy is essentially reactive. There are very few examples (Brandt's *Ostpolitik* being one) of leaders having grand designs in the foreign policy areas; most of the time leaders are reacting to events in other societies. Second, it is clear that the power structure of international society affects the behaviour of the units of that society. To give just the clearest example, states behave differently according to the polar structure of international society (see Weltman, 1973; Rosenau, 1969, Chs 27–31). The characteristic behaviour of the units of international society is different in a system dominated by two states (bipolarity) than in a system dominated by five or more states (multipolarity). This might at first seem an arcane point, but it has a central message for the focus of this chapter: the structure of the international system is one determinant of the foreign policies of states. We will return to the notion of role implied by this argument, but, for now, the implication is that the leaders of societies are responsive to the requirements of international society. Indeed, some theories of international relations treat domestic factors as exogenous to an explanation of foreign policy behaviour, since that behaviour seems to be most powerfully explained by the structure of, and distribution of power within, international society. To the extent that we can explain the foreign policy behaviour of states by utilizing a systemic perspective, this downplays the domestic factors that are deemed central to democratic theory, for, if the behaviour of states is really determined by the international power structure, then whether a political system is democratic or not is essentially irrelevant.

There are, then, good reasons why the orthodox literature indicates that the structure of international society reduces the impact of the form of democratic structure on the foreign and defence areas of a state's political life. Yet, in a very important sense, such a characterization is somewhat misleading. There are two reasons for this. The first is that the account so far has treated defence and foreign policy issues as unique, as different in kind to the issues found in other areas of politics. The structural analysis we have undertaken has led us to posit an international system that determines state behaviour in the foreign and defence areas; this implies not only a rather mechanistic account of human behaviour, but it also leads to the inference that domestic politics is a realm of free-will and choice. Yet each of these implications is unwarranted. With regard to the first, it is clear from the other chapters in this book that the relationship between structure and agency is a complicated, but certainly not a unidirectional, one. The point is not that agents have no choices because of the structure of international society, but that they will, because of their role, come to see the world in certain, structurally induced ways. This links to the second implication: there is a large neo-Marxist literature (for example, Habermas, Offe and O'Connor) that claims that there are considerable structural constraints on democracy arising from the nature of capitalism. The kinds of constraints that contemporary capitalism (or state socialism) imposes on democratic practice may well be similar in effect, if not in form, to those imposed on defence and foreign policy by the nature of international society. The result is that defence and foreign policy may well be one end of a continuum of the impact of structure on democratic practice, rather than a separate class of issues. In short, the dilemmas found in the foreign and defence policy fields may be best understood as the most extreme example of the relationship between structure and democratic practice, rather than a discrete and self-contained area.

The second reason why the orthodox account is misleading is that it relies on a notion of the state that is altogether too simplistic. This does not prevent systemic theorists from developing explanations of foreign policy behaviour, but they can only do so by defining that behaviour in a rather narrow way (for example, by concentrating on military aspects of foreign policy). Two sets of developments have occurred in the last twenty years that reduce the explanatory power of theories that treat domestic factors as exogenous. The first is that the state's predominant role in world society has been challenged by the rise in importance of non-state actors such as multinational companies and revolutionary groups. Put simply, although the state may indeed be the most important actor on the international political stage, it is by no means the only important actor, and in many issue areas it is not the major one. This is most clearly the case in the economic domain, but it is increasingly true of areas such as regional security and terrorism. While non-state actors may be unable to prevail in each and every conflict with states, they can significantly affect the costs of states getting their own way (Keohane and Nye, 1972). It is impossible to discuss the economic dimension of international relations without examining the role of multinational corporations, and to this extent theories based on states as the units for explanation can only be partial.

A second set of developments has occurred that serves to erode the distinction between domestic and foreign policy. These are those developments related to the growing economic interdependence between states.[3] The characterization of the role of the state in international society presented above relied upon a clear distinction between domestic policy and foreign policy for its explanatory power. The effect of increased economic interdependence between states has been to make that distinction less clear-cut. The leaders of states today cannot but define economic issues as crucial aspects of foreign policy. The increased connectedness between the states that comprise the Western capitalist economic system has changed the very notion of what foreign policy is. Economic issues are now very much 'high' politics, and much time is spent by leaders in an attempt to mitigate or control the effects of recession or inflation on the economy of their own society. The implication of this development is that the very notion of the state has undergone considerable change in recent years. It is no longer a hermetically sealed unit, the external behaviour of which can be defined in military-political terms and explained by reference to the structured features of the society in which it exists. Just as has occurred in domestic politics, the nature of the state has changed: it is now involved in areas and issues that were not historically seen as central to its international activity.

So, for these reasons, our characterization of the nature of foreign policy behaviour was a little misleading. The effect of this qualification is an important one for any discussion of the linkage between democratic theory and international relations. For, if the state can no longer be seen as the

dominant actor in all issue areas, and if the state is increasingly involved
in an attempt to manage a wider set of events than was previously the
case, then surely this opens up the possibility of democratic practice
affecting policy-making. There are two reasons for this assertion. First,
if the state is indeed having to deal with non-state actors, then this creates
a set of linkages that increasingly involve aspects of the domestic society.
Non-state actors, by definition, have to be based within states, and so we
can postulate a set of relations emerging between societies that might impact
on what are usually seen as domestic politics. In short, the state might
well have to negotiate with elements of its own society to manage aspects
of foreign (especially economic) policy. Second, the effect of increased
economic interdependence is to make international economic issues of more
salience to domestic politics. The widening scope of foreign policy results
in a situation in which governments are trying to control and manage
economic factors that become critical to the welfare and livelihood of
groups in the domestic society. As such, we can envisage the increased
concern of publics over areas now defined as central to foreign policy.
Although there are limits to the areas of this concern, the trend does seem
to be towards the increased salience for domestic political debate of issues
that governments see as critical components of their foreign policy. In
terms of economic issues, then, one can look to the increased participation
of populations in the formation of these aspects of foreign policy.

Having said this, however, it is important to point out that in the
other areas of foreign and defence policy democracy cannot penetrate so
effectively. The areas in which democracy seems least effective are those
concerning major defence issues, which is in a very real sense a paradox.
What seems to be occurring in the defence arena, certainly in Britain,
is the extension of state control of information and a widening network
of security controls over the activities of civil servants and citizens alike.
The recent prosecutions, brought under the Official Secrets Act, of Sarah
Tisdall and Clive Ponting indicate not only the extent of surveillance in
the defence area but also the ability of the government to define what is
in the national interest. In the Ponting case, the prosecution claimed that
Ponting had no defence by arguing that he was acting in the national interest
in leaking documents; the government's definition of what information
was to be restricted was final because only the government could be in
a position to judge the national interest. This raises crucial constitutional
issues, because Clive Ponting claimed that he chose to pass on the
documents to a parliamentary body (the Defence Committee). Yet the logic
of the prosecution's case was that Parliament could not offer an alternative
view of what was in the interests of the state; it could *only* accept (or,
constitutionally, reject by a vote of confidence) the government's view.
It thus raised the issue of the distinction between government and state.
In Britain, then, the defence area is one that sees the government in a

very privileged position with regard to Parliament when it comes to the control of information and the definition of what information it is in the national interest for Parliament to receive. The tortuous history of the reasons for the sinking of the Argentinian cruiser the *General Belgrano* illustrates the formidable problems Parliament faces in unearthing the truth in defence issues. There is now ample evidence that the British government is involved in an extensive surveillance operation directed at members of organizations such as the Campaign for Nuclear Disarmament, but the very cloud of secrecy just referred to prohibits open discussion of this, even in Parliament. So, although one might look forward to an increase in public participation in matters of international economic policy, it would be wholly mistaken to assume that other areas of foreign and defence policy are being likewise opened up to public scrutiny.

It is now necessary to examine the ways in which decisions are made in the defence and foreign policy arenas, so as to offer some examples of the limits of democratic control in these areas. There are two main examples that will prove instructive: the Trident decision in Britain and the decisions on MX in the United States. We will look at these two examples in order to compare and contrast the nature of democratic control in Britain and the United States.

### 8.3 The Trident decision in Britain

The decisions made by the British government between 1979 and 1981 to purchase the US Trident missile as the next generation of the British nuclear deterrent were, like all other decisions concerning that deterrent force, made in secret and by a very small group of people.[4]

The original decision to acquire nuclear weapons was taken by a sub-committee of the Attlee Cabinet in 1949; not only was over £100 million spent without informing Parliament, but also the matter was not discussed in full Cabinet.[5] Similarly, Parliament had no role in the British decision to acquire a fleet of Polaris submarines in 1962–3. By the early 1970s there was a feeling in defence circles that Polaris could no longer penetrate Soviet anti-ballistic missile defences around Moscow, and so a secret programme to modernize the 'front end' of Polaris was undertaken by the Conservative (1970–4) and Labour (1974–9) governments. The fascinating point about these programmes, codenamed Chevaline, was that the bulk of the expenditure was undertaken by the 1974–9 Labour government, despite explicit manifesto promises not to develop a follow-on programme to the Polaris force (Labour, in opposition, had spoken against the purchase of an improved US missile, Poseidon). By 1979, £1000 million had been spent on the Chevaline programme, with no public discussion, no parliamentary debate, and with the money being hidden in the annual defence estimates. All that the full Cabinet was told was that a Polaris improvement programme was being undertaken; there was, reportedly, only 'slight objection' (Freedman, 1980, p. 52). Even when, in 1977, it became clear that the programme (originally estimated to cost £220 million) was running into serious cost overruns, the small group of five ministers overseeing the project decided to continue it, since to do otherwise would require an explicit (and public) choice over whether to scrap the Polaris nuclear deterrent or to replace it with an improved force. As Freedman concludes, 'The tradition of secret and bipartisan policy-making, with its emphasis on continuity, was one reason why the Conservatives chose Chevaline in 1973 and why the programme survived in 1977' (Freedman, 1980, p. 55).

By the late 1970s the Labour government was advised that it had to make a decision on the replacement of Polaris, as that force would cease to be operational by the early to mid-1990s; given a fifteen-year procurement process, this required a decision by about 1980. As noted above, the Labour Party's manifesto for the 1974 election had carried an unequivocal statement about the nuclear deterrent: 'We have renounced any intention of moving to a new generation of strategic nuclear weapons' (Hennessy, 1979, p. 4). This commitment had been repeated in the 1975 Statement on the Defence Estimates (Cmnd 5976, para. I, 25D). Government ministers and senior civil servants maintained, as late as 1978, that no decision was required for several years. In January 1979 the Prime Minister, James Callaghan, announced in the House of Commons that a decision would need to be taken in the 'next two years' (*Hansard*, 16 January 1979, Col. 1500). Accordingly, the Expenditure Committee of the Commons began an investigation into the future of the British nuclear deterrent, but this was interrupted by the dissolution of Parliament in April 1979.

At the public level, then, by mid-1979 there was only a perception that a decision would need to be taken within two years, and the Labour government had reiterated its policy of not developing a follow-on force to Polaris. Yet this public version of events is very misleading. In fact, a good deal of preparatory work had been undertaken by the Labour government. In 1978 Prime Minister Callaghan had set up two working groups to examine the options for any Polaris replacement, and had set up a small secret sub-committee of the Cabinet to co-ordinate their work. Peter Hennessy claims that: 'In Mr Callaghan's judgement the matter was too delicate to put before the Cabinet's Defence and Overseas Policy Committee (DOP), upon which sat one or two sticklers who might have reminded him of the party's manifesto commitment in the October 1974 general election' (Hennessy, 1979, p. 4). The sub-committee was so secret that it did not have a Cabinet Office number, and comprised only the Prime Minister, the Chancellor of the Exchequer (Denis Healey), the Foreign Secretary (David Owen) and the Defence Secretary (Fred Mulley). The two working groups reported to this sub-committee in November 1978, and as a result the Prime Minister discussed the possibility of purchasing Trident with the US President, Jimmy Carter, during the Guadeloupe summit in January 1979.

On coming to power in May 1979, the Thatcher government set up a sub-committee of Cabinet, known as MISC 7, to examine the future of the British nuclear deterrent. On 24 January 1980 the government announced, in the first debate on nuclear weapons for fifteen years, that it had decided to replace Polaris; no system was named, but the estimated cost (£4–5 billion) indicated that it was to be Trident. It is not necessary to go into the debates that had taken place within the civil service and government as to the choices between a cruise missile force and a sub-marine force, and between different forms of a submarine force, since these were never public debates. At the public level, the government announced on 15 July 1980 that the decision would be to purchase four or five Trident 1 missile-carrying submarines. Parliament debated this decision on 3 March 1981 and approved it by 316 votes to 248. When the US government decided in October 1981 to develop a successor to Trident 1 (C4), known as D5, the British government decided to opt for that system, the memory of the need to upgrade Polaris with Chevaline acting as a powerful 'lesson of the past'. This was announced to Parliament on 11 March 1982. By the end of 1985 the cost had escalated to an estimated £10 008 billion.

This very brief outline of the history of the decision to replace Polaris with Trident D5 serves as a background to what is, for us, the more central issue, namely the role of democratic control over these decisions. What was Parliament's role in the Trident decision? In a constitutional sense, Parliament is, of course, the body that has the right to accept or reject such a large amount of expenditure, yet it is clear that its role was a very limited one. To start with, although the Expenditure Committee began a lengthy examination of the issue in January 1979, its evidence was never debated in the House of Commons. During these hearings the Committee was told that there were 'no plans' to replace Polaris. Defence Secretary Fred Mulley told the Committee, on the same day that the Prime Minister announced to the House that a decision would have to be taken in two years, that 'there are no plans for any successor system to the present Polaris force' (House of Commons Expenditure Committee, 1979, p. 2). Although this was literally correct, it was a very misleading answer, since a consensus had been reached in the small sub-committee that a successor force should be developed.

In the debate on 24 January 1980, although Defence Secretary Francis Pym announced that a successor system was to be developed, he argued that no decision had been made; again, this was misleading, since negotia-tions with the USA were virtually completed. In a debate on the Defence White Paper on 28 and 29 April 1980, the government refused a Labour Party call for the publication of a Green Paper on a successor system, saying that the government would make its decision and defend it before Parliament. At this point, the Defence Committee of the Commons became involved, opening a set of hearings on the British strategic nuclear force. Scarcely had it begun its examination into the choices available for a replacement of Polaris than the government announced its decision to buy Trident (15 July 1980). This critically pre-empted the work of the Defence Committee, which published its evidence on 20 May 1981. By then, of course, the government had obtained parliamentary approval for its decision (on 3 March 1981). Nevertheless, even the majority report (i.e. the Conservative members) of the Defence Committee stated that the Committee's work had been impeded because the Ministry of Defence had been unwilling to provide it with the information necessary to make an informed decision:

> We must record that it has been a matter of great regret to us that we have found the Ministry unwilling to discuss in any detail the opportunity costs of purchasing the Trident system. We cannot believe that the Secretary of State for Defence...did not ask for an assessment of the likely projects to come under pressure...We would have welcomed an indication of what these assessments were. (House of Commons Defence Committee, 1981, p. VI)

The minority report was more openly critical. It stated that:

> Parliament's role in the decision to procure a successor system to Polaris has been limited to endorsing a decision already taken. Decisions on defence, and on Britain's strategic nuclear deterrent, have historically been taken by a small elite of very senior Cabinet Ministers, Civil Servants and Service Chiefs, and this present decision was certainly no exception. (House of Commons Defence Committee, 1981, p. XXXVIII).

The Trident decision indicates very clearly the limits on public accountability in the defence area. The barriers to democratic control are formidable. First of all there is the question of secrecy. Virtually all the decision-making took place in secret. Parliament was only informed after decisions had been taken, and partially implemented. There was no discussion of the work in progress, and governments continued to argue that 'no decision has been taken' up until the actual announcements of them. This prevented Parliament from having the ability to debate the issues, even in the case of the Defence Committee. When that Committee attempted to examine the options, it was not presented with the information necessary to reach an informed judgement. Not only was much of the activity undertaken in secret, but there must also be constitutional implications of the size of the decision-making group. This group comprised four ministers in the Labour government and five in the Conservative government. It is uncertain to what extent Cabinet was informed, but it is probable that it, too, was presented with a consensus recommendation from a small group of very senior members of the government.

A second aspect of the limitation on democratic control was the ability of the government to set the policy agenda. The governments were able to decide when to announce the decisions; this was critical in the case of the 3 March 1981 debate, since this pre-empted the publication of the Defence Committee's report. The effect of this piece of agenda-setting was to set the limits to the kinds of questions that the government would have to consider. Parliament's role was therefore not one of participation in the decision-making process. Its role was simply that of *approving* a decision taken elsewhere. Now, constitutional theorists can point to the ability of Parliament to overturn this recommendation, but the reality of political behaviour made this an almost unimaginable prospect. Additionally, the government was clearly able to control the flow of information: not only did parliamentary debate and questions fail to unearth much information, but, more importantly, nor could the Defence Committee obtain this. A final aspect of setting the agenda was the government's ability to limit the brief of the Defence Committee to considering the options for a successor system to Polaris, not the issue of whether there should be one.

A third feature of the Trident decision was the extent of continuity in policy. Despite the statements of the Labour Party in opposition, it is evident that in government they acted in a very different manner. Within government circles, there was a great emphasis on the importance of continuing with an established policy. It is for that reason that the Labour government preferred to continue with Chevaline in secret rather than open up the question of whether Britain should continue or scrap its nuclear deterrent; it would have been a politically controversial issue for the Labour government to raise publicly. As Peter Hennessy noted in 1979, before the Conservative government decision on Trident,

> the people to watch...will be on the opposition front bench...if they baulk at the cost in an era of expenditure cuts, or suggest a cheaper (and less effective) land-based or air-borne system, it will represent one of those operations in hypocrisy that oppositions can so easily mount when their private intentions in Government remain concealed under thick layers of Whitehall secrecy. (Hennessy, 1979, p. 4)

This continuity in policy was aided by the crucial role of senior civil servants in the decisions. There was an overwhelming consensus within the top levels of defence civil servants and service chiefs that Britain should procure a successor system to Polaris, and also that this should be Trident. This was probably of significance in influencing the actions of the Labour government, and for both governments this consensus would have had considerable effect on the information made available to ministers. This is a good example of the general point as to how the structure of international society leads to advantages for certain bureaucratic groups in the making of defence policy.

Finally, there is the question of the role of wider public control. The first point to note is that there was very little public debate of the issue before the decisions were announced. This was partly because more public attention was concentrated on the 12 December 1979 NATO decision to deploy cruise and Pershing II missiles in Europe, but, more saliently, there was no indication of what options were being considered, and so there could be no real informed public debate. The second point is that the public lacked any mechanism for control over the outcome of the decision-making process. Of course, members of the public could lobby their MPs and could write to the newspapers attacking the decision, but in a critical sense this was too late. The realities of parliamentary government in Britain meant that the public was presented with a *fait accompli*. Democratic control, if by this we mean public control, did not really come into the picture; and, as we have seen, even parliamentary control over the outcome was minimal.

## 8.4   The MX decision in the United States

Having spent some time discussing the history of the Trident decision in Britain, we can now offer a contrast by looking at the way in which democratic control has operated in the United States over the decision to deploy the MX ballistic missile. Here there is a contrast to the situation pertaining in Britain, since Congress has been able significantly to affect the plans of successive administrations (see Holland and Hoover, 1985; Scoville, 1981; Edwards, 1982; and Office of Technology Assessment, 1981). The planning for MX dates back to 1963, when the US Air Force undertook preliminary studies into the 'Improved Capability Missile', a follow-on to Minutemen III (which was not itself deployed until 1970). By 1967 the Air Force had decided that this new missile should be a land-based mobile missile. In 1974 MX entered the advanced development phase. The problem was how to base it: after numerous studies it was clear that the issue of how to ensure its mobility would be politically contentious. Under President Carter, the plan was to base MX in a multiple protective shelter (MPS) arrangement: this involved 200 MX missiles, each deployed on a separate oval track.

The problem of this plan was that it required a large amount of land, and the proposal was to use the Great Basin region of Utah and Nevada. This led to a massive local movement to oppose the deployment of MX, not so much because of an opposition to nuclear weapons but more because of the huge environmental impact of the MPS scheme. It would have required an area of land the size of Connecticut and some 10 000 miles of heavy-duty roads: all of this would have had a serious effect on the fragile ecosystem of the area, since farming land borders on to desert there. There were also considerable economic objections: MX was calculated to be the most expensive weapons system in US history ($33.2 billion at fiscal year 1978 dollars). The result of these local objections was to add a crucially important set of Republican opponents to the liberals in Congress who opposed MX anyway (Holland and Hoover, 1985, Ch. 7). By the time President Carter left office in January 1981, MX was in trouble in Congress, and the MPS basing mode was in especial difficulty.

With the arrival of President Reagan, MPS was dead for another reason: during his campaign he had spoken against that basing mode, and on 2 October 1981 he announced that it would be dropped. Congress, by then, had determined that no money could be spent on MX until a basing mode was agreed. The President proposed that the first 100 MXs would be placed in existing Minuteman silos. Yet this received a sceptical response in Congress, since the whole rationale behind MX was to provide a mobile land-based system in order to close the 'window of vulnerability' of silo-based systems. Putting MX in the same silos that were vulnerable in the first place did not seem a very good idea. The history of MX from that date on is instructive of the power of Congress in the United States. President Reagan proposed a new basing mode, Dense Pack, in November 1982, but this was immediately attacked in Congress for its cost and its dubious strategic utility. Accordingly, in December 1982, Congress restricted expenditure on MX pending the approval of a basing mode. The President established a commission to examine this issue (the Scowcroft Commission) and this reported in April 1983, recommending that 100 MXs be deployed in Minuteman silos, with a new small mobile missile (Midgetman) to be developed in order to provide a mobile Inter-Continental Ballistic Missile component. The reaction in Congress was understandably one of confusion, since this basing mode, as noted above, was directly contrary to the original rationale for MX. During the 1970s the justification of MX had been precisely that it was mobile. The effect of this recommendation was to increase opposition in Congress.

Since 1983 the President has found it impossible to get congressional approval for the purchase of the 100 MXs envisaged by the Scowcroft Commission. The current situation is that Congress has limited to fifty the number of MX missiles to be deployed in Minuteman silos; there seems little possibility that the President will be able to get the 100 he originally requested, and certainly no possibility of the 200 planned for back in the 1970s. In fact MX has only survived at all by some considerable use of presidential persuasion, including the recalling of the Geneva arms control negotiators to Washington to lobby for MX in March 1985. In October 1985 a proposal to delete all funding for MX was only defeated by 214 to 210 votes (*Aviation Week and Space Technology*, 4 November 1985, p. 22).

What does the tortuous history of the MX tell us about democratic control over defence policy in the United States? The key point is a structural one: the separation of power in the USA does offer Congress a much more independent role with regard to expenditure than Parliament possesses in Britain. Because congressional approval is required and there is not the structural linkage between the executive and the legislature that exists in Britain, Congress can in practice stop the plans of the executive. The nature of party loyalty and the whips system in the House of Commons makes this almost impossible. Additionally, the fact that it is common for the President not to have a majority from his party in control of both houses of Congress makes such events all the more likely. Finally, the nature of congressional politics means that Representatives and Senators are likely to be far more responsive to local concerns than is the case with British MPs.

But this structural issue is only one aspect of the reasons for the different patterns of behaviour in the USA. It can be argued that it is equally important that Congress does not have to rely on the information provided by the executive. Congressional staffs are large, and commonly include specialists on defence issues. Congressional committees can call expert witnesses and subject them to much more intense questioning than occurs in the Commons committee system. Finally, the existence of the Freedom of Information Act has a critical impact on public debate: not only can members of Congress receive confidential information but also public pressure groups can gain access to a much more extensive amount of information than is possible in Britain.

It is fascinating to compare the public debate over MX in the USA with that over Trident in Britain. It is not simply that congressional members had access to far more detailed information (often supplied by the Congressional Research Service – an arm of Congress, not the executive) but rather that the detail included in public debate contained the kind of information over options, costs and implications that was almost totally absent in the debate over Trident in Britain. Public pressure groups could use the Freedom of Information Act to obtain information that would certainly be classified as secret in Britain.

The result of these factors is that Congress was both in a constitutional and a practical position to act against the wishes of the executive. Because they had the information, members of Congress knew the questions to ask and could see the various costs and benefits of each alternative. The President was unable to get his way on MX and, to this extent, he had far less power than was possessed by the small group of decision-makers in Britain who guided nuclear weapons policy. But before we run away with the assumption that such a pattern applies across the board in foreign and defence policy-making in the USA, it should be noted that MX was not entirely typical because of its cost and the serious difficulties the Air Force faced in finding a basing mode for it. The President still retains considerable power over Congress in his ability to make policy in either those areas that require immediate action (such as foreign policy crises) or those areas that can successfully be hidden behind the veil of secrecy (such as arms control negotiations). In addition, we should note that the President can sway members of Congress in those areas in which he claims that a programme is vital to national security: this is reinforced to the extent that the President is popular domestically and is able to mount a moral case for his proposals (such as the Strategic Defense Initiative, or so-called 'Star Wars' programme). MX was a tough product to sell to Congress precisely because it looked very much like a missile without a home. Perhaps a better example of democratic control will arise over SDI: will Congress be able to stop the project before it becomes self-sustaining? All the evidence indicates that while Congress can cut back the funding for SDI, there is no possibility of it being able to stop the programme – it is all too clearly the pet project of a popular President.

In summary, though, there are other examples of congressional action overturning presidential proposals (the development of the Anti-Satellite weapon is a current example), so the picture in the United States is a mixed one. Congress can act independently, but only to the extent that the issue is one that can be subjected to scrutiny over a period of time, that requires expenditure, and is one in which information cannot be hidden behind definitions of national security. As a final comment, it should be noted that it is by no means obvious that congressional involvement exactly equates with public control, given the power of lobby groups in the United States.

Before turning to discuss why the role of democratic control is limited in the ways indicated above, it is worth pausing to note that the situation over MX in the United States is in many ways the exception to the rule. The picture presented by the Trident story in Britain is much more typical of the role of democratic control in liberal democracies than is that of MX in the United States. There is not space to discuss the nature of democratic control in other countries, but it is clear that in the other European countries the situation resembles that of Britain more than it does that of the United States. The ability of the Dutch government to accept the deployment of cruise missiles despite sizeable public opposition is one obvious example; another would be the lack of domestic reaction to the sinking of the Greenpeace ship *Rainbow Warrior* by the French in 1985. The participation of European governments in the Strategic Defense Initiative and the history of NATO weapons deployment decisions are more extensive indicators of the ability of governments to make and implement decisions almost regardless of domestic concerns. In Britain, the decision of the Thatcher government in April 1986 to allow the use of US bases in Britain for the attack on Libya was a classic example of the limitation on democratic control. This was a decision opposed by over two-thirds of the population and by not only the opposition parties but also large numbers of Conservative Members of Parliament. It was also a decision that, reportedly, was not referred to Cabinet. Despite the controversy created by that decision, the government was able to claim that it had 'incontrovertible evidence' of Libyan culpability in terrorist actions, evidence that could not be made public because to do so would reveal the sources. A further argument was that the decision was the only one possible given both the close links between Britain and the United States and the debt owed to the Reagan administration for its help over the Falklands/Malvinas conflict. So although constitutionally Parliament could have voted against the government in a vote of confidence, this, given the nature of the party whip system, was not an available option. It would also, of course, have been after the event.

## 8.5   The limits of democratic control

Why does democratic control fail to penetrate foreign and defence policy areas? There are six main reasons.[6] First, foreign and defence issues are not of continuing importance to domestic publics. Although there are occasions when members of a society do express strong views about these matters, this is not the norm. For most societies there is at best indifference to most events in the foreign policy field, the exceptions being those instances which directly affect people. Public opinion surveys indicate that foreign and defence issues rank fairly low down in any list of the most salient issues. To the extent that publics do become involved, there is the critical fact that they have to find out information about events. This is important because the news media tend to concentrate on domestic events; most significantly, the reporting of foreign and defence policy issues that does occur tends to adopt an ethnocentric perspective. Think, for example, of reporting in Britain during the Falklands/Malvinas conflict, especially the staggering jingoism of all the popular tabloids. More recently, the reporting in the United States of the US raid on Libya was almost exclusively from a nationalistic stance. This may reflect a desire to sell newspapers or attract advertising, but there is an obvious structural factor at work, namely the ways in which the division of international society into states encourages a nationalistic standpoint. This same factor makes a resort into knee-jerk nationalism a very common response by domestic publics. So, except on those relatively few occasions when a foreign or defence issue directly affects the lives of people, foreign and defence policies are seen to refer to a very remote set of incidents. Even for those individuals who are concerned about these issues, the ethnocentric lens of reporting these events makes it difficult to obtain information that might challenge the conventional wisdom.

Secondly, and following on from this point, is the fact that very few elections are decided on foreign or defence policy issues. This is not simply because the bulk of the population is uninterested in those issues but also because elections are seldom single-issue events. Thus, even if someone was concerned about a foreign or defence policy issue they might either have no real option of choosing between parties that took different positions (since, as mentioned above, these areas are usually marked by considerable inter-party consensus), or feel that other, possibly more immediate, issues were more important in determining their vote. On the one hand the degree of party consensus has been a marked feature of British politics for most of the post-war period, thereby offering no real option to anyone wanting to use the democratic process to influence policy in these areas; on the other hand, surveys again show that although people may feel strongly about a foreign or defence issue, they tend to feel more strongly about economic or law and order issues. For example, at the time of his defeat by Ronald Reagan, Jimmy Carter was unpopular because of his handling of the Iranian hostage crisis, yet close analysis of the poll data indicates that this was not ranked in the top five issues that people gave as reasons for voting against him. Similarly, in the 1983 British general election, although there was considerable opposition to the pending deployment of US cruise missiles at Greenham Common, this was again not in the top five reasons given for voting against the Conservatives. The result, of course, is that parties tend to be far less interested in foreign and defence policies than in domestic ones; they are not seen as vote-winners. This places a considerable limit on the possibility of democratic (i.e. electoral) control being exerted in these areas, although we should note that foreign and defence issues may well be important aspects of the context in which elections are fought (for example the 'Falklands factor' in the 1983 general election).

Thirdly, within governments there is a marked tendency for executives to dominate legislatures in these policy areas, with the possible exception, as noted above, of the United States for certain types of issues. Because of the relative lack of public interest in foreign and defence policies, these come under far less parliamentary scrutiny than applies to domestic issues. Even when there are debates or enquiries by committees, the government has a formidable trump card in the use of the term 'national interest'. Its use allows governments to foreclose debate over some aspects, and to claim a kind of guardianship over the choices available in other issues; it has proven very difficult for oppositions to challenge this role. An added advantage possessed by governments is their role in controlling the flow of information: this was most evident in the Conservative government's attempts to restrict parliamentary enquiry into the events surrounding the sinking of the *General Belgrano*, but it is commonly found in debates on defence and foreign policy issues. This means that opposition parties, or even members of the government party, simply do not have access to the kind of information necessary to reach informed judgements; they may even lack the information they require to ask the right questions. This has fundamental implications for the ability of parliamentary bodies to oversee policy-making in these areas.

Fourthly, in contrast to the plethora of interest groups concerned with domestic issues, there are far fewer concerned with foreign and defence policies. The reason is simply that there is rarely the kind of direct connection between events in these areas and the daily lives of people. The exception here is in the economic field, and, as was noted above, there is an evident expansion of pressure groups concerned with the economic dimension of foreign policy. In the defence area the picture is more complicated: while there are sizeable groups concerned with issues such as nuclear disarmament, governments have been able to marginalize these somewhat, dismissing them as idealists (at best!) who would think differently if only they knew what the government did. There are also powerful interest groups among those who benefit from the defence industry and, certainly in the United States, these have been very effective: for example, there is little doubt that one reason the B-1 bomber pro-gramme survived despite formidable technical and strategic problems was that the contractors (Rockwell) had managed to sub-contract work on it to forty-eight states! When Congress voted on the B-1 there were significant pressures on the congressional members from these states to support it. The limitations on pressure group activity in these areas are, naturally, exacerbated by the difficulties faced in obtaining information: thus CND in Britain was pilloried for some of its early (inaccurate) statements about the role of cruise missiles as first-strike weapons.

Fifthly, there is a marked contrast between the positions adopted by politicians on foreign and defence policies while in opposition and those they take when in government. The Trident case in Britain illustrates this clearly, but the phenomenon is much more widespread, both within British politics and within other liberal democracies. The explanation for this is again the structural features of international society: being a minister responsible for policy in these areas involves being in a role that is influenced not only by domestic political factors but also by international considerations. Occupants of these roles talk frequently of the constraints imposed upon them by the network of complex rela-tionships between states; their freedom of manoeuvre is much less than might be envisaged when in opposition. It is instructive to note the extent to which Labour governments in Britain have been involved in developing the British nuclear deterrent despite very different statements when in opposition. Again, there are many examples from other countries. The factors restricting democratic control discussed above make this external impact on role-occupiers more likely to prevail. One does not have to adopt a conspiratorial view of politics to accept that the cobweb of bilateral and multilateral relationship in which any state is involved will suggest certain courses of action as 'obvious' or 'natural' to policy-makers. This is especially so because of the continuing need to co-operate with the leaders of other states to achieve policy goals in other areas: such linkages certainly pervade decision-making in organiza-tions such as the European Community and NATO.

Finally, there is the role of the civil service. The complexity of foreign and defence issues, especially because they involve negotiations with other states, means that continuity and predictability are much sought after by civil servants. Not only does this colour the information that they provide to ministers, but it also leads to the development of a policy hierarchy such that certain issues are accorded priority. There is also the phenomenon of bureaucratic politics, which refers to the tendency in governments for bureaucratic groups to adopt views on issues based on a narrow definition of what is in the interest of that bureaucracy. Decision-making, in this sense, is a continual set of compromises between various bureaucratic interests, and this bureaucratic battleground is essentially fixed. This further limits the ability of a minister to shift policy. This is obviously true of all policy-making, but it is especially important in issues such as foreign and defence policy because of the secretive nature of much of the information and the complexity involved in ongoing relations with other states.

For all of these reasons it is more difficult for democratic control to extend to foreign and defence policy areas than is the case with domestic politics. The final part of this chapter will turn to discuss whether there is any possibility of changing this situation: can we envisage ways of making these areas more accessible to democratic control or must they, because of the very structure of international society, be left to the 'professionals'?

## 8.6 Can democratic control be increased?

In thinking about the possibility of increasing democratic control over foreign and defence policies, it will be helpful to return to the comments about the nature of democracy and the link between democratic theory and international relations that were made at the start of the chapter. Broadly speaking, we can divide possible 'new forms' of democratic control into those that attempt to ameliorate structurally induced constraints on democratic control, and those that are more radical in character, which aim at more sweeping changes in both domestic and international societies. Recollect that earlier we introduced the distinctions between wide and narrow definitions of democracy (with the former being concerned with public participation and the latter with accountability and control) and between realist and idealist accounts of international society (the realist seeing foreign and defence policy being determined by the structure of international society, while idealists see domestic political factors leading to international outcomes). Accordingly we can imagine two major approaches to increasing democratic control: for the realists (who adopt a public accountability view of democracy) the best that can occur is for public control to be increased; for the idealists, the aim is to alter both domestic and international societies so as to make each more democratic. The literature of international relations has many examples of both the reformist and the radical view of how to increase democratic control, and we can now deal briefly with how these two perspectives deal with the question of how to democratize foreign and defence policy.

At the outset I should make explicit my judgement that the structure of international society acts as a limiting factor on the possibility of democratizing foreign and defence policy. It is interesting to note that the more radical accounts of how this democratization is to be achieved require a transformation of the structure of international society. A good example is to be found in the work of the World Order Models Project (WOMP), which deems as central the decline of the state, and its replacement by a trans-societal functionalist model (see Falk, 1975; Mendlovitz, 1975). For WOMP analysts, the structure of international society has to be changed precisely because it limits democratic control. Such a position is reflected in the work of many Marxist international political economists. For all of these writers the democratization of domestic society and international society are interlinked. This level of analysis is dealt with in John Burnheim's chapter in this book, where he is concerned with transformations in the international structure. The issue for our analysis is the extent to which such a trans-formation is achievable, since, paradoxically, the argument of many radical theorists indicates the limiting effect of international structure by their desire to transcend it. In short, the argument being advanced here is that there is indeed a body of literature that posits a radical path to democrat-izing foreign and defence policy, but this is to be achieved by altering the structure of the international political system. An earlier precursor of this approach would be the work of functionalists such as David Mitrany (1975). For Mitrany the states system was to be transcended by the growth of universal voluntaristic international functional agencies that would gradually take over the more technical aspects of state-to-state behaviour. Eventually they would create a 'working peace system' that undermined sovereignty. Yet the optimism of functionalists was misplaced because they relied on the states being willing to give up, or unable to prevent the erosion of, their sovereignty: neither of these has occurred. Thus, there is good reason to be sceptical about the likelihood of achieving radical democratization at the international level.

But this does not mean that we are condemned to pessimism and a return to systems dominance. This is because there are changes that can be brought about at the domestic level. For example, it is evident that the wave of protest that accompanied the NATO decision to deploy cruise and Pershing II missiles in Europe in the early 1980s has created a sizeable transnational pressure group. Within national societies these movements show signs of being able to challenge the ability of governments to manipulate public opinion, and in several cases they have contributed to significant shifts in the defence policies of opposition parties (for example, the Labour Party in Britain and the SPD in West Germany). New concep-tions of defence are being advanced, and it is likely that these will be put into practice in European countries before the end of the 1980s (especially in the case of non-nuclear defence policies). In terms of a wider notion of democracy, then, there has been a significant change in the nature of public involvement in defence matters in the last decade, and, in Britain at least, bipartisan consensus has been shattered. Certainly, as public expenditure programmes come under increasing pressure, there is good reason to expect an increasing salience of defence and foreign policy issues for domestic politics. Certainly, it seems that we are entering a phase in which decisions in these areas can no longer be kept out of the public gaze precisely because people see these areas as important, either directly or indirectly, for their lives. To take just the most obvious example, the current impasse in superpower arms control negotiations, combined with the Reagan administration's decisions on SDI and SALT II seem likely to maintain public concern over nuclear weapons, and, as the Greenham women have shown so clearly, this concern can itself lead to new forms of political activity. At the wider level of participation, then, there are strong reasons to believe that people are becoming more concerned with foreign and defence policies, and although the structure of international society might impose limitations on the degree of democratization that might be achieved, these areas are being brought more and more into the participatory arena.

Moving from the participatory to the public control or reformist aspect of democracy, what reforms might be undertaken to increase public control over foreign and defence policies? One development would relate to increasing the flow of information on foreign and defence issues; this would involve legislation such as the Freedom of Information Act in the United States. There is no doubt that a major impediment to the exercise of democratic control is the ability of governments to hide behind a shield of secrecy when it comes to releasing information. Legislation such as a Freedom of Information Act, while protecting those areas that genuinely did concern national security, would change a situation where governments can classify information as secret and face no challenge to one in which they would have to justify any such classification before a non-executive body. While it would be naive to think that such legislation could lead to democratic control on its own, since in practice the Freedom of Information Act still allows the US government to claim reasons of national security to prevent the release of information, it is clear that access to information is a necessary prerequisite for democratic control; after all, if the information is not available, the critical questions cannot be asked.

A second area which would aid the democratization of foreign and defence policy concerns the executive-legislative relationship. A basic reason why democratic mechanisms cannot control policy-making in these areas is that executives tend to be able to dominate discussions. There is, of course, a limit to such reform, in that the nature of executive-legislature relations is, in many countries, deeply embedded in a constitution. Thus, for example, although it might aid democratic control if there was a split between the executive and the legislature in Britain, it is very unlikely that such changes could occur. Nevertheless, one possible change would be to increase the power of the purview of legislature committees so that they can operate more on the lines of congressional committees in the United States. A very desirable, related development would be for the establishment of an independent research service for these committees, and for members of the legislature generally – a service free from executive control and able to have access to classified materials. As it stands, all the resources of the state in the official information area are at the service of the executive; altering this situation could be of significant importance in developing an independent source of analysis and information for members of legislatures to draw on. Finally, it seems crucial that committees of the legislature have sufficient professional staff. In the Commons Defence Committee's enquiry into Trident, all it had was three part-time staff. There is no way in which such a small staff can hope to match the large numbers of professionals working in those areas in the civil service and armed forces. These developments in bolstering the role of the legislature could do much to give it some independence in its relations with the executive, and this might strengthen democratic control and accountability.

A final area of possible development relates back to the proposal for a Freedom of Information Act. If this was passed, it might be easier for pressure groups to present more informed cases, not only to governments, but also to publics. In short, it seems critical that the public can be made aware of the impact of foreign and defence policies on their lives. In one respect this is a rather optimistic alternative to posit, given the earlier comments about the lack of interest shown by the public in these areas. Yet, in many ways, it seems that unless public interest can be aroused, then our notion of democratic control will have to be limited to the role of the legislature in its relations with the executive. Certainly, that would be an improvement on the current situation, but we must face up to the fact that unless people can see how events in these areas might affect them, then we are defining democratic control in a classically pluralist sense. There are areas where such a wider public interest is being developed – nuclear weapons, NATO and European Community issues being examples. If the developments in the information area and in executive-legislature relations occur, then public awareness would have a channel through which democratic control, in this wider sense, might be exercised.

In conclusion, then, we can see that there are two ways in which democratic control over foreign and defence policy might be increased: the reformist, or accountability, route and the radical, or participatory, way. In each of these ways, the public can increase its involvement in, and control over, foreign and defence policy – the power of Congress over MX being an example of the former, CND and the alternative defence movements in Britain serving as an example of the latter. But these are only possible developments, and the overall nature of defence policy-making in the USA is a powerful reminder of the limitations of reforming the system. So although it is possible to outline radical and reformist schemes for increasing public control, it is important that the forces working against these should not be underestimated. Although progress has been made in the last century in opening these areas to public control, that progress has been slow. The situation is still one in which policies in these areas are not vote winners for political parties, either since people are uninterested or because elections are not single-issue: the result is that the usual mechanism for exercising democratic control in a liberal democracy, the party system, is not responsive to these issues. This returns us to our starting point, the structure of international society. That structure does, in an important sense, make states (at least psychologically) separate units, and does place individuals in leadership roles within states in a position whereby systemic factors act as powerful constraints on their freedom of manoeuvre. What this survey indicates is that the view of traditional democratic theory, that the existence or absence of a democratic structure leads to certain forms of control on policy-making, is a very misleading one when it comes to foreign and defence issues. A person from another planet would surely notice the similarites in the ways in which all types of states made foreign and defence policies much more than any differences related to the existence or absence of a democratic political system. Thus, despite the possibilities for creating alternative, and more democratic, policy-making processes in the foreign and defence fields, we must recognize that there are powerful factors serving to limit the extent to which democratization can occur. While the development of economic interdependence and increased concern about the nuclear threat may alter the domestic variable, by making people more interested in these areas, and thereby parties and legislatures, the structural factor of the nature of international society remains as a parameter, limiting the extent to which democratic control might be possible. However, recognizing the limits is no reason for not trying to reach them.

## Notes

1. I would like to thank the editors of this book, the D308 course team and, above all, Tony McGrew for their most helpful and incisive comments on an earlier draft of this chapter.
2. For examples of the distinction between liberal democracy and totalitarianism see Crick (1973), Lively (1975), Finer (1970), Blondel (1973), and Almond and Powell (1978).
3. The 'classic' treatments of interdependence are Cooper (1968), Keohane and Nye (1977), and Morse (1976). For recent discussions see Jones and Willetts (1984), and Maghroori and Ramberg (1982).

4. This section is based on my much more detailed forthcoming account (Smith, forth-coming).
5. For useful sources of the history of policy-making in the nuclear weapons area see Freedman (1980) and Malone (1984).
6. The relationship between foreign/defence policy and domestic politics is discussed in Rosenau (1967), Wallace (1971), Barber (1976), Cohen (1963, 1973), and Barber and Smith (1974, Part Four).

## References

ALMOND, G. and POWELL, G. B. (1978) *Comparative Politics*, Boston, Little Brown.

BARBER, J. (1976) *Who Makes British Foreign Policy?*, Milton Keynes, Open University Press.

BARBER, J. and SMITH, M. (eds) (1974) *The Nature of Foreign Policy*, Edinburgh, Holmes McDougall.

BEITZ, C. (1979) *Political Theory and International Relations*, Princeton, Princeton University Press.

BLONDEL, J. (1973) *Comparing Political Systems*, London, Weidenfeld and Nicolson.

BULL, H. (1977) *The Anarchical Society*, London, Macmillan.

BUTTERFIELD, H. and WIGHT, M. (eds) (1966) *Diplomatic Investigations*, London, Allen and Unwin.

COHEN, B. C. (1963) *The Press and Foreign Policy*, Princeton, Princeton University Press.

COHEN, B. C. (1973) *The Public's Impact on Foreign Policy*, Princeton, Princeton University Press.

COOPER, R. (1968) *The Economics of Interdependence*, New York, McGraw-Hill.

CRICK, B. (1973) *Basic Forms of Government*, London, Macmillan.

DAHL, R. (1971) *Polyarchy*, New Haven, Yale University Press.

DONELAN, M. (ed.) (1978) *The Reason of States*, London, Allen and Unwin.

DOWNS, A. (1957) *An Economic Theory of Democracy*, New York, Harper and Row.

EASTON, D. (1953) *The Political System*, New York, Knopf.

EDWARDS, J. (1982) *Superweapon: the Making of MX*, New York, Norton.

FALK, R. (1975) *A Study of Future Worlds*, New York, Free Press.

FINER, S. E. (1970) *Comparative Government*, London, Allen Lane.

FREEDMAN, L. (1980) *Britain and Nuclear Weapons*, London, Macmillan.

HENNESSY, P. (1979) 'Planning for a future nuclear deterrent', *The Times*, 4 December, p. 4.

HOLLAND, L. and HOOVER, R. (1985) *The MX Decision*, Boulder, Westview Press.

HOUSE OF COMMONS DEFENCE COMMITTEE (1981) *Fourth Report from the Defence Committee, Session 1980–1: Strategic Nuclear Weapons Policy*, London, HMSO.

HOUSE OF COMMONS EXPENDITURE COMMITTEE (1979) *Sixth Report from the Expenditure Committee, Session 1978–9: the Future of the United Kingdom's Nuclear Weapons Policy*, London, HMSO.

JONES, R. J. B. and WILLETTS, P. (eds) (1984) *Interdependence on Trial*, London, Frances Pinter.

KEOHANE, R. and NYE, J. (eds) (1972) *Transnational Relations and World Politics*, Cambridge, Mass., Harvard University Press.

KEOHANE, R. and NYE, J. (1977) *Power and Interdependence*, Boston, Little Brown.

LIVELY, J. (1975) *Democracy*, Oxford, Blackwell.

MAGHROORI, R. and RAMBERG, B. (eds) (1982) *Globalism versus Realism*, Boulder, Westview Press.

MALONE, P. (1984) *The British Nuclear Deterrent*, London Croom Helm.

MAYALL, J. (ed.) (1982) *The Community of States*, London, Allen and Unwin.

MENDLOVITZ, S. (ed.) (1975) *On the Creation of a Just World Order*, New York, Free Press.
MITRANY, D. (1975) *The Functional Theory of Politics*, Oxford, Martin Robertson.
MORSE, F. (1976) *Modernization and the Transformation of International Relations*, New York, Free Press.
OFFICE OF TECHNOLOGY ASSESSMENT (1981) *MX Missile Basing*, Washington, Government Printing Office.
ROSENAU, J. (ed.) (1967) *Domestic Sources of Foreign Policy*, New York, Free Press.
ROSENAU, J. (ed.) (1969) *International Politics and Foreign Policy*, New York, Free Press.
SCOVILLE, H. (1981) *MX: Prescription for Disaster*, Cambridge, Mass., MIT Press.
SMITH, S. (forthcoming) 'The Trident decision', in GREENAWAY, J., SMITH, S. and STREET, J., *Decision-making in British Government*, London, Croom Helm.
WALLACE, W. (1971) *Foreign Policy and the Political Process*, London, Macmillan.
WELTMAN, J. (1973) *Systems Theory in International Relations*, Lexington, Lexington Press.

# 9 Democracy, Nation States and the World System

*John Burnheim*

Democracy hardly exists at the international level, and it is difficult to see how it could in the context of existing institutions and practices. At best in some international organizations we have a democracy of states in which each state, formally at least, has an equal vote, and some of those states in turn have claims to be democracies. Granted that there is already an enormous problem for electoral democracy in existing states, especially large ones, because of the remoteness of central government from the individual voter, it is very difficult to imagine international authorities being controlled effectively by a mass electorate, through very distant representative bodies.

Moreover, it seems impossible to envisage electoral bodies on a world scale. Mass electoral democracy tends to work only where the electorate, however large, is relatively homogeneous in religious, cultural, political and economic background. Otherwise opposing parties tend to be mobilized around religious, ethnic, linguistic, regional or class differences in ways that undermine the possibility of peaceful alternation of competing political teams in office. There is little possibility of there being an accepted political morality, a common core of public opinion or any common purpose between such heterogeneous groups as, say, Calcutta unemployed and Sydney bourgeoisie.

In any case, I believe, as I have argued in *Is Democracy Possible?* (1985), that significant though their achievements are, both the nation state and electoral democracy are inadequate as the vehicles for democracy under modern conditions. In the emerging global order we are less and less identified with any particular 'total' community. Each of us has a range of changing interests, differing in scope from the very local to the inter-national, with which we are involved in varying degrees. It is not possible for any one representative to represent any electorate in all its diverse interests, nor is it possible for anybody to take an active part in all the affairs that affect them, or even to be tolerably well-informed about them. Moreover, if one's vote is only a drop in an ocean, it is hardly worth-while trying to vote responsibly, or even to vote at all. These problems are extremely serious for democracy at any level. At the international level they seem quite insuperable. A radically different approach is needed. I shall begin by asking whether a stable international order demands a world state (Section 9.1). Having rejected that, I shall outline a different con-ception of public order in general and international order in particular

(Section 9.2), look at the main problems that an international order needs to deal with (Section 9.3), explain how democracy is possible in an international context (Section 9.4) and how its authority might be enforced (Section 9.5); I shall then speculate on how my proposals might be put into practice (Section 9.6) and answer some objections (Section 9.7).

## 9.1 A world state?

The traditional argument for a world state is that the states of the world are in a 'state of nature' analogous to that postulated by Hobbes as the situation of individuals or households before the emergence of the state. There are significant differences, notably that, unlike Hobbesian individuals, they are not substantially equal in power, and their interests are much more complex and diverse. Nevertheless, they are inclined to war and other forms of conflict that may well seem to demand a world state to impose order on them, especially in view of the destructive power of nuclear weapons and the likelihood that they will become more generally available.[1] While it is unlikely that a world state will emerge, even in the face of such dangers, from a free contract among most existing states, it would certainly be in the interests of a superpower that achieved clear dominance to impose one. It would even be in the interests of the superpowers jointly to do so if nuclear proliferation posed a greater threat to both of them than either did to the other. Interest might override ideology, allowing each to stabilize its hegemony in its own sphere more cheaply and effectively than at present.

Such a world state might have certain trappings of democracy, but it clearly could not be democratic in any substantive way, even as a federal entity of component states like the USA or Australia.

It would have to operate more on the model of the UN Security Council than of the General Assembly. Much less could it be democratic in the sense of being responsible to and representative of individuals and groups that are not themselves states. Clearly a world state would make such governmental functions as it assumed more remote from, and impervious to, most particular non-state interests than they are already. Nevertheless, it might well result in some increase of welfare for those at present worse off by controlling local despots, eliminating some barriers to trade and development, and engaging in some redistribution of resources. In doing these things, it would both expand its functions and increase its legitimacy in the ways in which federal bodies usually do. The very diversity and number of the forces opposed to it might make it relatively easy for such a state to divide and rule in the classical imperial mode without much use of military force. Economic and legal sanctions orchestrated by an effective world authority would be extraordinarily powerful.

Athough a world state might eventually come to have even greater power over the lives of individuals and small groups than most existing states, that power might sit comparatively lightly on most people. Unlike the nation state, which is under pressure to eliminate cultural differences in the interests of national unity against its enemies, the world state could be pluralist, presenting itself as the protector of minorities. Its interest would be to break up other forms of centralization in order to rule a disaggregated complex of subjects better. Again, it might even simplify a great deal of the red tape connected with migration, trade and many other areas. To some extent, a lofty and universal authority tends to be less open to *petty* corruption and chauvinism than smaller and more particular authorities. Even where the superpowers are concerned, they might acquiesce to regulation that removed problems from their plate without obviously constraining them. Politicians readily buy immediate advantage even at the cost of their long-term interests.

Nevertheless, there can be little doubt that, in spite of many relatively short-term advantages, a world state would, in the long run, constitute a dead hand on social change and individual and group freedom. It would spawn an uncontrollable bureaucracy with an inbuilt tendency to closer and closer regulation, an enormous inertia and no constructive countervailing political power. It would end up being extremely conservative, not only because it might be expected to perpetuate itself principally by co-option, but also because that would always be the easiest thing for it to do. Regularization, homogenization and the subordination of the particular to the recognized 'universals' would be entrenched not only in its philosophy, its conceptions of justice and of 'humanity', but also in the structure of its bureaucratic practice. Reducing all particular interests to 'private' or 'special' interests, it would entrench the interest of its own effectiveness, efficiency and universality as the 'common interest of mankind'. The spontaneous and experimental character of individual variations would be eliminated in favour of a rationality based on requirements of uniformity in all 'essentials'. Both traditional legal theory and the necessities of bureaucratic administration push strongly in this direction.

The absence of any effectively organized internal or external constraints on the inherent tendencies of an authority to glorify itself by grandiose schemes, expand its power and appropriate more resources, would pose a constant threat to liberty, diversity and even the living standards of its subjects. We are driven, then, to ask whether there is no better alternative solution to the problems of international peace and world development. The key to such an alternative involves questioning both the necessity of the state at any level and the accepted procedures of democracy, especially free elections.

## 9.2   Public order, co-ordination and public goods
One of the great fallacies of political theory is the assumption that a centralized monopoly of power, and especially of military force, is necessary to

assure public order, co-ordination and public goods. In fact, all that is required are specific authorities that deal with specific kinds of order, co-ordination and goods. The need for states is the result not of any absolute necessity, but of the system of nation states. There is no inherent reason why we should not set up specialized authorities, co-ordinated among themselves by negotiation, or failing that by recognized arbitrators, to ensure the production of various public goods, including the repression of various forms of crime. Each such authority would derive its legitimacy basically from its possessing general, democratically generated recognition, and enforce its decisions by sanctions, and it could mobilize in co-operation with other recognized authorities.

One familiar sphere in which authorities of this sort already exist is sport. Each major sport has its international authority that regulates a variety of matters ranging from the rules of the game to the administration of competitions. Such bodies are, of course, open to schisms and rivalries, but these are rarely a major problem, in spite of the fact that they have no sanctions to enforce their authority other than excluding competitors from participation in events they organize. What is less commonly realized is that there are very many international authorities in other areas, most of them resting formally on agreements to which states are signatories, which exercise considerable powers in specialized areas with a large degree of stability and autonomy. Many aspects of air, sea and land traffic, health, trade, policing and international law are regulated, in some degree, by such bodies. That there are not more of them is mainly a matter of the reluctance of nation states to surrender their powers and the dangers of their being dominated by very powerful states. If only nation states could be dissolved into specialized authorities, there is every reason to believe that most world problems could be handled by appropriate specialized authorities.

That such a dissolution of nation states is possible I have argued at length in *Is Democracy Possible?* (Burnheim, 1985). To summarize very briefly, the vast range of public goods we have come to want has been provided mainly by expanding the role of the state, because the state, with its powers of taxation and legislation, has been the easiest way in which to establish the requisite bodies authoritatively, to fund them and to co-ordinate them. State provision has been contrasted with either commercial or purely voluntary non-commercial provision of goods and services, both in theory and in social practice. Ideologies of the state as exemplifying *the* common good or the general will or democratic control have powerfully reinforced the inherent tendency of the state to appropriate more power to itself. I shall return to this question in Section 9.4 below.

Meanwhile I shall take a closer look at the existing international agencies. Most of them are formally part of the UN organization, but many of them originated prior to it and have strongly defended their independence within it. From our point of view the most useful comprehensive study remains Evan Luard's *International Agencies: the Emerging Framework of Interdependence* (1977). The principal advocate of a 'functionalist' approach to international authorities is David Mitrany, whose work is summed up in his book *The Functional Theory of Politics* (Mitrany, 1975; see also Groom and Taylor, 1975).[2] Very roughly, international agencies have tended to be efficient, effective and uncontroversial to the extent that they have been concerned with problems that are primarily technical. Prominent among these agencies are the Universal Postal Union, the International Telecommunications Union, the International Civil Aviation Organization, some of the international shipping authorities, the World Meteorological Organization, and various scientific bodies. At the other end of the spectrum lie bodies whose activities are much more obviously social and political: UNESCO, the World Bank, the International Monetary Fund, and the various aid and trade bodies such as the General Agreement on Trade and Tariffs and the United Nations Conference on Trade and Development.

The reasons for the difference are simple and obvious. The technically based agencies work mostly on small budgets and predominantly technical staff. By and large it is clearly in the interests of all nations to use the services they supply, and the developed nations profit most from them, getting good value for their contributions. Even where such agencies supply various forms of technical assistance to poorer nations, it suits the rich nations for them to do so. On the other hand, although there is a good deal of talk about the importance of aid to developing countries through organizations dealing with educational, financial, agricultural, health and trade matters, the pay-off is much less clear and the costs incomparably greater. There is a continual struggle for control of policy in such matters between rich and poor, capitalist and socialist, producer and consumer blocs. These struggles often take the form of attempts by the poorer nations to bring policy under the control of the UN Assembly, where each nation has an equal voice, rather than under specialized arrangements that reflect the relative power and contributions of the richer states. The recent withdrawals of the USA and the United Kingdom from UNESCO also reflect these conflicts, as does the refusal of the USA to ratify the agreement on the use of the sea bed.

The salient problem of international order at the present time is the prevention of war, especially of global war involving nuclear weapons. I shall not attempt to address this problem directly, partly because I want to concentrate not on the problems of relations between states but on the possibility of setting up an international order that largely bypasses nation states altogether. To set up such an order would be to exclude the very possibility of war by diffusing people's loyalties among a variety of different authorities, none of which could claim their absolute allegiance or the resources for military action.

Even now it seems almost inconceivable that war should break out betwen any of the major democratic states. The kinds of issues that could arise between them are hardly things for which their people are going to risk destruction. Even conflict between the superpowers is likely to arise not out of any genuine interest of the peoples of either, but from their roles as states attempting to shape the destinies of other states. The USA and USSR do not impinge directly on each other at all. They have no boundary dispute, and each is so self-sufficient as to have no need of the other. Their conflicts arise out of their interests as superpowers each trying to maintain a dominant position in the world system of states. The ultimate solution to the threat of war is to replace the system of states with a system of specialized authorities, where appropriate on a global scale.

My main concern here is to show how such a system could deal with the major problems of the modern world, whether they exist independently of the state system or are functions of it, and to outline the sort of democratic control that might be exercised over such specialized agencies. However, I should also want to claim that even if such a system did not lead to the complete whittling away of the capacity of states to wage war, it would make war both more difficult to orchestrate and much less likely to succeed from the point of view of the aggressor. Many of the causes of war would be removed to the extent that there were other means of dealing with them that had a strong democratic legitimacy. Moreover, the effective conquest of another nation would become much more difficult to the extent that its workings were decentralized in a number of independent agencies instead of being under the centralized control of a state bureaucracy.

The task of one nation exercising control over another is greatly facilitated by the state apparatus of the subject country. The conqueror does not have to attempt to control every aspect of the public life of the conquered by installing its own officials in a host of specific authorities. All it has to do is to maintain a firm control of central government and insist that it control the details in the interest of the conqueror. It is rarely very difficult to find 'patriots' who will co-operate in this task on the pretext of preserving some residual autonomy for the conquered people. Vichy France and contemporary Poland are clear examples of this process. If, by contrast, the public affairs of a nation were controlled by a complex of independent authorities, the task of a conqueror in attempting to control each of these authorities would be much more difficult, costly and precarious.

This perspective is, of course, a very long-term one. It offers no immediate solution to the urgent problems of peace and disarmament. It needs to be supplemented by the development of means of non-violent resistance to aggression (see Sharp, 1973). A community that understands and is committed to these techniques can make the task of a conqueror an extremely daunting one, especially if that resistance is backed up by the determination of other communities to bring peaceful pressures to bear against the aggressor in every way possible. I am not suggesting that we should relax our efforts to find interim solutions to our problems within the framework of existing institutions and negotiations, but that we need to develop strategies that go to the root of the problem.

### 9.3   The problems of development

International efforts to stabilize production of marketing of primary products have not been very successful. Such authorities rarely succeed in bringing together all producers, never have the resources to tide them over difficult periods, and lack any effective sanctions to enforce even the few agreements that are made. Perhaps least successful of all have been the efforts of international authorities to deal with local wars, their causes and their effects, apart from some very limited successes in alleviating the plight of refugees. Even famine relief still depends very heavily on voluntary aid from states to states and on private voluntary agencies. Aid programmes have proved utterly inadequate. Most poor nations are now relatively poorer in relation to the richer nations than they ever were, and are often poorer in absolute terms than they were, saddled with hopelessly high levels of debt and intractable problems of population and production (see Tinbergen, 1976).[3]

The most pervasive and systematic source of these failures is the system of nation states itself.[4] Even the most liberal and democratic of states in which there is also a good deal of generalized sympathy with poor nations are inevitably under strong pressures to use international agencies to promote their own political and economic ends. At the very best they conceive of the problems of international aid in a very paternalistic manner. Even states that pursue some degree of socialism at home tend to behave, and in a sense have to behave, according to the requirements of short-term 'national interests' in matters of trade, at least where this is not overriden by 'reasons of state' and ideology. More radically, the world system rewards past success, both economic and political, with the resources that ensure an oligopoly of resources needed for future success. The poor are largely deprived of access to the means of production necessary to market commodities profitably on the world market.

In these circumstances there is little prospect of the poor countries accumulating capital, and in the short term the immediate effect of injecting capital into their systems is to disrupt production and produce disastrous unemployment. The labour liberated is labour nobody wants at any price, especially when there is a surplus of relatively educated, experienced and disciplined labour in the world economy. In these circumstances the worst off in the advanced countries want to exclude such labour from their markets, and even international capital finds little incentive to exploit it in ways that would provide substantial relief to the problems of Third World unemployment. Robots are becoming cheaper and much more reliable than even the cheapest of such labour, and are free from the political complications that attend its use. The growth of international trade has tended to take place among the rich nations to the virtual exclusion of the poor.

In a sense the problem is not so much that the rich exploit the poor, but that they do not even give them the option of being exploited, except in the case of a few marginal or over-supplied products. There seems to be no prospect at all of an economic development on the world scale that would raise the living standards of Third World workers in ways analogous to the advances in First World countries.[5] The poorer countries will have to rely mainly on internal development, attempting to use labour-intensive technologies for the most part, insulating their economies to a large extent from the world economy, maintaining tight control over imports and the movement of capital, and attempting to mitigate the destructive social effects of rapid economic change.

The immediate prospect for the development of international economic co-operation is bleak. Both political and economic forces in all countries seem to be pushing towards a minimal degree of co-operation designed to avert the more catastrophic kinds of trade wars and military confrontations. Nevertheless, even in this unpromising situation, and especially in the absence of realistic short-term policy options, it is necessary to think through how a viable international order might work. Such a relatively utopian approach can, I believe, suggest initiatives that at least offer a hope of planting seeds that may germinate in more propitious circumstances. The very absence of solutions to immediate problems should lead us to concentrate our attention on taking the first steps towards subverting the system that blocks the possibilities of constructive short-term solutions, the system of nation states, and the identification of democracy with nationalism.

It is probably too much to hope that the nexus between democracy and national autarchy can be broken in the first instance in those countries that have only recently gained their political, though not economic, independence. Their will to achieve national identity and independence is too deeply entrenched in their struggles against their colonial past and neo-colonial present. For them, democracy means primarily popular power rather than diversified participation or individual and group liberties. They aspire to strong and stable governments that can tackle their problems by effective mobilization of all the resources available to them. The first steps towards a democratic order will have to come from the more affluent states, and especially from those middle-sized countries that most need to break the overarching power of the superpowers, and which have most to gain from a more democratic international order. Such initiatives, however, are wholly dependent on a concomitant will in the peoples of these states to reverse their internal tendencies towards state-centred democracy in ways I shall now attempt to indicate.

## 9.4  Principles and procedures of democracy

The problems of war and of development are by no means the only important problems that face us on a global scale. Ecological problems that threaten our environment and the destruction of natural resources – soil, forest and fisheries, for example – are equally urgent. What kinds of functional authorities, then, do we need? And how can they be controlled responsibly and democratically? There is no possibility of analysing these questions fully in this chapter. Instead, I shall sketch a somewhat utopian solution and then ask how we might make some progress towards it.

Individually and collectively, especially in the economically advanced countries, we are utterly prodigal in our use of non-renewable resources. Those resources are the concern of all human beings, including future generations. Granted a global market economy, how can they be managed responsibly? The obvious answer is to market them at a price that is high enough to force us to use them more sparingly. If such prices were charged by a set of international authorities each having a monopoly in certain specific resources, these authorities would generate a substantial revenue which could be used to fund development projects. Moreover, such monopolies could put conditions on the use of materials derived from the resources they control so as to ensure that ecologically and socially harmful results were minimized.

Such authorities could maintain their monopolies if they were prepared to enter into a very tight agreement that any country or firm that stepped outside the monopoly of any authority would attract the strongest possible sanctions from every other authority. Their tasks would obviously be very complex and difficult. They would need to assign production quotas, license distributors and refiners, and make suitable arrangements for prospecting and investment. Nevertheless, orderly arrangements in the long run would be of enormous benefit to all concerned. Producers could rely on stable and assured revenues, consumers could plan effectively to develop resource-saving technologies, and substantial funds for development could be generated in a fair and assured way. Such a system would not so much replace the market as feed into the market mechanism those long-term global needs that cannot be registered in the market at present.

Analogous arrangements might be set up for many agricultural products that are at present subject to price fluctuations which can have catastrophic effects on the economies of nations that are very dependent on them. They would incorporate insurance against crop failures, technical and financial assistance to disadvantaged producers, and soil protection and environmental safeguards. The objective in the case of arrangements for the marketing of agricultural products would not be so much to generate public revenue, but to ensure reasonably cheap supplies to consumers while guaranteeing reasonable stability to producers and facing the problems that orderly production would in turn create. There would be a need, for example, to assist marginal producers who were put out of business to transfer to other branches of production and retrain or relocate workers displaced by bringing in more productive technology.

It is absolutely essential for the good working of authorities such as these that they be quite independent of states in their operation. States have too many interests and are subject to too many pressures, internal and external. Some governments will be under overwhelming pressure from well-placed lobby groups to protect domestic producers, while others may be prepared to sacrifice certain internal interests in order to please some other state on which it depends. Once states are involved, every decision becomes a matter of power-trading with a view to a wider context of issues that are quite irrelevant to the specific matter in hand, but very important to it in other ways. Agreement is made much more difficult, and the compromises reached are unlikely to be optimal for the specific interests in question. Great powers and power blocs tend to have quite disproportionate influence, even where they are not greatly affected.

If not only the specialized authorities I have been talking about, but authorities at every level, from the very local to the global, are to be controlled democratically, I believe it is necessary to adopt an entirely new form of democracy. Some aspects of my view have already been expounded and examined in Christopher Pollitt's chapter on democracy and bureaucracy, and there are many other aspects that cannot be examined here. In general, I believe, the traditional mode of representation by geographical areas has to be abandoned in favour of a system of representation of interests. More radically, I want to reject the idea that democratic control should be exercised through central authorities elected on the basis of one person, one vote.

That system gives people too little and too much: too much, because everybody has a say even in matters that do not affect them; too little, because it gives them only a generalized say through voting for a political party, and no great influence in the specific matters that are important to them. People in effect hand over everything to power-brokers, professional politicians, who trade off votes on various issues more in accordance with the needs of maintaining alliances and access to power than in accordance with the needs and desires of those affected by specific issues.

The rational alternative would be a system in which *each citizen or group would have a say in each specific area of decision in proportion to its material interest in that area.* The mere fact of having opinions about the matter or even some moral principle about it should not entitle one to a say in it. For reasons I have set out at greater length in *Is Democracy Possible?*, I do not believe that it is either practicable or desirable to attempt to express these diverse interests through a complex system of differentiated voting rights. Voting in elections or referenda is a very unsatisfactory way of arriving at a decision. Even in most matters that affect me I have no well thought-out, informed opinion. I do not know enough about the alternatives or the candidates, and granted that my vote counts for so little, it is hardly worth my while to spend time and effort in finding out. In mass voting I have to decide between a few pre-set alternatives. I have no input into framing the questions. Moreover, a vote records very little information. It does not express strength of preferences or degree of interest. In fact, it is a reasonable device for terminating discussion and arriving at a decision in committees where the discussion must come to an end. In other contexts it is of very dubious value or validity.

The procedure for arriving at decisions on matters of common concern should be so designed as to maximize the chances of arriving at an optimal decision for the various interests involved. Many matters where conflicting interests are involved in 'prisoner's dilemma' situations, in which each party is pursuing its own interests without regard to the other interests involved, will result in each being worse off than it would have been if it had settled for the best available compromise. In order to work out solutions to such problems and enforce them, it is necessary to eliminate irrelevances and establish a strong working relationship among those affected or among representatives whom they can trust. In practice, since this sort of work must be done in committee, the problem is that of arriving at committees that are both representative and authoritative. The simplest way of arriving at a committee that is representative of the diverse interests in a particular population is to take a *statistically representative* sample of that population. If that committee is comprised of members who have indicated their willingness to serve on it, they are likely to be people who have an active interest in its work. Each member would have a significant say in its decisions. So it would be worth their while to inform themselves as fully as possible about everything relevant to their decisions so as to be able to influence debate on the committees. Since they would not represent political parties, they could look at specific matters on their merits, even adopting unpopular decisions if it appeared necessary to do so. I call such a system *demarchy*.

Demarchic committees would rest their authority on their representative character, on their relative expertise and on their attempts to achieve optimal solutions. They would allow the diversity of interests full weight. It is most unlikely that any one person or party could represent adequately my interests in all public matters. Demarchic procedures would give a strong likelihood that *each* of my interests would be represented by somebody who shared it and had an interest in promoting it effectively. If democracy is a matter of maximum popular participation in public decisions, it would vastly increase the opportunities of ordinary people to participate. The membership of these committees would change one at a time over an appropriate period, ensuring both continuity and change. They would, of course, be subject to rigid demands for full disclosure of their proceedings. Anybody could nominate. There would be no place for professional politicians.

The higher level functions of apportioning public funds between such bodies, hearing appeals against these, adjudicating demands for changes in formulae by which they were chosen and arbitrating disputes between them, would be vested in committees chosen by lot from a pool of those nominated by their peers on lower level committees as having the requisite skill and dedication for this kind of work. These higher level committees could not interfere in the work of lower level committees except where a dispute was referred to them. The lower level committees would normally co-ordinate their activities as appeared desirable by negotiations among themselves, joint working parties and specific agreements. I believe that this system could operate at every level, from the municipal to the international. In the case of international bodies, the representatives would be an appropriate statistical sample of those who had shown promise in their work at more local levels.

A crucial problem would be the generation and disbursement of funds to finance the work of these committees. In the absence of a sovereign state at any level, taxation as we know it would be impossible. In some areas it might be possible for committees to charge or impose levies for their services, but most would have to rely on public funds. I believe that the appropriate way for such funds to be raised in a market economy is by vesting common resources, ultimately all major natural and accumulated resources, in specific trustee committees which would lease them to firms under conditions designed to provide for ecological safeguards, the interests of posterity, and a substantial public revenue. The bodies entrusted with public revenue would then be required to contribute most of it to various fixed commitments. However, they might retain a certain amount that they could disburse according to their own judgement to various official and unofficial organizations for public purposes. The prices they charged for the use of public resources would feed into the market system, for the most part being borne by those who made most use of those resources.

Not only productive and rule-making bodies, but also various policing agencies could all be controlled by demarchic committees. Bureaucracy would be minimized and decentralized. Since demarchic committees would be difficult to corrupt, many operating functions could be let out to tender. For expert advice such bodies might tend to rely on professional consultants rather than a permanent corps of bureaucrats. The whole system would be very much more flexible and responsive than our present forms of public organization can be. It should also be much more efficient, cutting fixed overheads and constantly reviewing budgets. It would be easy to disband obsolescent organizations and set up new ones and to change patterns of representation in response to changing situations and problems. A variety of forms of expertise in discussing or assessing public activities would become much more widely disseminated throughout the community, and political rigidities of all kinds would be undermined. Groups with a special case to put might expect to get a readier hearing, irrespective of their economic or political clout. There would be much more scope even for those who were not chosen for office to influence decisions.

## 9.5   Enforcement of authority

While other forms of authority rarely hold up against those backed by military force, if military force is eliminated or kept at a distance, there are many ways in which an authority can secure compliance with its commands, norms, requests or rules. Evan Luard (1977) distinguishes many of these in the distinctive modes of operation of existing international authorities, none of which is in a position to exercise military power. The basic power that a recognized authority has is that of rule-making. Where rules are needed and there is no rival authority with the standing needed to make them, the authority in possession of the field normally succeeds in getting its rules accepted and obeyed. Rules may vary greatly in binding force, in flexibility and in scope. In technical matters they are often precise and demand exact conformity. At the other extreme, for example in such matters as the elimination of racially and sexually based discrimination, they are more a matter of the spirit than the letter. There is a presumption in favour of the rule that is difficult to ignore if the matter is public and obedience expected. Disobedience needs justification. It has intangible costs. Closely related to rules is the setting of standards, for example of working conditions or safety or environmental protection, which, though not mandatory, give a basis for interested groups to appeal to in attempting to influence practice in such matters.

Co-ordination is a third method of acquiring and enhancing authority. It is, in a sense, a subdivision of Luard's fourth method, the administration of common services such as those provided by the International Civil Aviation Authority or the World Health Organization. In the same grouping comes the production of knowledge, not only through specialized research and information-gathering, but through collating, standardizing and publicizing relevant information in a systematic and continuing manner. Refusal to supply or receive knowledge is difficult to justify, unless there is a very particular reason. Once the right of an authority to knowledge in some area is recognized, there are few limits to it expanding its scope.

Finally, authorities establish themselves by providing assistance to those who need it. Almost every international authority supplies some material, technical or educational services to some of its members, thus increasing its authority over them and perhaps, too, over other members who recognize the need for such aid for the functioning of the system as a whole. Even outside of intergovernmental bodies, voluntary organizations like the Red Cross or Oxfam succeed in establishing a certain authority because of the needs they meet.

All of these normal processes of entrenchment of authority can be reinforced powerfully by mutual assistance and orchestration of sanctions between related bodies. At present the explicit orchestration of sanctions is inhibited by the fact that most international bodies depend directly on the nation states. Independently constituted bodies would be much freer and more effective in imposing sanctions even on nation states, let alone on specialized authorities of a more limited kind. The crucial problem from a practical point of view is to change the status of international bodies from that of intergovernmental bodies to genuinely supranational status. By and large, the processes we have just mentioned tend in this direction. The more the origins of an organization recede into the background and its authority comes to rest on its actual performance, the less easy it is to delegitimize, and the more autonomous it becomes. That is all to the good, providing that it is sensitive to the interests of those its activities affect.

Thus in most of the existing agencies there is a contraction of the role of general assemblies of the members in favour of the operating councils, reflecting a shift in authority from the contracting powers to their creatures, especially in the case of the more successful and less contentious bodies. Formally speaking, this involves a diminution of democratic control in so far as the contracting nation states are appropriate agents for representing the real needs involved. However, it often seems that the interests nation states are most apt to insist on are their own interests *as states* rather than the specific interests of those affected by the operations of the agency. Often the administrative and technical staff of the agency seem better placed to take account of these specific interests than the politicians. Nevertheless, there is a very real danger of the professional interests of the agency and its staff dominating their decisions, and of the perpetuation of an unaccountable bureaucracy by co-option. It has proved very difficult to change the structure and scope of many agencies and to eliminate duplication and conflict between them. Clearly demarchy offers a promising solution to these problems. It would ensure closer control of the agencies by those affected by their operations and a flexible means of restructuring them that would respond to specific needs rather than the play of power politics.

## 9.6 The road to Utopia
If demarchy is ultimately to prevail as the dominant form of democratic decision-making, the crucial problem is to find opportunities for it to get a reasonable trial. It is not inconceivable that once it became established

as a practical and effective procedure, pressures would be generated to introduce it into more and more areas. Such hopes may appear utopian, since demarchy runs counter to virtually every entrenched interest – economic, political, bureaucratic and professional – as well as to the dominant liberal and communist ideologies. Moreover, it is not the sort of proposal that lends itself easily to mass mobilization. Initially at least, it will depend on specific groups pressing its claims to solve specific problems, and on broadly based support for giving it a trial. Nevertheless, it may, once successfully launched, gradually erode the power of traditional authorities in much the same way as electoral democracy has triumphed over monarchies and dictatorships in so many parts of the world. It may suit the short-term interests of existing powers to get rid of problems they find intractable in the hope of consolidating their power in other areas.

Even in the absence of demarchic structures within nations on which an international order might be built, some approach to demarchy might be instituted in the case of many international organizations by choosing representatives from existing professional, consumer and even political bodies in accordance with demarchic principles. Imperfect though it would be, such a policy would at least bypass to some extent the nation states and perhaps set in train a process of functional democratization. Initially the main support for such moves might come from professional elites that are frustrated by the present system of power politics in international organizations and forums. It is in their interest to reduce the influence of the internal politics and external rivalries of the member states, the proliferation of talk at the expense of action, and the dead hand of politicians who have little understanding of the problems, even where they have a certain interest in seeing them solved. The hope of bringing these professional elites under control from below would then rest on the development of demarchic institutions within nation states.

Such a development from below is not inconceivable. Even in the highly centralized communist states, concessions to demarchy might prove a much more attractive way of responding to popular pressures for democratization than traditional multi-party parliamentary institutions. The ruling party would not have to abdicate its monopoly as the only party. The prospect of general political destabilization could be minimized while introducing by degrees the flexibility and decentralized initiative these countries so badly need. In parliamentary regimes demarchic institutions might appeal particularly to those parties that are forced to look for a fresh and distinctive approach to difficult problems such as those of health, education and welfare, where present bureaucratic structures cause so much discontent. It might also gain a good deal of support at the level of municipal government.

In the international field there is not much immediate prospect of restructuring existing agencies, with the possible exception of those that have suffered most severely from inter-state politics and from their own internal problems, notably UNESCO. The most promising approach seems to be to identify areas where new organizations are clearly needed and to promote demarchy as a way of overcoming some of the resistances to their formation. Some obvious areas are the sea, the sea-bed and Antarctica, where there are great resources that should be regarded as the common responsibility of all mankind and no adequate frameworks for dealing with them in ecologically, legally and economically acceptable ways. The problems raised by the exploitation of these areas grow daily more pressing, and the incapacity of traditional forms of international co-operation to deal with them has been amply demonstrated. Properly developed by genuinely supranational authorities, these areas might generate substantial revenue for world-wide public purposes and set a pattern for the responsible management of natural resources that might eventually be extended to break down the 'private property' of nation states in important natural resources. Ultimately, for example, one might envisage a world oil authority that would control the production and marketing of oil, charging a high price for it in order to conserve it and generate common revenue. The traditional owners might submit to such an arrangement if it offered them a better and more secure income than present marketing arrangements. If it was a genuinely independent authority, it would not derogate from their sovereignty much more than concessions to oil companies do. Similar arrangements might well prove to be in the interests of other exploiters of non-renewable resources, following the repeated collapse of 'private' arrangements for 'orderly marketing'.

The problem in matters of resource management and the possibilities they suggest are well illustrated by the history of the UN Conference on the Law of the Sea (UNCLOS III). Until its proposals were rejected by the Reagan administration, it did indeed seem possible that an operating authority might be set up to control all exploitation of the sea-bed outside of the Exclusive Economic Zones (EEZ) of the coastal states in the common interest. However, it is questionable whether the proposed set of laws was entirely satisfactory even from the point of view of the poorer countries. Moved by the insistence of a few coastal nations with very particular interests such as Kenya and Peru, the bloc of poorer countries forced the acceptance of a 200-mile EEZ for coastal states, thus putting virtually all of the immediately available resources in the hands of coastal states, especially such prosperous islands as Australia and New Zealand, with their very long coastlines (Clute, 1982, p. 198).

This decision exemplifies crucial weaknesses in efforts to deal with such matters on the basis of representation of national states. It seems that on several matters many of the less developed states were ill-informed about their interests, voting out of solidarity with their allies rather than in their own specific interests. From this point of view it would have been better if *interests* had been represented rather than states in the negotiating process. In such matters states often have several interests that conflict. So they may be both consumers and producers of various maritime products in various degrees, as well as having political interests in the form of control of these matters and an economic interest in the revenue generated by the exploitation of common resources. If these interests, most of which would be shared by other states, were represented adequately, it is much more likely that an optimal and generally acceptable solution could be found than under the present system of power-trading. Instead of having to sacrifice their interests in some matters in order to maintain a power bloc of those who share certain of their interests, they could hope that *each* of their interests would be fully represented. Moreover, many of the smaller countries cannot afford delegations with the requisite expertise and support facilities to mount an adequate case on the issues that affect them.

An initial move towards fairer and less futile structures of representation of interests might be made by asking each country to nominate the major concerns it has about, say, the law of the sea-bed and a panel of nominees, not necessarily its own nationals, whom it regards as suitable representatives in the case of each of its major concerns. A committee of a reasonable size would then be chosen by lot from these nominees which would determine a structure of working parties on various matters, attempting to give proportionate representation to the various interests expressed. The working parties would then be chosen to reflect these interests. Conjointly they would hammer out a proposal, which they would no doubt attempt to represent as the best available compromise. The various states concerned would then have the opportunity of accepting or rejecting the proposal. It would, however, have a better chance of acceptance than a proposal that was largely imposed by a majority.

In time it might be possible to induce most states to delegate their rights of nomination to relevant scientific and other bodies, if it could be established that representatives chosen in this way were more likely to be effective than political nominees. Gradually it might be possible to build on the professional interests of expert opinion to freeze out political interference. The next and more difficult step towards democratization might come with non-expert representatives of consumer, worker and environmental interests being chosen by a statistical procedure from a pool of nominees from grass-roots bodies in the various countries affected in a way that reflected the interests involved. Appeal courts could be set up to consider the fairness of the sampling procedures and make adjustments to them.

Of course, none of these things will come about automatically. A great deal of argument, education and agitation would be involved. Although the law of the sea-bed well illustrates the problems and the ultimate advantages of a demarchic solution to them, it may not be a good place to start, since many countries have no committed positions on the matter. Perhaps a more promising case might be some more specific matters of environmental protection, where many of the more developed middle-sized countries might be expected to take the lead and be willing to push for the setting up of relatively impartial agencies to tackle such issues as acid rain, the pollution of waterways and the protection of animal habitats. It is even possible that such moves might be initiated not by nations or the UN but by voluntary agencies that would set out to establish for themselves a recognized status as impartial authorities in certain areas by setting up joint committees on important matters on the basis of demarchic representation of all those affected. Such a policy might win for an organization such as Greenpeace more lasting and solid support than its present rather flamboyant interventions. Again, some of the voluntary international relief and development agencies might find it appropriate to set up demarchic structures among those they assist as channels for their aid which might provide a durable nucleus of developing self-help in the communities they assist. Demarchical organizations would, I believe, be likely to work better than co-operatives, which are very vulnerable to the apathy of much of the membership. Once they reach a certain size they tend to be taken over by permanently installed entrepreneurs.

### 9.7 Objections to demarchy

1 'If authority is devolved into autonomous, functionally specialized bodies, there is not going to be a well-formed public opinion about their activities. Such a public opinion is one of the most important elements in democratic control.'

Part of the answer is that if each agency is controlled by committees of those affected by its decisions, and if it is relatively easy for those who are interested to have access to the committees, then specific publics centred on each activity are likely to be developed. There would be a constant turnover of membership of these committees. Ex-members would no doubt keep a vigilant eye on the ways in which their successors 'ruined' what they had built up and would be quick to mobilize pressures against such vandalism. One might expect that such pressure would have a good deal more effect on demarchic committees than it has on professional politicians or bureaucrats. At the highest levels of government in most specialized matters, what counts most is specialist opinion in the ordinary course of events. Public opinion intrudes only when some storm is aroused over a 'sensitive' issue. What I would suggest we need is less of this somewhat arbitrary and often contrived intervention and more informed and continuous supervision and assessment by the relevant public.

2 'Demarchy amounts to putting power into the hands of the technocrats and professionals. Even those who nominate as potential popular representatives

are likely to be either quasi-professionals or inexperienced people who are easily "snowed" by the professionals and their allies.'

To a large extent this objection stems from unrealistic ideals of popular control. The amateurs are never going to be able to subject the professionals to their complete control, nor is it desirable that they should try to do so. Professional work of any sort is impossible without a good deal of autonomy and room for initiative. Ideally one would hope that a dialogue might develop between the lay people and the professionals of the sort that often takes place between patients and their doctors or architects and their clients. Less idealistically, demarchic committees might operate much more than present institutions do by hiring and firing teams of professionals rather than building up standing bureaucratic structures, with their entrenched permanent professionals. They could do so more easily because they would be less vulnerable to corruption than professional politicians and bureaucracies.

3   'Demarchy is anti-political. It takes the politics out of public decision-making. It removes the possibility of our taking an overall view of the direction in which we are heading and facing clearly the value-decisions that are being made.'

In one important sense demarchy is indeed anti-political. A great deal of political activity under centralized regimes, whether democratic or authoritarian, consists in power-trading: 'You side with me on this and I'll side with you on that'. The substance of politics in this sense is building alliances, and what is often called 'log-rolling'. In this process genuine interests are often sacrificed, simply for the sake of the power strategies of various agents. Functionalism is an attempt to undercut this process and bring genuine conflicting interests into negotiation with each other, with a view to arriving at solutions that are acceptable to each.

Demarchy, however, is also anti-political in a sense that touches more nearly on a more honorific sense of politics. There is in much thinking about politics a deeply entrenched assumption that the whole community, national or global, needs to define and rank its priorities and values in a comprehensive way and attempt to order its practical decisions in the light of that overall conception.

I believe, though I cannot fully argue the case here, that this conception of politics is deeply illusory. In practice it leads to claptrap and ideological thinking. In principle it is not possible to articulate hierarchies of values in a well-grounded way. Various values have very different importance in different contexts and from different points of view. Sometimes security will be salient, at other times liberty; here equality, there diversity; and so on. The only rational way of looking at questions of what is important and what is not is to look at the specific problems that arise in connection with specific interests.

This is not to claim that such questions are reducible to technical considerations, but rather that conflicts of values in specific matters have to be articulated and resolved in relation to the specific problems in connection with which they arise. If a particular interest group is most concerned about equality, they ought not to be overridden simply because most people in the society are most concerned about liberty, for example. A public political morality is indeed of great importance, but it must grow out of the efforts of responsible agents to arrive at morally defensible solutions to specific problems. There does have to be a strong consensus about the moral rules that place limits on what individuals, groups and public authorities can do. But moral ideals and values are much more various and contestable, especially in regard to their relative weighting. In an open society no specific moral ideal can be imposed. To the extent that there is a convergence towards one, it will tend to be articulated in a demarchy not by collective decision about it but by various agents bringing it to bear on the specific issues that affect them. This is particularly important in international affairs, where there are very deep differences in such matters.

4 'Demarchy makes very strong assumptions about human nature, specifically about the rationality and responsibility of those who are chosen by statistical procedures to represent the various interests concerned.'

In a sense this is true. However, any democratic proposal does have to rely on the rationality and responsibility of ordinary people. I should argue that demarchy provides a more favourable context for the development of these qualities than electoral democracy, which can easily generate irrational and irresponsible behaviour, even where people are individually responsible and rational. It is often in the interests of political parties to manipulate irrational hopes and fears, to agglommerate distinct issues, to reduce issues to personalities, and so on, leaving voters with the choice between alternatives that are all unacceptable. The more issues can be faced by those involved in specific and concrete terms, the more likely they are to be faced rationally and responsibly, especially if those making the decisions are typically affected by those decisions.

5 'Demarchy must take the actual interests of people as given. It works on the assumption that proper decisions are to be reached on the basis of negotiation between those interests. But this is to entrench an existing pattern of interests that itself is a product of a radically unsatisfactory social order. It inevitably perpetuates that order.'

A great deal here hangs on the questions raised by Marxist analyses of the dynamics of market societies. I have said something about these issues in *Is Democracy Possible?*, but a great deal more remains to be said.

In general this appears to me to be the strongest objection, and an extremely serious one. Clearly, demarchy *could* work in this way, and there is no way of demonstrating *a priori* that it would not. Nevertheless, I believe that the alternative, namely to attempt to remake the social order by centralized planning, is more dangerous, and that it is more likely that demarchy would result in a desirable restructuring of social relations than any other alternative. Clearly, in deciding which interests are to be counted as legitimate and what relative weighting in representation is to be given to each in a specific context, the second-order committees that decide such matters will have a very difficult task. But there is no reason why they should not give great weight to those who are adversely affected by the present distribution of power and resources. So, for example, I would hope that committees concerned with resource management would be so structured as to give predominant weight to those who need the resources rather than to those who presently control them. The cumulative result of many such decisions might be expected to be a massive shift in power in favour of the disadvantaged, which would eventually result in a radical change in the overall pattern of society.

## Notes

1.  It is not necessary to suppose that individuals, social groups or the state are 'by nature' aggressive or even wholly self-interested. Wars and other forms of conflict can arise not so much from a 'need' or 'will' to conflict but from distrust and the absence of any way of resolving real or imagined problems. Hobbes himself, incidentally, emphasized not universal aggressiveness or cupidity but distrust as the key problem in the state of nature.

2.  Functionalism is a somewhat vague theory, and although I endorse its main theoretical and prescriptive features, I believe that both it and what I am contending in this essay require a great deal of further elaboration. While functionalists have generally favoured democracy and argued that functional organizations tend to be more democratic than multi-functional ones, they have not paid much attention to the problems of how democratic control can work at the international level, which is the main concern here.

3.  The following remarks on the problems of development are very sketchy. There is an enormous literature on the subject and radical disagreements about it, not only between various schools of economic analysis, but even among Marxists.

4.  It may well be true that in some sense it is not the system of states but capitalism that is the ultimate cause of the problems. My point is that most nation states can do something to mitigate them within their own borders, but those same borders put almost insuperable obstacles in the way of doing so on the international scale. At the same time I would deny that world socialism conceived of as an international 'planned economy' is an appropriate solution to the problems to the extent that it would entail a world state.

5.  There seems little to be hoped for from the development of 'multinational' corporations. The word is misleading, since such corporations are almost invariably wholly dominated by their home base. The result is that they invite political intervention by their country of origin to 'protect its citizens and interests'. Very rarely do they have the effect of inducing the home country to take a constructive interest in assisting their host countries. No doubt they do often contribute to stimulating economic activity in the host countries, but only in very limited ways. They typically want to tie up markets for their products

or sources of cheap raw materials. Quite apart from questions of exploitation, they are not usually equipped to bring to the underdeveloped countries the kinds of technology and organization that are most needed to make best use of their human and natural resources, such as very simple agricultural, construction and processing equipment, and small, low-capital enterprise.

## References

BURNHEIM, J. (1985) *Is Democracy Possible?*, Cambridge, Polity Press.

CLUTE, R. E. (1982) 'International Future', in G. K. BERTSCH (ed.) *Global Policy Studies*, Beverly Hills, Sage.

GROOM, A. J. R. and TAYLOR, P. (eds) (1975) *Functionalism, Theory and Practice in International Relations*, London, University of London Press.

LUARD, E. (1977) *International Agencies: the Emerging Framework of Interdependence*, London, Macmillan.

MITRANY, D. (1975) *The Functional Theory of Politics*, Oxford, Martin Robertson.

SHARP, G. (1973) *The Politics of Non-violent Action*, 3 vols, Boston, Mass., Poster Sargent.

TINBERGEN, J. (co-ordinator) (1976) *Reshaping the International Order*, London, Hutchinson.

# Index